The Red Wedding

R. B. CARIAD

Disclaimer

This book contains strong language and scenes that may offend sensitive readers. This is not a sweet romance book. It contains graphic sex and dubious consent scenes, scenes of a disturbing and violent nature, pertaining to suicide, and references to mental health issues.

Recommended for readers over 18 years old.

This book is a work of fiction. Characters, names, places, and incidents are products of the author's imagination or used fictitiously. Any resemblance to actual events, location, buildings, events, institutions, or persons living or dead is coincidental.

Published by R. B. Cariad

Copyright © 2023 R. B. Cariad

All rights reserved. No part of this book may be reproduced or used in any manner, including photocopying, recording, or other electronic methods, without the prior written permission of the copyright owner, except for the use of brief quotations in a book review.

To request permissions, contact rbcariadauthor@gmail.com

Website: http://rbcariad.com

First paperback edition

Edited by Katherine Tate

Cover art by Arcanicmedia and Virtualrover

Other titles in the series

Connect With R B. Cariad

Join R. B. Cariad and The Cascade of Lies by signing up for her newsletter and giveaways at

Home—R. B. CARIAD author (rbcariadauthor.com)

Follow RB on Facebook
R. B. Cariad

Instagram
@rbcariadauthor

Tik-Tok
@rbcariadauthor

Acknowledgments

To Lucy and Nathan, thank you for the love and support from day one of my journey. I'll be forever grateful to you both.

To Christine Miller, (Mother!) Thank you for making me your daughter, so I would always have a mother. Your support has been amazing!

To my father's adopted son, Dave Peacock. I couldn't write a book about Viking Bikers without thinking about you and the strength you gave our father when he needed it most. He cherished that necklace, and it went with him when he passed.

To the beautiful soul who entered my life recently. Tinman. Thank you for your continuous inspiration.

For the daring Celts, those who defy limitations and for those who love getting lost in a dark and dangerous biker world.

This one's for you.

CHAPTER ONE
Diagnosis

Zander sat outside the doctor's office in the pouring rain, crushed by his diagnosis.

The sun shone through the heavy shower as if it was trying to brighten his day, only nothing could console him in his moment of sadness. He had believed he and B were finally going to receive their happily ever after until they received another devastating blow.

The rain lashed upon him as if the Almighty was punishing him, making Zander collect his karma for his past digressions. The hurt and anger formed knots in his stomach as he rested his head against the pebble-dashed wall.

B shouted to him in desperation as she ran towards him, but Zander's tsunami of pain deafened him.

"Here you are," she said, panting to catch her breath.

He couldn't look at her as she palmed his cheeks.

"You scared me, running off like that. We run towards each other, remember?"

Zander closed his eyes, the disappointment at himself for failing her again etched over his face.

"Listen, this doesn't change a God damn thing, you hear me?"

He faked a smile, removing her hands with his. "How can you say that? It changes everything."

"Not for me, handsome. I love you just the way you are."

Zander drew in another sharp breath. "Welsh Cake, I've been waiting all my life for you. I allow myself to believe we'll be happy, and yet another whirlwind of shit strikes us, ruining our life plans."

B slipped her hands inside his cut, holding his chiseled torso.

"I believe in us, Scottie. This will happen!"

He shook his head, frustration making him grimace. "Dinnae do that, darling. I know you mean well, but hope is dangerous when the outlook is dismal."

B narrowed her eyes, squeezing his sides. "It's not dismal!"

"A 23 percent chance of conceiving in two years, coupled with our age Welsh Cake. Come on. I've let you down. What kind of man cannae get the woman he loves pregnant? Low sperm count, for fuck's sake. Christ, I feel like I've been castrated; I dinnae deserve this Prez flesh," he said, tugging on his cut with pain ripping from his throat. "I'm less than a fucking man!"

"Scottie, you have a low sperm count, not a death sentence. Besides, we've not even started trying yet and I'm glad we got health checks. We're aware of the challenge ahead now."

Zander ruffled his hand through his hair, shirking away from her, "Aye, but we're always up against it darling. I just want us to be happy."

"I thought we already were. Scottie 23 percent isn't a no. It just means it may take a while."

The rain continued to crash upon them as B sat on the edge of the sidewalk. He watched as she tapped her feet in the puddles, arms stretched out behind her, propping herself up.

Zander jammed his hands onto his hips. "What the fuck are you doing? It's pissing down with rain, and you look like you're fucking sunbathing."

"Maybe I am."

Confusion painted his already tormented face. "What?"

"Well, it's a matter of perspective, Scottie. I choose to see the sun amidst the rain. This is a tiny bump in a big, fuck off-road. We've hit them before, and we'll probably hit them again. Are you going to stop riding because of a few bumps, Scottie?"

Zander kicked the puddled water across the road and plonked himself onto the wet concrete next to her.

"You're an asshole."

She laughed, noticing the growing smile on his face. "Yeah, but I'm *your* asshole."

Zander retrieved a packet of cigarettes from his inside pocket, attempting to open them when B snatched them from his hand, launching them into the road, where a car promptly drove over them.

Zander glared at her in disgust. "Thanks very fucking much!"

"Well, they're not going to help you, are they?"

Zander allowed a chuckle to escape. "I suppose fucking no'. So, what now?"

B relaxed back on the concrete, "we carry on as planned. I have arranged for my birth control to be removed, and you need to make some lifestyle changes. We're getting married and starting a family."

Zander gazed upon her, astonished by her resilience. "You really believe we can grow our family?"

B grinned. "I know we can, good boy. See, when people throw obstacles at me and tell me I can't, I do it twice just to show them I can. Call it oppositional defiance or whatever, I'm not giving up until I have what I desire."

Zander planted his palm on the concrete, hovering over her wearing a tooth-filled smile. "Fuck, I'm so fucking mad at you."

B narrowed her gaze, the soft undertone in her voice questioning him, "why?"

"For making me feel better when I just want to be pissed at the world."

B sat up, forcing him to sit up too, wrapping her arms around his neck. "You can be mad, tough guy. Down, depressed. Just don't live there. Have your moment, transmute that shit, then straighten that bloody Prez crown. I got you, Scottie, just like you always have me."

Zander swallowed the lump in his throat as he leaned in to kiss her, his hurt dissipating as he did so.

"Apologies for my behavior. Storming out was a shit move," he said, pulling back to meet her gaze.

B ran her fingers through his mop of wet hair.

"I'll let you off, but no dwelling on this Scottie. There's no pressure here. We'll get married next week, and you'll get your Celt babies, I promise."

Zander hugged her tight, kissing her neck. "I love you darling."

"Love you too, handsome."

While lost in each other's arms, Zander unexpectedly flinched. "Shit!"

"What's wrong?" B asked in a panic.

"Talk about babies. We better go pick up our adult baby's birthday present. We're due to collect it at noon."

Zander peeled himself off the concrete, dragging B to her feet.

"Well remembered. I had forgotten with all this crazy."

Zander squeezed her hand. "I'm still mad at you, though."

B laughed. "How can I compensate you?"

"I'm sure I'll think of something," he said, winking at her.

B shook her head, changing the subject. "Do you think Tyr will like his birthday present?"

Zander threw his head back, laughing. "You've seen him. He's obsessed. He even has one as his lock screen."

"I'm so excited to see his face. That boy deserves happiness."

"Aye, he's a good lad. I saw it the moment I laid eyes on the laddie. He was a lost boy when I found him brawling with four men in a bar. He dinnae say much when I sponsored him, but I could tell he appreciated it. Tyr just wants to belong, darling, and since you've arrived in Sunnyville, I think he feels more at home."

B unlocked the truck, "how?"

"You've welcomed him into our home, placed a loving arm around him. That boy needed nurturing, and you're doing that for him. Tiny is like an older brother to him, and when he left for Uskiville, I assumed Tyr would leave, too. Surprisingly, he stayed. He said Sunnyville felt like home to him."

"Aww, that's so lush! I love him like he's one of our own Scottie."

"Yeah, me too, darling."

THE RED WEDDING

B rushed around the house, readying everything for Tyr's arrival. The patched members requested she host Tyr for the night, allowing them preparation time for his surprise birthday bash at the club the next day. It wasn't out of the ordinary for Tyr to stay at B's. They had become close since Tyr landed the role of bodyguard prior to Jericho's attack. He stayed over often when Zander was busy trying to track down Jericho.

B noticed Tyr was relaxed in her home. He once fell asleep while working, waking in a panic, providing B with an embarrassing and apologetic smile, requesting she didn't inform Prez that he was sleeping on the job. He confided in her that her home was the only place he could relax, confessing that being around her family relieved his anxiety.

Since then, B clarified that Tyr was welcome to stay whenever he felt he needed to escape the chaos of the MC dorms. B prepared the spare room in the far wing of the farmhouse with Nordic décor, aware of Tyr's pride in his heritage.

Madoc and Rhys both loved having him around, too, as Tyr always made a fuss of them, offering to help with their homework, playing video games, or playing pool in the den with them. B and Zander found it refreshing, watching Tyr wrestle and play fight as if he was their older sibling. He was coming out of his shell at last, and B loved she could provide a safe space for him to be himself.

After setting the cake on the counter, she left Madoc and Rhys to finish the decorations while Zander followed her into the kitchen.

"You're gonnae ruin that boy," he said, whispering into her ear and wrapping his enormous arms around her.

"Good! He deserves it!"

Zander kissed her neck. "Tell me again why you love celebrating so much."

"I lacked that as a child, Scottie. Watching everyone else around me have banners, balloons, parties, and ponies was traumatizing when I was lucky if I received a card. I vowed to be better, sparing loved ones of my hardships."

"And you, my darling, will experience nothing of the sort again." He tapped her sternum, "that beautiful heart of yours is beyond special, magnificent even. The love you show to people is miraculous, and I feel like the luckiest guy on the planet that you chose me to love."

B swallowed hard. "Aww, you'll have me crying now in a minute, handsome. It's me who's lucky,"

Zander took her hands. "Now, in a minute. Your Welsh isms crack me up. Seriously though, you don't realize how bright you shine. You illuminate every room you enter. I just wish you could see yourself as I see you."

"And that's why I love you. You make me feel like no one else has. Scottie, I've never felt special or loved until I met you."

"Whoa! Not even by Irish, the perfect bestie?"

B shook her head. "I used to feel something for Mackie, but I was broken, Scottie. I wasn't ready for love or to be loved. You taught me those things. Mackie will always be my bestie. Like Frankie, he's all I've known. We got each other through some tough times, but you?" she said, tugging at his shirt and grinning. "You took everything I knew and turned it on its head. You pulled my heart out, put it in the wash to remove the hurt and the self-limiting beliefs, and filled it with a love I've never experienced before. Scottie, Mackie may be my bestie, but you will always be my world."

Zander fixed on her gaze. "Thank you, beautiful. I suspected there was something between you both and I appreciate you opening up and being honest with me. I understand how difficult that is for you. You are the only light I want in my life, and I hope I'll always be yours."

"Always," B whispered, "and just to be clear, nothing has ever happened with Mackie. I want to reiterate that before we marry because I'm in this for keeps, lover boy, and I don't want you ever doubting my love for you."

Zander picked her up, sitting her at the breakfast bar. "Oh, I dinnae, darling. In fact, I think there's just enough time to show you how much I love you," he said, slipping his hand up her skirt.

B's naughty laugh escaped her throat. "Scottie, the boys are in the next room."

Zander scooped her up, carrying her down the hallway. "Then we'll slip upstairs for a minute. You've bought enough decorations to keep them occupied and fill the town hall. Boys," he bellowed. "I'm just stealing your mother for half an hour. You'll be alright without her for a bit, won't you?"

"Yeah, we're fine!" chimed Madoc and Rhys.

Zander carried on up the stairs. "See, all good. So let me please you, woman!"

CHAPTER TWO

It was early evening when Tyr left the club to head for B's. He welcomed the tranquility of the farmhouse, a stark difference from the club. The only noise at B's came from the den when Madoc and Rhys battled each other in their latest video game.

Tyr seized every opportunity to visit there. He loved the sense of harmony the house and its occupants fostered. The house was always full of love and laughter, whether it was Zander chasing B around the kitchen, pool and game nights in the den or simple movie nights. Tyr appreciated the effort B made to create the most holistic and wholesome family home, a far cry from Tyr's, back home in San Diego.

Tyr's upbringing was one of survival. The youngest of three brothers, his father would often pick them off against one another. Erik, the oldest, was the most formidable, just like his father, Leif. He strove for greatness, desperate to follow in his father's footsteps. Tyr watched how he would mimic his father's actions in the hope of one day becoming the next President of The Rus Reapers MC. Tyr got along with Erik despite how hard he was on him, Tyr's only annoyance being when he showed off to impress his father Leif, making Tyr the butt of his fist and his jokes.

Ragnar, the middle son, had a jealous streak. He often whined and moaned about looking more like his mother with his brown eyes and fuller facial features and less like his father, who had long red hair, green eyes, and a bushy red beard. He was also jealous of Erik and Leif's relationship. Leif would set challenges to determine the honorary champion of the day, with Tyr coming last because of his age and smaller size compared to his Viking brothers. His father would reward his brother Erik with treats and lessons in combat for always winning, leaving Ragnar in a fit of rage. Tyr often fell onto the receiving end of Ragnar's temper, choosing to beat his baby brother every time he lost against Erik. Tyr once made the mistake of crying to his mother, Revna, only for Leif to step in and clip Tyr around the ear, calling him weak and bellowing 'Vikings don't cry, boy.' It angered Tyr that his mother didn't stand up for her children, he didn't blame her, rather left himself wondering if his mother was as terrified of Leif as he was.

Tyr was the runt of the litter, with his father constantly pressuring him to be better and providing an ungracious look of disapproval every time Tyr failed to match the strength of his older brothers.

Erik often gave him a sympathetic glance, understanding Tyr never stood a chance, being eight years younger. Ragnar loved to tease and gloat, underpinning the low self-esteem Tyr had for himself. Tyr always felt less than in the family home.

Tyr understood that the family would never accept him, but it didn't deter him. Instead, it lit a fire inside him, driving him to be better. At twelve, he joined the school wrestling team and after puberty hit, the strawberry blonde-haired Viking boy beat his brother Ragnar in a home wrestling match, forcing his father to notice him.

Tyr assumed his life would get easier after that; however, it became quite the opposite. His father created challenges Tyr could not win, ensuring Ragnar had victory over him to save face with the patched members in his club. Leif wanted his club to view his older boys as future leaders, knowing that Tyr would always be regarded as too young to be taken seriously by the elders.

Tyr brought more disappointment to his father when he studied Applied Sciences in college, rather than follow in the family footsteps and working for his father's joinery business. Revna, his mother, never offered much sympathy, questioning why Tyr always riled his father by making, in her opinion, the wrong life choices.

After college, Tyr couldn't wait to escape the family home, choosing not to return after his last semester, instead he hit the road, winding up in Sunnyville, resentful and angry, choosing to pick a fight with anyone and everyone until Zander offered to sponsor him as his prospect.

Tyr felt an overwhelming sense of gratitude towards Zander for supporting him, and towards Tiny for their brotherly friendship. Now, years later, Tyr enjoyed time with Prez and his beloved family.

He was in the MC parking lot donning his helmet when "unknown caller" flashed across the screen of his cell phone.

Who the hell is this?

"Hello?"

"Tyr, it's time to come home, son. You're needed here!"

Panic swept through him. His hand trembled at the sound of his father's insistent, demanding tone.

"Faðir?"

"You've had your tantrum. Now heed my call. You are a Rus Reaper Viking, not a wolf! Your family needs you."

Tyr inhaled a hard breath, coughing and struggling to inhale. "No, Faðir! I will always be a Rus Viking, just not a Rus Reaper Viking, and I'm also a Gray Wolf and proud of it!" He exhaled. "Wolf's blood runs through my veins as much as Viking blood does. Zander is my Jarl. He sponsored me, accepted me as his own kin when my blood couldn't. I didn't abandon the Rus. You all abandoned me, Faðir."

A raspy, venomous tone reprimanded him. "You will come home and play your role in this family. Your brodir, Erik, is missing. It is your duty to help ensure that he returns to us."

Tyr stepped off his bike, pacing the parking lot. "He probably realized how sadistic your environment is and ran just like I did. I'm not going back to that prison you call home. Goodbye Faðir."

He was about to hang up when Leif bellowed down the line. "You dare defy me, Tyr, then watch your club burn!"

Tyr hung up, shaking. Turning in a fit of uncontrollable rage, he lashed out, punching the wall several times, busting his knuckles open before doubling over in anguish.

Shit!

Hyde, who had just stepped out for a cigarette, rushed to his aid. "Hey, man, what's happened? You alright?"

Tyr brushed him off. "Fine, I'm due at Prez's. Catch you later."

"Are you certain you don't want me to examine your hand? It looks nasty."

Tyr jumped on his bike, revving the engine. "It's just a scratch!" he said before driving off.

CHAPTER THREE

The doorbell chimed around the house, with B rushing to answer the door. Opening it, wearing a beaming smile, she grinned at a nervous Tyr. "Happy birthday eve, handsome boy! You know you don't have to knock; this is your home too, remember."

"Thank you, Mrs. Prez," he said, deflated, embracing her. "Sorry I'm late."

Releasing her, he reached down to remove his boots; B had a strict no outdoor footwear in the house rule.

B waited for him to change into his comfy slippers, casting her eyes to his split knuckles.

"Hey, are you alright," she asked, leaning against the stair pillar. "You look a little off color."

Tyr rose to his feet, towering over her and clearing his throat. "Uh, yeah. I'm just not used to people making a fuss on my birthday. We didn't celebrate my birthday back home and I've hidden it until now."

B smiled, rubbing his arm. "You should know by now nothing gets by me. I was like you, Tyr, and that's why we always celebrate here. You are part of my family, and we want to celebrate the gift that you are, lovely boy, so suck it up, buttercup."

A chuckle escaped his raspy throat as she took his hand, dragging him to the kitchen.

"Come on, everyone is waiting."

The house smelled amazing as the Gravlax, hearty Viking stew and Viking flatbread decorated the dining table like a fine banquet. Zander had even spent the last four weeks brewing mead for Tyr and purchased matching Viking horns for himself and Tyr to drink from.

"Happy birthday, lovely boy," B said, joined in by Zander, Madoc, and Rhys.

Tyr stood dumfounded as B tracked his movement around the dining room. "Wow! Mrs. Prez, this is amazing. Thank you for making my birthday special."

B smiled, rubbing his back. "Tyr, when will you call me B? You should know you don't need to be formal with me."

Zander stood to greet him, slapping his back. "It's a respect thing, isn't it, pal? Tyr likes to show respect for the chain of command within the club. I admire that in you, son."

Tyr's cheeks flushed. "Thank you, Prez."

"Fair enough," B said. "Now please sit so we can eat."

Zander poured two horns of mead, handing one to Tyr. "Happy birthday, Tyr!" he said, tapping horns before they both knocked back their drinks.

"Wow! That's superb," Tyr said. "Did you brew it yourself?"

"Aye, Welsh Cake bought me the kit online," he said, giving her a cheeky wink. "Now dig in. Welsh Cake has slaved over this for you."

After sharing laughter over B's home-cooked meal and celebrating with birthday cake, B directed Tyr to the decorated sitting room. She welcomed the warmth washing through her, seeing Tyr smiling as his eyes darted around the banner and balloon-filled room and back to the pile of presents sitting on the sofa.

"Open mine first!" Rhys said with the excitement of a five-year-old, thrusting a rectangular-shaped gift into his chest.

"Thank you, Rhys," Tyr said, humoring him by shaking it.

Rhys wore the biggest smile, watching Tyr open the latest zombie video game.

"Oh, this is awesome. Thanks," he said, high-fiving Rhys.

"I thought we could play it once you've opened all your presents?"

"Sounds great!" Tyr gushed.

"Mine next," Madoc said, handing him another box.

Tyr smiled, sitting to open it as Zander grinned, threading his arm around B's back to clasp her waist.

"A model Viking long boat kit. Man, this is special. Thank you, Madoc," he said, annunciating the 'c.'

"Now ours," Zander said, tossing Tyr a red, square, jewelry box.

Tyr took the box, fumbling with nervousness. opening it, his pupils dilated at the solid gold wolf necklace. His gaze shifted from the jewelry box to B and Zander, and then returned to the precious jewelry, leaving him speechless once more.

Zander beamed at B, kissing her cheek, before turning to Tyr. "That there is 24 carat gold. Only the best for you, Tyr. We're lucky to have you as part of our family, son."

Tyr struggled to compose himself. "I-I- thank you!"

B could tell Tyr was overwhelmed already, and he still hadn't received his grand gift yet. Kneeling in front of him, she took the box from his trembling hands. "Here, let's see how it looks on you," she smiled, taking the necklace, and placing it around his neck. Clasping it, she ran her fingers along the fine gold chain, ensuring it sat at his sternum and delivered a kiss to his head. "A special person needs a special gift."

Tyr stifled back the tears, making B panic. She had always handled him with care after noticing the trauma behind his beautiful eyes, and although he tried to maintain his tough Viking biker exterior, she knew he required a nurturing hand. To B, Tyr's mental age in terms of personal growth didn't correlate with his physical age.

B stroked his head. "Sorry Tyr, we didn't mean to overwhelm you. We just wanted to show you how much you mean to us. We feel honored to have you here."

Tyr ground his teeth and cleared his throat, composing himself. "No, thank you. I am blown away by your gratitude. I've never received such precious gifts or had a kind family like this."

Zander approached him, sitting and clasping a loving arm around him. "You'll always have a family here, Tyr, and dinnae forget it."

Tyr nodded, peering up at B with nervousness once again. "Mrs. Prez.... I would like to call you something if that's okay?"

"Of course."

Tyr swallowed. "It would be my honor to call you Móðir if you'll allow it?"

A puzzled smile flashed across B's face. "*Móðir?*"

"Yes, it's Nordic for mother."

B's mouth dropped open in awe of the young man who sat before her. Battling back the tears, she swallowed against the boulder-like lump in her throat, whispering his name. "Tyr."

Tyr's face flushed scarlet red. "You've made me feel more like a son than anyone. You welcomed me into your home, accepting me as part of your family. I would like to honor you with that title, please?"

Shocked smiles surrounded them as B dragged him into her embrace, hugging him and kissing his cheek. "The honor is all mine, lovely boy. I love you, Tyr!"

Tyr held her tight enough for B to feel his heart slamming into his chest. She hadn't realized the depth of the bond they had built this year.

Dragging herself away, she grinned. "Do you think you can handle one more surprise?"

Tyr's eyes widened as if he was about to have a heart attack.

"There's more?"

Zander and the boys roared with laughter. "Welcome to the Blethen Jones birthday experience," Zander said. "Honestly, just role with it. You'll come back down to earth soon, I promise."

B rushed out of the room with excitement flooding her veins, eager to see Tyr's face upon her return.

"Ready to meet your new daddy?" she said, reaching into the puppy cage in her garage and picking up the husky puppy sporting a red collar. She returned to the sitting room, peeking inside to show off Sigrún.

Tyr gasped.

"Tyr, I want you to meet Sigrún the Valkyrie. She's from your ancestral hometown and needs a home."

Tyr was beside himself with joy as B handed him the blue-eyed, husky puppy. Shaking his head and wearing the biggest grin, he chuckled as Sigrún licked his face. "Hey, girl," he said, fussing with her before turning to B, who had plonked herself on the floor between Zander's legs.

"She's for me?"

"Sure is!" B said, brimming with pride.

"And she goes where you go!" Zander said. "I've cleared it at church, so she can stay at the club with you, and you're welcome to bring her here when you stay over."

"You better!" Madoc said.

"Yeah, we want to play with her, too!" Rhys teased.

Tyr hugged her tightly. "How did you know?"

B and Zander laughed. "Everyone knows!" Zander said. "You cannae take your eye off your cell phone screensaver, so we figured you might like the real thing. We have the papers and a puppy starter kit in the garage, too. Welsh Cake will drop it all off at the club tomorrow morning."

Tyr's grin was wider than ever. "I'm speechless! I don't think I've ever been this happy."

Zander tussled his hair. "Let's just call it your official welcome to our family."

After an evening of fun, laughter and video games, everyone headed off to bed, the excitement proving too much as tired eyes said goodnight.

B slept for a couple of hours before waking. She wasn't sure what woke her from her sleep, putting it down to a dry mouth and wandering downstairs to fetch a glass of water.

B stepped onto the cold marble hall floor when Tyr caught her eye sitting on the sofa with Sigrún, stuffing his face with his favorite cookies, like a manic depressive.

I knew something wasn't right!

"Hmm, stress eating, good boy?" she said from the doorway.

Tyr jumped out of his skin as B took steps toward the sitting room's sofa, placing an arm around his shoulder.

Tyr appeared a little embarrassed. "Sorry I can't sleep."

"How about I make us a nice chai latte and you tell me what's bothering you?"

Tyr sighed into a smile.

B returned minutes later with two mugs, handing him one.

"Now, I don't want to pry, but from my experience, a problem shared is a problem halved."

Tyr took a sip of his latte before placing it on the coffee table. His hands fidgeted in his lap until B took hold of them.

"Take your time."

Tyr nodded, taking a moment to compose himself.

"My father called my cell tonight."

B leaned in, providing her undivided attention. She was aware of Tyr's estrangement from his family. "Oh."

Tyr stared at his hands, unable to make eye contact.

"He told me I have to go home."

B narrowed her eyes.

"And is that something you want?"

Tyr shook his head. "I told him my family is here now, but he's dangerous and I know he'll come for me. I can't go back there. The memories still torment me. I want to be rid of them and the torture they inflicted on me.

Upon her return from Marshalls, Tyr had recounted his upbringing to B. They chatted for hours over breakfast the day after B's return, with Tyr opening up a little, providing enough details pertaining to his ill treatment back home.

B placed her arm around his shoulder. "Hey, if you're happy here Tyr, you know we'll fight to the death for you."

"Yes, but I don't want any wolves getting hurt because of me. I'd rather go back to hell than see that happen."

"You're no' going anywhere, son," Zander said, startling them, appearing, shirtless, in the doorway.

Tyr sat up straight, watching his Prez sit beside him on the sofa.

Tyr averted his eyes, his apparent nervousness getting the better of him.

"Look at me, Tyr," Zander said.

Tyr raised his head with hesitation, looking like someone had instilled the fear of God into his fragile soul.

Zander gripped the back of his neck. "You have become a son to us, Tyr, and you belong here until you decide to leave. It's your choice whether you stay. No' us and no' your bully of a father."

Tyr pursed his lips as his face crumpled with emotion. He wasn't used to being showered with love and attention. "Prez, you don't understand, my father... My father is Prez of The Rus Reapers. If he says I need to go, nobody can stop him. He'll rain hellfire on the club like you've never seen."

Zander's facial expressions resembled a deer in headlights, shooting B a glare of concern while pulling Tyr into his embrace.

"Your father can be the King of bloody England for all I care, Tyr. You're my boy now, and I'll no' let him take you away. We'll have a church meeting in the morning, and you'll see that everyone's behind you."

Tyr held Zander like a scared child.

"Thank you, Prez."

Zander squeezed him, with a desolate look on his face, forcing B to shake her head in disgust for the situation as she stroked a sleeping Sigrún. Her heart ached for Tyr as she watched Zander console him.

Zander broke away first. "Right, get yourself and the pup to bed, busy day tomorrow and dinnae worry. We got this, pal, okay?"

Tyr nodded, scooping up Sigrún as B cupped his cheek. "Good night, my lovely," she said, watching him head upstairs.

Zander remained silent, standing to fetch a whiskey, and clattering the decanter in the room's corner. Knocking back a shot, he woke B from her troubled thoughts.

"Jeez, if it doesnae rain, it pours!"

"It's not his fault, Scottie. The boy is terrified."

Zander faced her with a serious rasp in his tone. "And he should be. I've heard the stories of Leif the Viking. His father's a psychopath."

B's face hardened. "Then I strongly suggest you diffuse this situation. Scottie, Tyr is hurting."

"What do you mean?"

B sipped her chai. "Tyr informed me of his treatment back home and let's just say, I'd happily behead the bastard for how he treated his son, and I'd love to tear out his mother's heart for allowing that shit to happen."

Zander became stern. "Darling, I'm ordering you to stay out of this."

B laughed. "I don't take orders, good boy. I give them, remember?"

Zander stepped forward, grimacing. "Welsh Cake, this is club business, and I'm the fucking Prez."

"Not in this house you're not, and not regarding my family. In this house, you're Scottie; the man who I adore. So, don't start with that misogynistic bullshit here!"

Zander palmed her cheeks. "Leave this alone. I dinnae want you getting hurt."

"Then I suggest you deal with this away from the club because if I see any of his family, I'll scratch their fucking eyes out."

Zander threw his hands in the air, turning his back on her. "God, you're so fucking impossible sometimes."

B approached, wrapping her arms around him and nibbling his earlobe.

"Dinnae do that Welsh cake! I'm fucking mad at you, remember?"

"Oh, come on. Really?" she said, leaving a trail of kisses down his neck. "But my new tattoos are all healed, and I want to play."

Zander's grimace transpired into a soft groan. "Fuck's sake. You've got me whipped, woman."

"Nope," she teased, reaching down into his boxer briefs.

Zander's mouth fell open as he gazed upon her. "I'm still pissed at you," he breathed.

"Oh, I know," she said, biting her lip and dropping his boxer briefs around his ankles.

"Fuck woman! You're gonnae be the death of me," he said, lifting her silk nightgown over her head. Tossing it onto the plush, cream carpet, he picked her up, wrapping her legs around his broad torso.

"Yeah, but you'll die happy!" she whispered in his ears while running her fingers through his hair.

"Yes, I fucking will! But I'm still gonnae drill you to this wall to ease my frustrations with you."

"I deserve that!"

"Hell, yeah, you fucking do! You've been a bad girl, Dragon, and now I need to punish you!" he said, pinning her against the wall next to the fireplace.

B stared into his lusty, frustration filled eyes. She understood his burdens regarding their potential baby dilemma and didn't want to add to his troubles with the Tyr situation.

"I'm sorry, Scottie," she whispered.

"For misbehaving. Dinnae worry, I'll soon set you right," he breathed through rugged breaths.

"No," she said, stopping him in his tracks.

Zander's brow furrowed, providing an inquisitive stare. "That there's a high chance we're about to endure another shit storm."

He tilted his head to ponder her words. "We play the cards we've been dealt, darling, and right now, I have a cracking hand. So how aboot we forget tomorrow because it's no' happened yet, and you allow me to release our tensions from today."

"Release away, big guy," she said, biting his lip.

"That's what I like to hear," he said, adjusting his grip to enter her.

Zander covered her mouth with his delicious lips, making her gasp into his mouth by filling her. It was as if she was unprepared for his size when he penetrated her and pressed his chest against hers.

"Too much too soon?" he teased, thrusting again and growling into her neckline.

"Scottie," she gasped.

"It's Prez tonight, darling! I need to do some unimaginable things to you and you're gonnae take it for me, aren't you?"

B's body quivered at his commanding tone. She had never experienced this level of arousal as he thrusted again, teasing her. "aren't you?"

"Yes," she moaned, glimpsing the determination in his eyes. Knowing Zander's recent doubts about his masculinity, B was determined to make him feel like a man tonight.

Zander nuzzled into her neck, kissing and sucking hard while increasing the tempo of his lusty thrusts with enough to force her to twitch with excitement.

Her body clambered to him, with her hands instinctively adopting a mind of their own, raking his back and pulling him close so he could devour her mouth; his tongue had never explored her mouth with such force.

Thrust after pleasurable thrust forced symphonic cries from her vibrant body as Zander became lost inside her. His vexation was clear as he stared into her eyes.

"Prez!" she whimpered, struggling for breath as his heavy chest rattled against hers. "I can't breathe!"

Zander peeled her off the wall, withdrawing from her long enough to drop onto one knee and lay her down on the carpet, next to the slow-burning fire. Spreading her legs with his, he lowered himself to gaze into her eyes, winking at her. "Better?"

B nodded, still in a state of shock from the way he took her, she struggled to collect herself as Zander penetrated her again, stretching her sex with his hard cock.

"God, you're beautiful," he said gruffly. His glowing, dilated eyes bored into her as he hovered over her, palming either side of her head.

B's body quivered at his heavy thrust, turned on by his rugged handsomeness, and Zander slowed, as if to calm himself, settling into a comfortable stride. "I'll start slow so you can catch your breath, but then I'm giving you everything!"

B shifted her hips to meet his, surprising him. "Don't hold back on me now, Prez. Finish what you started," she beamed.

Zander released a rough, growling laugh before dropping onto his elbows. "That's my woman," he said, driving himself into her.

B gripped his backside and circled her hips, encouraging him to rebuild his stride.

Zander became merciless, delivering thrust after mind-blowing thrust, making B writhe beneath him.

"Fuck, yes!" he growled, increasing his tempo. His bulging blue vein threatened to explode out of his forehead like a man possessed, taking her over and over as if his life depended on it.

B's toes curled and body twitched, her impending orgasm promising to rip through her body as Zander covered her lips with his, moaning hard into her mouth.

Overwhelmed by her senses, B bit into his chest to stifle her screaming; her orgasm spreading through her body like a euphoric disease, clenching around Zander and forcing him to bellow a thick, gravelly roar.

"Christ!" he roared in desperation, thrusting into her, encouraging his own release.

B did her best to aid him. Almost convulsing in pleasure, her body bucked, matching his chaotic rhythm with her hips until Zander released with his thunderous, Scottish tone. "Dragon, darling!"

He jerked in uncontrollable fits, his climax subduing him, making him pant into jagged breaths.

"Fuck!" he coughed, stilling with closed eyes above her and struggling to catch his breath.

B panted into her satisfied afterglow, vibrating on a love frequency for her Prez.

"Jeez!" he continued, opening his eyes, his breath steadier, "darling, you have no idea how much I needed that!"

B stroked his back. "Oh, I have a fair idea. I may not walk tomorrow."

A self-satisfied grin spread across Zander's face, his eyes twinkling with delight. "Full marks for me, then?"

"Damn right! Bloody hell, Scottie. I thought I was going to die."

Zander kissed her, "Good job you bit down. I've never heard you scream so loud. Fuck me, what a turn on!"

Staring at his chest, nervousness consumed her. "Shit, I've broken the skin. You're bleeding!" she said, sitting herself up to study his wound.

Zander rolled onto his back. "If that scars, I'll be over the fucking moon!" he teased, caressing her cheek.

B giggled, covering her hand with her mouth. "Sorry!"

"Dinnae be sorry, darling. I'm no' complaining," he said, pulling her on top of him. "In fact, I may just demand you do it more often."

"Take me like that again and I'll bite whatever you want, good boy. Just make sure I'm breathing afterwards. The kids need me."

CHAPTER FOUR
Brother!

Mateo sat at his older brother's bedside, watching him struggle to breathe. Anton had become a shell of a man since a crazed- Irishman attacked him outside his club a couple of years previously.

Anton had got handsy with a woman close to the Irishman, who reeked revenge on the club, leaving Anton with a broken jaw, nose, three broken ribs, a collapsed lung and a ruptured spleen.

Mateo's flashback corrupted his mind as he sat next to his sleeping older brother's bedside. He had just secured another deal as a pharmaceutical conglomerate when he received the call from his mother requesting his presence at the hospital. The doctors quickly took Anton to surgery for a splenectomy and to repair the damage to his lung.

His eighty-year-old mother's frail face and distraught eyes flickered at him as she fought back heartbreaking tears. She always worried about Anton following his COPD diagnosis a week after his fortieth birthday.

Wrapping his mother in his jacket and holding her in the cold waiting room chair for 7 hours was torture for him. Unbeknown to them, Anton would never be the same following the brutal attack.

Upon his release from hospital, Mateo hoped Anton would forgo his duties as the president of the Greyhound MC, only to receive his brother's angry wrath, branding the idea ludicrous. Anton was determined to ride again, despite his declining health.

The club planned to vote him out on account of the fact he could no longer ride or breathe without oxygen. Instead, Mateo threatened their lives and business, ordering them to stand down.

Mateo provided ninety-five percent of the club's revenue from his illegal distribution of fentanyl and methamphetamine in unadulterated form. His business allowed for him to make millions by hiding his shipments amongst other drugs, pressing them into pills and packaging it in plain sight within his pharmaceutical cargo. His products came directly from the cartel in Mexico, entering the US through legal ports of entry unchallenged. However. Mateo ensured his man on the inside, working for the US Customs and Border Protection Agency, always diverted any unwanted attention from his illegal cargo, providing him with an abundance of wealth for his troubles.

The role of the Greyhound MC was simple: distribute his drugs from their factory, a few miles from their clubhouse.

Mateo had a series of MCs doing his bidding. A graduate, he was smart, pushing his drugs across the US via street-level thugs like the Greyhound MC.

Staring at his weak older brother's strained face, witnessing his struggle fueled him with rage. Anton's injuries and ill health had slowed the distribution of Mateo's illegal drug production, resulting in Mateo seeking and employing other one-percenter MCs to ensure his products remained in a state of supply and demand. The unknown Irishman had not only left his brother with life-changing disabilities, but he had also cost Mateo a pretty penny, and to Mateo, that was unacceptable.

CHAPTER FIVE
Birthday Bash!

Tyr's birthday bash was in full swing at the packed MC. His adrenaline-filled consciousness was still recovering from the surprise he received upon entering the club. Tyr indulged in copious amounts of alcohol and his pick of women before steadying himself at the bar.

He smiled, allowing himself a moment of happiness as he sat digesting his surroundings and joy filled the air as everyone celebrated his birthday. He ushered to a prospect to fetch him a beer while waiting for Tiny to finish engaging with his latest bunny. Twisting the cap off, he shuddered as uneasiness swept through his Viking bones. Tyr shifted his attention to the club's entrance, cowering as a familiar face swaggered through the club toward him with two other burly men.

Tyr couldn't breathe, paralyzed to the bar stool and trying to muster the courage to compose himself.

"Hello little brother," Ragnar said, gripping onto his shoulder, sneering at him.

"I'm n-not going anywhere," Tyr stammered. A first since high school.

Ragnar laughed as he played with the matchstick between his teeth. "I'm not here for you," he said, swaggering over to Zander's table and studying B in his lap as if she was a prize pig at a fair.

Tyr gulped watching B, Frankie, Tiffany, Jimmy and Marshall give him the evil eye.

"You need an invitation to enter my club, boy," Zander said, glaring up at him.

"I'm the VP of the…"

Zander slid B off his lap, standing and towering over him. "I know who you are, and if I ever catch you looking at my old lady again, I'll rip your wee face off."

Ragnar snorted, nudging his company as if he was mocking Zander. "Easy old man, I come with a message to inform you of my father's request to meet."

Zander puffed out his head and cracked his neck. "If your father wants to meet me, tell him to go through the proper channels and tell him I dinnae appreciate unwanted visitors at my club. Appointment only, asshole," he said, poking his chest.

Ragnar smirked. "Alright, have it your way," he said, turning to leave.

Tyr's head remained fixed on his beer as Ragnar and his entourage passed the bar.

Ragnar whispered in his ear, "see you soon baby brother. I look forward to watching you feel faðir's wrath." Slapping the backside of the honey closest to the exit and laughing, he strutted out of the building.

Zander approached Tyr, sitting on the stool next to him. "You okay, son?"

Tyr stared at his beer bottle. "I hate him!"

"Dinnae ever be scared in your own home, Tyr," Zander said, placing an arm around him. "He cannae hurt you here, my boy. No one can. Besides, that lanky streak of piss isn't fooling anyone. Behind that false confidence, there's a scared wee boy. I can see it in his eyes."

Tyr glanced up at him. "You think so?"

Zander reached over the bar for a beer, twisting the cap off. "I know so. I also know you'd wipe the floor with him, if only you would work on your inner demons and show up for yasel'. Tyr, you're no' a wee boy anymore. You're twice the size of him and you're a wolf. My wolf!"

Tyr sighed. "Thanks Prez. It's just that I've spent my life beaten down by him."

Zander stood to head back to his table, "then maybe it's time to stand up for yasel' and show him you're no' wee anymore. The next time he picks a fight with you, Tyr, show him exactly who you are. Show him the man you've become, and I promise you, he'll no' bully you again."

"Thanks Prez. Thanks for mentoring me and helping me grow into a man. He won't push me around anymore."

"That's the hammer! Now come on, this is your party. Go have some fucking fun."

Zander tossed and turned that night as B slept next to him. Frustration wreaked havoc in his mind, thinking about Tyr and his family. Zander wanted to protect Tyr. Only he and B had had their fair share of trauma, and Zander became desperate for peace. On the verge of marrying his soulmate, the fear of another war loomed in his mind. An unnerving, cold pang in the pit of his stomach repeated like an old alarm clock, creating wave after wave of anxiety, as if intuition was warning him of the troubled waters ahead. The fear of the unknown stopped him from sleeping, forcing him to climb out of bed with volatile restlessness. He chucked on his jeans and boots, making way for the bar with the eeriness of the night sky following through the passing bar windows.

Despite the stench of booze and passed out bodies crammed in every crevice of the bar; Zander felt at peace, knowing everyone slept soundly tonight.

He dragged his feet around the bar, reaching for the absinthe to pour himself a double, hoping the toxic-looking liquor would be enough to help him sleep.

The wind rattled against the window, providing a welcoming distraction from his troubled mind as he sat on his favorite bar stool and knocked back the shot. Taking one last glance over his shoulder to ensure the security of the club, he turned to see Jimmy entering the bar.

"Cannae sleep?" he asked.

Jimmy shook his head. "Nah, man. All the pussy in the world couldn't help me shake that jumped up prick waltzing into the club tonight."

He stepped behind the bar, retrieving a clean glass from the counter shelf. "What are you drinking that shit for?"

Zander shrugged. "I figured it might knock me out."

"Wreck your liver maybe. Put that shit away and grab the whiskey."

Zander stepped off his stool to switch out the absinthe for the whiskey then poured them both a drink.

"What are your thoughts on tonight, Prez? That smarmy prick looked like the cat who got the cream."

Zander raised an eyebrow. "The wee prick has balls; I'll give him that. Did you see Tyr mind? He was like a scared wee bairn. I've never seen him look so small. I mean, he welcomes a good brawl, only big brother scared him shitless."

Jimmy threw his drink down his open gullet, raising his glass to Zander to pour him another. "Yeah. I don't get it, Zand. Tyr is huge compared to him."

"Aye, but Leif has conditioned that laddie into believing he's weak." I had a chat with him about standing up to his brother. Whether he takes the advice is another thing, mind."

"And what about his dad? We've heard the stories, man. He's a whack-job! We need to play smart here."

Zander rested his elbows on the bar countertop. "I'm no' giving him Tyr. Tyr is afraid of them. He's ours Jimmy!"

Jimmy nodded. "Well, we've been to war over less, and I have every faith in our pack. Might be worth drafting Uskiville in to show strength in numbers if Leif appears."

"Aye, good call," Zander said, now tapping his fingers on the bar.

Jimmy narrowed his eyes to him. "What's up with the fucking tapping? You've been doing it for days now?"

"I quit smoking and I'm desperate for a cigarette. I cannae seem to calm my shit since I stopped."

"Why did you quit?"

Zander stared into his whiskey. "Welsh Cake and I had a check-up. I'm desperate for a bairn since becoming part of her family."

Jimmy beamed with pride. "That's great man! I'm happy for you."

"No, pal. It's no'"

Jimmy's puzzled expression rippled across his face. "I thought you wanted a family?"

Zander pinched his nose between his thumb and forefinger, "Aye, it's all I want." He turned to face Jimmy with a desolate frown. "I've got a low sperm count, Jimmy. Our odds of conceiving are pretty fucking low. So, cigarettes are out."

Jimmy dropped his head in despair for his brother. "Shit. I'm sorry man. How did B take it?"

Zander laughed, almost choking on his drink as Jimmy stared in amusement. "Oh, she sunbathed in the pissing rain. It dinnae faze her Jimmy. She has this blind, fucking belief that everything is gonnae work out. I tell you, whatever she's on, I want some because I feel like a failure, yet again."

Jimmy gripped his head, squeezing it. "Brother, whatever's meant for you won't miss you. If you and B are meant to have beautiful Celt babies, you will, regardless of having a low sperm count."

Zander nodded into a smile. "I see my old ladies' faith is resonating throughout the club these days."

Jimmy climbed off his stool, collecting their glasses to place in the bar's dishwasher. "Well, it's better to have faith than to feel miserable, man. Look at me. I can't even get a woman?"

Zander tapped the bar as if he was recalling a memory. "Speaking of which, B is bringing someone by the club tomorrow who she thinks you'll like."

Jimmy stopped in his tracks, his eyes screaming with excitement. "Okay. Who? Is she fit?"

"She's no' my cuppa tea like, but Welsh Cake thinks you'll hit it off."

"Oh, great! She's fuck ugly then?"

Zander backtracked. "I dinnae say that! I said she's no' my cuppa tea. You may like her. She's a nice enough lassie. Curvy, and she has massive boobs!"

"So, she's big?"

Zander headed toward the dorms. "It's rude to talk aboot a lassies' weight, brother. Just give the lassie a chance. She's a braw wee lass, and you might like something other than the skanks you fuck!"

"So, she's a hog with a personality, then?"

Zander spun around to face him. Exasperation leapt from his face. "Look pal. She's an honest lassie. I'm just no' sure you're ready for nice. You seem to like them filthy bunnies too much."

"Yeah, because they're young, hot, and do as they're told."

Zander rolled his eyes. "Aren't you fed up with false and dirty pussy, pal? What I will say is fill your boots while you can. Anyone no' snagged by a patch this week is gone. I'm sick of seeing them to be honest and I'll be glad when this club no longer looks like a whore house!"

CHAPTER SIX
Meeting With the Enemy

Zander and B emerged from Zander's room a little after ten a.m. to the smell of bacon ushering them into the kitchen, where Jimmy stood over the grill.

"Morning, lovebirds!" he teased. "Grab yourselves a plate before feeding time at the zoo turns into chaos at the club."

Zander laughed, watching B, who couldn't move quickly enough. She loved Jimmy's breakfasts. He would brush his bacon with maple and make poached eggs like she'd never tasted. Helping herself, she loaded her plate, missing the sausage and mushroom while Zander shook his head.

"The two best bits of a breakfast and she dinnae eat them, Jimmy."

"I know, man. Are you sure you want to marry her?"

"I think I may have to rethink my options," he teased, receiving a clip around the ear from B.

"Ow, I'm kidding!" he chuckled.

"Fine by me, asshole. You can stay here tonight. Find yourself a bunny before they leave for good."

Zander heaved. "No thanks, darling. I have all I need," he said, kissing her cheek and sitting opposite her at the table.

"No point groveling now, Prez. I'm heading to the Sultry Slalom after this."

Zander's mouth fell open. "That's no' fucking funny!"

B shrugged, chewing her bacon. "If you can't handle the heat, good boy, get out of the kitchen!"

Zander's head shook in dismay, grimacing as Jimmy laughed.

"Dinnae fucking laugh. You started this!"

Jimmy placed his hands over his heart. "Me? I did no such thing. You came out with that awful comment, Prez, not me. Welsh Cake knows I was joking," he said, adding extra bacon to her plate and winking at her.

"Of Course! Jimmy is an angel. He would never do me dirty like that," B teased, stifling a giggle.

Zander chomped on his sausage. "Oh, you bacon slut! If I knew you were that easy over bacon, I would have joined Noah on his ride outs to Uskiville with a pig on my back to win you over!"

B spat her tea everywhere, choking in laughter.

Humorous roars erupted in the kitchen as they sat at the end of the redwood table.

"You pair get fucking worse," Jimmy said, wiping hysterical tears from his rosy cheeks. *"Bacon slut!* Fucking hell, where did we get you two from?"

"Across the pond in Celt land. Only special people come from there." B grinned.

"Oh, you're special alright. Psycho fucking special. It's why you both work so well together."

Zander reached across the table, grabbing B's hand. "And soon, she'll be Mrs. Fucking Special McGovan. Isn't that right, darling?"

Tiny popped his head into the kitchen with a grumpy demeanor. "Having a fucking tea party without me? The bar phone has been ringing like fucking crazy. I had to climb out of my pit to get it. Clean your fucking ears out, will you? Some prick is on the phone asking for Prez!"

"Aye, alright? What's the matter? Woke you from your beauty sleep, did we, pretty boy?"

A bare-chested Tiny grunted and stumbled back to his old room.

Zander took the last sip of his coffee and wiped his face on a paper napkin before heading to the bar to take the call, leaving B to finish her breakfast.

"Hello," Zander said with enthusiasm.

"Zander McGovan?"

"Aye."

"Leif Erling. I've heard a lot about you, Celtic Warrior!"

Zander's tone turned serious. "Then you should know I dinnae like unannounced visitors!"

"I apologize. My son, Ragnar, can be a little hotheaded. My instructions were explicit. Make contact prior to visiting. The boy's ignorance of etiquette is his downfall. Please? I'd like to arrange a meeting halfway between our clubs."

"Oh, aye, and what's this about? If it's regarding Tyr, he's old enough to decide where he lives, and as his Prez, I'll support whatever decision he makes," Zander said, making his point clear.

"And I respect that. Tyr is grateful for your guidance, and I owe you a debt of gratitude for taking him under your wing. He's become a man under your reign."

"Oh, he was already a man!"

The phone line went quiet, making Zander narrow his eyes. "If it's no' Tyr you're wanting, then how can I help?"

The gruff voice rippled down the line in a jarring tone. "Make no bones about it. My son belongs to The Rus, but right now I have more immediate concerns. I want to propose a business opportunity between The Rus Reapers and The Gray Wolves."

Zander's eyes bulged from his head as he kicked the fridge door. "No offense, pal, but we're clean. Been straight for a bit now. Drugs might've been The Pitbull's bag but allow me to be clear. It's no' mine. Never will be!"

"Ah, we no longer move in that production line. See, my son Erik, crossed the line with our wholesaler, almost got himself stitched up by NARCO. We're looking to follow in Sunnyville's footsteps with legit business. You're building an empire, Zander. Teach me how to do the same with The Rus Reapers."

Zander grew mute, scratching his head. B would never sign off on any business with The Rus Reapers, knowing how they had treated Tyr. He, too, was not keen.

Leif continued. "My club is dying, Celtic Warrior, and we have mouths to feed. I have had members disappear and not return. I need to secure the club's future. Now I have some promising ideas moving forward with my joinery business, but I require help with the capital in exchange for a percentage of the business. If you would allow me to show you my business plan, I think we could both become very rich."

Zander reached into the fridge for a can of soda, cracking it open and taking a gulp.

"And if I agree to meeting you, you'll back off Tyr?"

Leif went quiet once again.

"Hey, take it or leave it, pal."

"Deal. Tyr can remain in Sunnyville for now."

Zander smiled. "And to be clear. There's no obligation to commit to any business. I'll listen, but if it's no' in alignment with us, no hard feelings, yeah?"

"Agreed! I will honor our agreement like you honor my son."

"Right, time and place?"

CHAPTER SEVEN
Clarabelle

B headed across the parking lot after spending an hour in the office, catching up with gym paperwork. Excited to greet her friend, she walked toward the mustard, clapped-out beetle parked near the bistro where Clarabelle was emerging from.

"Morning Belle, how are we this morning?"

Clarabelle's bright green summer dress clung to her voluptuous frame, as she greeted B with a warm, southern smile, wearing red lipstick and a yellow flower in her hair.

"Morning! Ahh, I'm so excited," she screeched, shaking B. "B, I can't thank you enough for this. My first job since Chase started school. You have no idea how grateful I am. I won't let you down, I promise! Now where's m-"

B placed her hands on her shoulders. "Breathe, lovely girl. Take a moment to compose yourself," she said, sensing the nerves emanating from Clarabelle's aura.

Clarabelle pursed her lips into a smile. She took a breath and exhaled, flicking her long, black hair over her shoulders. "Sorry, you're right. Oh, who am I kidding?" she gushed. "I can't help it! B, you've given me a chance to better myself and I'm just so happy."

B laughed, placing an arm around her shoulder, directing her toward the bistro. "Now, remember, there's some big characters here, so you need to adopt the same attitude you do at school. Imagine yourself at another school bake sale. I've seen you keep those stroppy teenagers in line. You need to apply that here."

"Oh, they'll be fine!" Clarabelle said, brushing B off as an overprotective friend. "Now, I have my portfolio of baked delights. What do you think Jimmy would like me to start with?"

"Well, he's about to find out you're working with him, so let's get over that hurdle first."

Clarabelle stopped in her tracks, flopping like an upset teenage girl. "B, you promised you'd talk to him."

B grinned into her humorous tone. "I am right now," she said, ushering her toward the bistro's entrance. "So, haul ass woman."

She stomped her feet. "Wait! What if he doesn't like me?"

"Jimmy loves everyone. He's a big pussy cat when you get to know him. He'll love you!"

Clarabelle stepped closer before hesitating again. "What if he doesn't?"

B shrugged into a chuckle. "You'll figure it out. Belle, you got this."

Clarabelle's panicked face threatened B with tears until B stepped toward her, taking her hands. "Why do I call you Belle?"

She blinked into a nervous smile. "Because I'm your beautiful baking friend whose cheeriness wakes everyone like a bell tower."

"Exactly. I understand this means a lot to you. Putting your stamp on the world with your amazing baking talent. I wouldn't have brought you in if I thought it would go wrong. The world needs to see you shine, lovely girl. You've been hiding at the school bake sale for too long. Volunteering your time is honorable, but now it's time to fill your own cup first. Now get your ass in the bistro."

B took her hand, practically dragging her inside where Zander and Jimmy sat eating breakfast.

"Morning darling," Zander said, jumping up to greet them and kissing B on the cheek. "Sorry, I ran out on you early this morning. Urgent club business."

"And is that sorted?" B asked.

Zander took her by the elbow, escorting her across the bistro and leaving Clarabelle to introduce herself to Jimmy.

Zander's stern face wreaked of trouble. "We're riding out this morning to meet Leif. After he made contact this morning, I called a church meeting. The club has agreed we need to hear him out. He has a business proposal."

"Fuck right off!" B snapped in anger, her face turning all shades of red.

"Now, hold o-,"

"Uh, no! You may be Prez, good boy, but this is my fucking business. If that prick steps one foot on my property, I'll smash his bloody face in, and don't tell me you're taking Tyr?"

"Hey, Clarabelle," Zander said, acknowledging her and trying to distract B from releasing her Dragon eyes.

Clarabelle and Jimmy exchanged glances.

"How about I get you a coffee, doll face?" Jimmy said, escorting her into the kitchen.

B scowled at Zander.

"Dinnae look at me like I'm a monster!"

B's venomous face stared him down. "I'm not looking at you like you're a monster. I'm looking at you like you're an absolute prick! You're seriously making me question whether I should bloody marry you, asshole!"

Zander gripped his jaw in disbelief. "Really?" he snapped. "What fucking choice do I have, Welsh Cake? He wants to meet and let me tell you, nobody refuses a meet with Leif, especially when his son is in the mix."

B paced the bistro. "You're not taking Tyr. You will literally have to go through me, sunshine. Feel free to meet Leif the prick, hear him out, whatever, but let's be clear, I'm not doing business with him."

Zander gripped the edge of the dining chair before ruffling his hair. His face resembled an angry steam train. "You're making my life difficult. This is club business."

B snarled. "I've told you, not when it comes to my family or my finances. He's rotten to the core and I won't stand for it!" Her chest pumped frantically as she sensed a loss of control wreaking havoc on her body.

Zander placed the chair to one side, stepping forward and taking her hands. "Welsh Cake. I know you're pissed, and I love how you protect him like a dragon protects her fucking eggs or whatever, but he must go to that meeting."

B attempted to pull away as Zander tugged her back. "Listen. If he hides here, he looks weak. We all look weak, darling, and Leif will crush us like a bug. Tyr needs to show his family he's no' afraid of them and so do we. I will let nothing happen to him. You have my word."

B inhaled hard, squeezing her eyelids together. "I don't like it!"

Zander wrapped his arms around her waist. "Neither do I. Look, I'm leaving Jimmy here and taking Frankie and Marshall to show our wealth of experience. We'll be back before you know it, and that's it. We'll get married and forget about that dickhead."

B closed her eyes and Zander kissed her lips, offering her inside his mouth as B reciprocated.

"Promise me you won't do business with him, Scottie."

"I cannae do business with him, anyway. You're my sugar momma, remember?"

"Less of the sugar, momma. I'm younger than you."

Zander burst out laughing. "What, by a whole two fucking minutes?"

"Six months, actually, but who's counting?" she said as he pulled her in, leaving a trail of kisses down her neck.

Her mind scattered like puzzle pieces as Jimmy's shouts echoed from the kitchen.

Zander rolled his eyes at the ceiling before they both rushed in.

"You're replacing me!" Jimmy barked at B.

Confusion splashed across her war face. "What the fuck are you dribbling now? No! I've invited Belle to join us. She's a fantastic baker Jimmy, look at her portfolio. She's gonna work across the compound and I'm hoping you can both come up with a menu for the live lounge bar and grill and we'll see how Belle's baked goods fit in with the bistro menu."

Belle appeared terrified as Jimmy cast her a look of disgust. "Consulting me would have been nice."

B pressed her hands into the stainless-steel counter, "Oh, and how many times last week did I tell you we needed to talk? About fifty-fucking-three! A Welsh woman only has so much fucking patience. Now do us all a favor, stop whining like a bitch, so we can sit down, and I can introduce Belle properly. And as for you," she said, turning to Zander, "you leave without finalizing the details this morning, you'll be eating wedding cake on your own and I'll be on our honeymoon as a singleton."

Zander and Jimmy glared at one another like a pair of sulking, misbehaving teenagers in the principal's office.

"Well, come the fuck on, then?" B snapped, sending them back into the bistro's dining area.

Turning to Clarabelle, she gave her a sympathetic smile. "You, okay?"

Clarabelle's eyes were wide as she giggled with nervousness. "Whoa! You're scary when you're angry."

B couldn't help but calm around her, smirking. "Seriously, good girl. That's what you took from that shit storm?"

Clarabelle shrugged. "When men speak, I just zone out. I just saw his mouth move, but honestly, all I heard was yadda, yadda, yadda."

B whipped her head back in laughter, wrapping an arm around her. "You're gonna be just fine here. Come on."

B and Clarabelle left the kitchen to sit with Jimmy and Zander in a booth near the window. Both Jimmy and Zander had faces like bulldogs chewing a wasp as B and Clarabelle made hot beverages.

"Right," B said, sliding into the booth. "Jimmy, you're going to work with Clarabelle over the coming weeks to ascertain new provisions for the live lounge and how her baked goods fit into your menu. I asked her to create protein bakes for the gym and shake shack. She'll shadow you until the wedding, and then you can discuss future arrangements together.

"Great!" Clarabelle cheered.

"Fantastic!" Jimmy teased.

B glared at him. "Jimmy, nobody is replacing you. The two of you can create something amazing together. Maximize profits."

Jimmy leaned onto the table. "You know the saying, too many cooks in the kitchen?"

B bit her tongue. "What's the matter Jimmy? Scared my girl is going to upstage you?"

Zander choked on his bagel, making Jimmy blow a gasket. "No. No. Why would I? This is my fucking bistro. I'm the manager!"

"Then you won't fear a little healthy competition? You never know, you might just learn something," Clarabelle piped up, surprising B with her newfound confidence.

"Fine!" Jimmy spat through gritted teeth.

"Great," Clarabelle said, pushing her portfolio across the table. "Go ahead, explore and select what you want, okay?"

B tried to hide her smugness. The laughter inside threatening to release in a roar.

"On that note, I'll leave you to it. I have business to address at the gym."

"Oh, great! So, you get to play with weights while I babysit," Jimmy snapped.

"Oh, Jimmy. You've got me all wrong," Clarabelle said with innocence in her tone. "No, sweetie, I'm about to show you how it's done. You won't find anything better than my corn bread and apple pie," she said, giving B a wink.

CHAPTER EIGHT
Ride Out

Zander straddled his motorcycle ready to leave, watching B straighten Tyr's cut like a proud momma bear, saying farewell to her son getting drafted until Frankie nudged him, distracting him.

"She still pissed at you?" he asked.

"Nah, no' really. Welsh Cake knows I'm right. She just hurts for him and wants to protect him."

"She's always been like that. B knows, hurt people, hurt people and her gift in this world is to guide them onto an alternative path. I've seen what's she's like with him. She was the same with me when I arrived at Uskiville."

Zander tilted his head inquisitively. "Aye?"

Frankie nodded, straddling his own motorcycle. "Your future wife is an empath; in case you haven't noticed. She senses other people's pain and while she's become a master of transmuting that shit, she's well aware when the people she loves can't."

"Aye. Then she protects them with her scary fucking Dragon temperament."

Frankie reversed his motorcycle, lining it up with Zanders. "You know it! What bothers me is her selflessness; she charges in without assessing the situation first. Bull in a china shop springs to mind."

Zander pulled on his riding gloves. "Aye, it's a worry. That dragon fire will land her in trouble one day and it scares the hell out of me!"

Frankie cast him a firm stare.

"Dinnae worry. I've learned better than trying to change her. That lassie burns a fire in my soul and if helping people is her bag, then I'll no' stop her being herself and doing so. I'm just glad she'll always have us to protect her from the fiery side of herself."

Frankie grinned. "Glad to fucking hear it!"

Marshall and Tyr approached them as Zander watched B from afar.

"We ready to go?" he asked Tyr.

Tyr nodded with uncertainty.

"Dinnae worry, pal. You're coming straight back home to Sunnyville. Otherwise, *Móðir* over there will tear me a new one."

Tyr laughed as Frankie gripped his shoulder. "Besides, I'm still training you up. The club's security won't sort itself and me and my old man can't do it alone, can we, dad?"

"Nope. You're needed in the dream team," Marshall added.

Zander burst out laughing, "dream team, oh, aye! More like, queen team," he teased. "Come on, let's get the fuck out of here!"

Zander and the Gray Wolves sped down the highway full throttle, knowing it would take most of the day to reach their destination. Opting for a more neutral territory, Zander and Leif agreed to meet in a busy parking lot in central Fresno, after Zander turned down the idea of meeting in a location suggested by Leif. He didn't trust Leif, so meeting in a busy theatre parking lot at four p.m. seemed logical. Leif would be less likely to cause a scene in broad daylight.

The pack had just met the Uskiville chapter at a local rest stop to ensure they showed the strength of their MC, with Mack more than happy to oblige, taking his place just behind Zander as they headed out.

Zander felt free, favoring his hightail, open face helmet, allowing the wind to dance across his face as he pelted down the open road. Rideout's were always a thrill to him, the adrenaline always lighting a fire in him as his machine roared between his legs. Riding was escapism for him, meditation that couldn't be replicated elsewhere. It was just him, his brothers, and the open road today, providing an exhilarating sense of pride as he led his pack.

They had made multiple stops for gas and food before finally reaching Fresno, with Tiny being the vocalist every time they passed a fast-food outlet, causing frustration within the ranks. They were two miles out when Zander called Tyr.

"Time to put your big boy pants on, son. Ride up front behind Mack and me," he spoke through his microphone.

Tyr made his way to them, overtaking his brothers, placing himself where Zander instructed before they reached the parking lot.

"This isn't right, Prez," Tyr said, calling him back.

"What do you mean?"

"My Faðir has a powerful pack of over sixty men. There's about ten here."

"Dinnae worry, pal. Remember what I said. They cannae hurt you anymore," Zander said, pulling up in the parking bays opposite The Rus Reapers.

Stepping off his bike, Zander removed his gloves and helmet and walked toward Leif with Mack, Tiny, and Frankie, leaving Tyr and the rest of the pack straddling their bikes.

"A strong pack you have, Celtic Warrior," Leif said.

"Leif," Zander said, shaking his hand. "This is Mack, President of our Uskiville chapter, Tiny, his VP. Frankie, here is my SOA and Marshall."

"No VP of your own here?" he quizzed, casting his eyes to Zander's entourage.

Zander grinned, "I've a strong enough pack to leave plenty at home,"

"I didn't realize your pack had grown so large."

"Aye, with our empire expanding, we've had to increase our membership capacity. You know, needs of the business," he shrugged.

"And does my son have permission to talk to his father?"

Zander glanced over his shoulder at Tyr's tight jawline. "Tyr doesn't need my permission, Leif. If he wants to talk to you, he can. Now, let's focus on business, shall we?"

Leif paused before extending his arm ahead of them. "Walk with me. Allow us to discuss the future."

Zander walked across the parking lot with Leif to a nearby cafe as Mack, Tiny, and Frankie walked a couple of yards behind them, accompanied by Ragnar and the two burly men who followed him into the bar the night before, leaving both The Rus Reaper and Gray Wolves remaining pack members in the parking lot, staring each other down.

"So, what do you want with my club?" Zander asked, adding sugar to his coffee.

Leif sat back in the creaking cafe chair, his weight placing strain on the furniture. "I want to extend my joinery business. San Diego provides enough to put mead in my belly but not the financial security the powder used to bring. I need stability, and I think your club can help with that."

"How so?"

"You have somehow developed an abundance of wealth yourself, yes? Your old lady, she is wealthy?"

Zander swallowed his coffee, refraining from allowing his blood to boil. "Aye, she's a grafter with a good business head on her. Sensible with her investments."

"Hmm. Why did she choose Gray Wolves? Protection?"

Mack released a chuckle, diverting Leif's attention from the conversation.

"Something funny?"

Mack waved his hand, smiling out the window. "Sorry, just ignore me. Somebody fell over outside. Carry on. Pretend I'm not here."

"You laugh at other's misfortune?"

Mack turned to face him. "Sometimes. What business is that of yours?"

Leif smiled. "No judgment. Perhaps it tells me something about your character."

"And what's that then?" Mack enquired, stretching into a grin.

"How about we discuss what we drove five hours to discuss? He doesn't concern you, Leif. You want my help? Out with it!" Zander barked.

Leif's attention returned to Zander. "You're a born leader, Celtic Warrior. I like the way you demand respect. You may want to strengthen your bonds with stronger brothers."

Mack stood from his chair, stopping as Zander raised a palm. "Take a walk Irish. I've no' time for bullshit today, and you," he said to Leif. "You want my help, remember? I dinnae come here for advice. Now, what do you want?"

Leif stroked his mustache between his thumb and forefinger, watching Mack whistle as he left the cafe. "I would like to meet with your old lady. Discuss a proposal. I wish to expand my business across California and Oregon. Provide profitable housing under The Rus Reaper brand. The market is there for the taking. I just need help to raise the capital."

Zander sat back in his seat, folding his arms across his chest, aware he was being tested by Leif. "You dinnae need to talk to my old lady. She'll do as she's told! It's my club, my rules. Keeping the business in her name is for legal reasons. She bends to my will. Now what's in it for The Gray Wolves?"

Leif grinned, slamming his hand on the table. "I knew it!" he cheered. "Ragnar said you had forsaken the ways of old. He said your club has gone soft in the Mauler's absence. You prove him wrong. I see you," he said, pointing at him with glee. "You're smart. Marry rich, build strong! Women need to know their place. I am glad that rings true in your MC."

Zander smirked, shaking his head. "Well, we're not married yet. That's next week, my lassie understands the needs of the MC."

"Oh, this is splendid! The Rus Reapers will attend! We'll discuss this further at your MC. I would like to meet this old lady of yours. I will bring my plans to your club so we can talk further."

Zander's heart sank. "Hold your horses, Prez. What's in it for us?"

Leif's smile vanished. "Well, five percent, of course?"

Zander laughed. "And how much capitol are we fronting you?"

Leif's head swung like a pendulum, mulling over the question. "Shall we say half a million to start?"

Zander burst out laughing and stood to leave. "Do I look fucking stupid? Come on, lads, this joker is wasting my time."

Zander attempted to leave, and Leif dived up from his chair to stop him. "Alright, alright. Fifteen?"

Zander stuck out his hand. "Goodbye Leif. Goodluck with your business. I'm rooting for ya, pal!"

Zander pushed his way outside, eyeballing Ragnar, and started back to the parking lot.

"Twenty-five percent!" Leif shouted after him.

Zander turned with a sparkle in his eye. "Call it fifty and we'll talk. Until then, I'll keep Tyr safe," he said, swaggering down the road.

"That went well," Frankie said, laughing. "I thought you fucked it, and he was coming to the wedding for a second there."

"Dinnae even joke, pal. That was our initial test from that bastard. He would have crushed us like a bug if I'd made one wrong move. He's trying to figure us out!"

Frankie looked both ways before heading across the road. "You handled it, though."

Zander huffed. "He'll be in touch, and we'll be ready when he does!"

Zander climbed on his motorcycle, a little unnerved by Leif and his pack observing him preparing to leave.

"Well?" Mack asked.

"Get on ya fucking bike. We'll discuss back at the club, you stupid prick?"

"What?" he joked. "Come on, protection? That shite was funny!"

Zander laughed. "Get on your fucking bike, knob head," he said, starting his motorcycle and glancing at a fearful Tyr.

Giving him a wink, he signaled his pack to move out, only to be hailed by Leif.

Stopping a whisker from a white-faced Leif, he witnessed the relief across his face, making Zander a little uneasy.

What's his game?

He switched off his engine, raising his hand to halt the pack. "Can I help you with something, pal?" he asked, basking in control without testing Leif's patience.

"Fifty percent. We'll take it! Now, I'll bring my plans to your MC on Monday morning. We shall talk about the future then and celebrate our alliance at your wedding. Until then," he grinned, startling Zander, who climbed from his motorcycle to embrace him.

"Pleasure doing business. Your business plan better be sound, brother," he warned.

CHAPTER NINE
We Have Real Problems

Shit! Shit! What the fuck is he up to?

Zander cursed himself as he sped up the highway. His phone rang in his ear. "Yeah."

"What the fuck, Prez. You can't bring him back to Sunnyville. And the wedding? He'll have a field day when he sees B and all her sass," Frankie shouted.

"You think I dinnae know that? Jeez, what the fuck was I supposed to say? Cross him and he crushes us, invite him, he fucks us."

"Fucking hell. We have real fucking problems. Convincing B to act like an old lady when he arrives, for one, and resolving this deal without starting a war is another issue."

"Let's just return to church and discuss!"

CHAPTER TEN
Bistro Bitching!

Clarabelle led the conversation, trying to convince a grumpy Jimmy to take an interest in her portfolio. In contrast, Jimmy prioritized preparations for a busy day at the bistro.

Clarabelle thrust her portfolio under his nose, disturbing his onion chopping. "If you'll just take a minute."

"Listen Doll Face, I'm sure your food is great, but I've got prep to do and a bistro to open soon. If you want to help, grab an apron, and fix up something I can add to the specials board. Nothing too fancy. People here like homemade grub!"

Clarabelle snapped her portfolio closed. "I can do that on the condition you spend some time on my portfolio when it goes quiet?"

"Ha! I'm guessing B hasn't told you how busy the weekends are?" he mocked, reaching for the garlic. "It's Friday, sugar. The start of the madness. We'll be full of pensioners as soon as that door opens, then we'll get the lunchtime rush, followed by the passing truckers. We'll die off for about twenty minutes around three p.m. then the high schoolers will be in for their burgers and shakes. I got up before sunrise to prep for today. It'll be chaos here within the hour and I don't have a waitress anymore. So, step up or step out!"

Clarabelle grabbed the apron. "Fine! Pressure is my middle name. You want something special. I'll bring the heat!"

THE RED WEDDING

Clarabelle's Creole Jambalaya went down a treat with the regulars, along with her bubbly personality. She grafted through her morning, waiting tables, washing up and promoting her southern dish. The pensioners even commended Jimmy on employing such a cheerful soul, saying Clarabelle's presence was the bistro's missing link.

She had just retrieved her homemade pecan pralines and King cake from her car to add to the dessert menu when Jimmy roared at her.

"Where the hell have you been? I have lunch orders coming out of my ass here. I don't do lazy. We rest when the work's done!"

Clarabelle placed the boxes on the counter, taken aback by his rant. "Jimmy, I've been gone two minutes. I told B I was bringing some cakes with me to add to the menu. I went to fetch them while you were fixing up the latest order."

"Well, they're getting fucking cold. So, deliver the damn meals for fuck's sake,"

Clarabelle stamped her feet, making Jimmy step back in surprise.

"Tantrums? Not on my watch, sugar. I thought you could handle the heat?"

"Heat, yes! Bullying, no! You haven't eased up on me all day and frankly, you're being a bit of a dick!"

Jimmy turned to the chicken on the grill. "You know where the door is!"

Clarabelle snatched the plates from under the heat lamp. "I don't give up that easily!" she said, backing out of the kitchen.

Moments later, she returned to her cakes.

"No time to fanny about with them. You got a stack of dirty dishes to put through the washer," Jimmy snapped again without casting her a look.

Clarabelle glared at the pile of dishes, knowing Jimmy had left them to ruffle her feathers. "You know what? No!"

"What the hell do you mean, no?"

Clarabelle stepped towards him, untying her apron then tossing it at him. "No! I'm not your slave. I came to collaborate, not to face mistreatment."

Jimmy stared at the apron littering the floor and glared back at her. "I don't need to collaborate. Look around. My bistro is booming. Now take your southern food and fuck off!"

Rage swept through her bubbly body. Trembling, she picked up an open bag of flour and flung it in Jimmy's face, covering him from head to toe.

"Asshole!" she said, storming out of the kitchen with her cakes, leaving Jimmy looking like a ghost.

Stepping into the bistro, Clarabelle held back her tears as she placed her treats in the dessert cabinet. Her hands shook, placing her King cakes and Pecan Pralines in neat rows next to Jimmy's double chocolate chip cookies and blueberry muffins, catching the eye of her hungry customers. Deciding to remain in front of the house, she served hot beverages and cakes and conversed with her customers, leaving Jimmy to bring out his own orders and do his own washing up.

A couple of hours had passed when Jimmy appeared from the kitchen, the flour in his hair and coating his double-breasted jacket still lingering as he perched himself behind the counter, staring at her. Clarabelle pretended not to notice him, continuing to joke with the club's prospects about their taste in music.

"Uh, Belle," he uttered, tapping her shoulder.

Clarabelle stood to attention; her arms crossed firmly over her chest, providing Jimmy with her best death stare.

"Don't Belle me. You haven't earned the right to be my friend. You've looked at me like I'm ugly and treated me like dirt because of your own insecurities. And you know what? I've seen men like you more times than I can count. I know you're only happy when those darn beautiful young girls are stroking your ego at the bar, but that's not me. And no, I don't resemble them, and you know why?" she said in her southern accent. "Because I'm a real darn woman! Yes, I'm strong, ballsy and say it like it is! I embrace my curves and those who don't accept me can walk on by."

Clarabelle wailed on, and Jimmy stood like a naughty schoolboy, feeling taken aback.

"And I'll tell you something else for nothing. I wouldn't pick you out of a line up. Real women have standards Jimmy. We like guys who show respect and celebrate us. We seek devoted men who will go above and beyond for us, so we can love them in return, but please, you play with the inexperienced young girls that only please you because of your title because I'm sure as hell that won't get old," she said reinforcing her statement with her enthusiastic body language. "And let's just be clear, B believes in me, and I believe in myself, so I'm staying put. You wanna speak to me? Come correct or not at all!" she warned, storming off to the kitchen.

Jimmy's guilty conscience consumed him all day. He stayed quiet through the afternoon rush. Jimmy hadn't meant to hurt Clarabelle's feelings. Despite Zander's vague description, he still thought she was quite pretty. A genuine woman scared him, his self-esteem battered by all that had happened with T.

Clarabelle was strong-willed and self-assured. She was an all-rounder, funny, straight to the point, with a soft side capable of melting anyone's heart.

He watched as she continued to charm the customers, her bubbly personality shining bright like a star. She made him laugh with her jokes, catching her attention before she tiredly returned to the old man, flattered by her wit.

"Right, let me get you Jimmy's favorite apple pie," she said before waltzing past him and heading into the kitchen.

Jimmy stood in the doorway, blocking her path. "Clarabelle, wait."

"We have customers, Jimmy," she said, pushing past him to prepare the dessert.

Jimmy's nerves got the better of him. "They can wait two minutes for a piece of pie. They've already eaten everything on the menu today."

Clarabelle stopped in her tracks, cracking a smile.

"Come on, even that deserves a laugh," he tried.

Clarabelle shook her head with humor. "They have eaten a lot," she said, placing the cream on the counter. "Where do they put it all?"

"Beats me, but your food is damn good. You can't blame them."

Clarabelle pretended to faint. "Did you just compliment my food?"

Jimmy smiled, avoiding eye contact as he scratched his head.

"Yeah, I did. Look, I'm sorry. I've been a total ass, and I promise it has nothing to do with your shape, size or culinary skills, for that matter."

Clarabelle shrugged. The tone in her response became low and less defensive.

"Then why the hard time? You've been horrible to me, and I didn't deserve that."

Jimmy gave her an apologetic smile. Ramming his hands into his pocket, he leaned against the cold tiled wall. "The last woman in this kitchen was pure evil. She made me feel like we had something special until I discovered it was all lies. She was full of smiles and compliments until I discovered she was a sadistic lunatic." He gave her a longing glance; his sincerity caught her off guard.

"Clarabelle, I have nothing against you, doll face. You're ballsy, kind, and witty, as much as it pains me to say it, Welsh Cake was right. We can make a good team. I need to get my head out of my ass and remind myself you're not the woman who shredded my heart."

Clarabelle tried to find her words, taking a breath to compose herself. "Well, alright then. How about we start over?"

"I'd like that."

She nodded into her smile. "I better get these pies out," she said, collecting the pie from the fridge.

"Allow me please? You've rushed around all day. Take a break in the sunshine. I'll deal with these."

Heat bloomed in Clarabelle's cheeks. "Well, okay then," she said with a smile as big as Baton Rouge.

CHAPTER ELEVEN
Fear of the Dragon

Zander dragged his feet into the club, kicking his chair out from under the table. Frankie rushed behind the bar, grabbing a couple of bottles of whiskey and a handful of shot glasses on his way into church where everyone took their seats. Tiny and Tyr grabbed extra chairs from the bar for the Uskiville pack, ensuring everyone crammed into the room.

Jimmy rushed in just as the meeting began. "What did I miss? I've had a hell of a day, and I could do with some good news."

"You'll no' find it here, pal," Zander said, gesturing to take his seat.

Zander cast his eyes across the packed room, seeing the waves of uncertain eyes waiting for his guidance. Tapping his fingers on the table, he snapped himself out of his frantic slumber. "Right. We have no choice but to let Leif the prick come to Sunnyville," he said, nodding at Tyr. "No offense, son."

"None taken. To be clear, I am a wolf. My loyalties remain here. I am bound to them by blood, not by brotherhood or heart."

Cheers of camaraderie rattled the room.

"Aye, we know. You dinnae have to convince us of your loyalty. We know where you belong. Now we need to be clinical here. Leif is expecting a one-percenter club when he arrives, so that's what we're gonnae give him. Anything less, he'll steamroller all over us. Now I dinnae doubt we can hold our own, but I'm no' wanting a war in Sunnyville. We've worked too damn hard to ruin what we've built."

Ayes echoed in agreement until Frankie silenced them all.

"We can make everyone conform, no problem. Wives will obey patches here, and Jimmy controls the remaining bunnies, but tell me, Prez, what the hell do you plan to do about my sister? Not to mention he's planning on attending the wedding. It's her wedding too, for heaven's sake."

Zander ran his fingers through his hair, digesting Frankie's words and leaning forward in his chair. "That's the million-dollar question. Fellas, I want to marry that lassie next week. If she sees Leif here or he attends the wedding, she'll lose her shit, and not because she doesnae like one-percenters but because she's like a lioness protecting her cub and Tyr there is a cub, she will fight to the death for."

Tyr hid his head in his cut with embarrassment.

"Dinnae get embarrassed, Tyr, you're lucky, pal. She wouldn't piss on some folk if they were on fire!"

Tiny, clasped Tyr's pack. "I'm glad Dragon is looking after you, mate. Gives me peace of mind in Uskiville."

Jimmy chirped in, "So we're clear. Our boy Tyr stays, no matter what. Zand, you can't keep this from Welsh Cake this time and expect her to be fine. You know, keeping shit from her isn't an option anymore. Just pull on your Prez pants and explain the situation."

Tiny coughed into his drink, "dead man walking!" creating a rip-roar of laughter amongst the club members.

Zander grinned. "You have met my old lady, Jimmy?"

Jimmy laughed. "Oh, we've met! I don't want to retrace those steps, thanks very much!"

Frankie slid the bottle of whiskey across the table to Zander. "Here, drink your liquid courage and if you're not back in the morning, we'll vote Jimmy in as Prez again."

"Fuck off!" Zander chuckled, catching the bottle before it slid off the table.

Mack, who'd remained quiet until now, piped up. "I'll talk to Dragon if it's too much. She'll listen to me. Just tell me, Prez, who do you fear more, Leif, or my bestie?"

"Ooh," the bar chimed in.

Zander dropped his head in a grin of defeat, biting his tongue. "I dinnae fear that prick. I can beat the shit out of him. My old lady. she's a different kettle of fish because I enjoy breathing, and I love her riding me."

"Oh, we've seen you both in action!" Hyde teased.

Zander stood. "Right, you've had your fun. I'm gonnae face the music and hope I'm no' divorced before I'm married. Please talk to your old ladies and make sure they fall in line when Leif arrives on Monday."

"I got the bunnies," Jimmy said.

"Of course you do," Zander teased.

"Not like that. I'm not in the mood tonight."

The silence became oppressive as a pin drop could have been heard. Frankie placed a palm on Jimmy's forehead. "You alright?"

Jimmy swiped it away. "Fuck off! I'm just getting bored with the same pussy."

Zander sat back down, crossing his legs. "I'm intrigued. You dinnae hit it off with a certain busty baker by any chance, did you?"

Jimmy shifted in embarrassment. "No! Quite the fucking opposite, to be frank."

Zander belly laughed, holding his stomach. "She's a good woman, Jimmy."

Jimmy's beetroot face couldn't take Zander's teasing. "I thought you had to leave. Welsh Cake's probably waiting to beat the crap out of you and tell her thanks. I've had a wonderful fucking Friday!"

Zander rose from his seat again. "Aye, I'm away. Behave the lot of you." He turned to Mack. "Make sure you're all back here before Leif arrives on Monday morning. I need bikers swarming the MC until I figure out his intentions. There's no way anyone agrees to giving up fifty percent of their business so easily."

"That's a fecking power grab, and you damn well know it. You should have told him to get bent!" Mack cussed.

"Not until I gather all the facts. This isn't aboot Tyr or aboot Leif's bullshit business proposal and I'm gonnae find out what he's up to."

"Fair enough! You sure you don't want my help with Dragon?"

Zander grimaced. "I can handle my old lady, Irish. Thanks!"

CHAPTER TWELVE
Unhappy Dragon

"I can't bloody believe you, good boy. We're getting married in a few days, and you want to invite the worst one-percenters from this side of the country into our home. Not to mention their treatment of Tyr."

She paced the bedroom. "You just couldn't allow our wedding day to run smoothly? It's bad enough I must hide who I am and act like a fucking bunny on Monday and now I'm expected to do so at our wedding?"

Zander took her hand only to watch B rip it away. "Don't fucking touch me. You've ruined our wedding day before it's even happened."

"Blethen please, darling. Don't be like that?"

"Don't you fucking dare?" she glared.

"What?" he grinned.

"You know what? Saying my name like that, trying to turn me on so I forget about how bloody angry I am. Piss off!"

B tried to leave the bedroom.

"No, you dinnae. We are gonnae talk like adults," he said, picking her up and pinning her down onto the bed.

B wriggled, trying to break free. "Get the fuck off me, asshole."

"Not until you let me speak!"

"I swear to God if you don't move, I'll knee you in the nuts so hard, you'll have no chance of ever impregnating me," she snapped.

Zanders stilled, stunned until he sat up away from her.

B softened. She'd kept him waiting for so long, telling him how she wanted to be married before they tried for children. Zander had begged her for months to stop her birth control, but B wouldn't budge and now he wasn't even sure if he could impregnate her.

B nestled up beside him, softening her hard face. "I'm sorry. I'm just so angry. I wanted everything to be perfect, even down to our wedding night."

Zander remained mute until she reached into her drawer and handed him an appointment card.

Zander peered down at the gynecology appointment card. "What's this?"

"My appointment to have my implant removed. I spoke with Dr. Taylor; all my tests are excellent. She started me on a pregnancy multivitamin, and I wanted our wedding night to be the first night we tried."

Zander stared at her in disbelief.

"I just wanted everything to be perfect. I'm leaving for Uskiville after your meeting with Leif, so I won't see you until our wedding day," she huffed. "Removing the implant was my priority on Monday morning. It was meant to be a surprise, but I want you to understand why I'm so angry with you. I'm hardly going to be in the mood after seeing Leif parade around like a bloody king on our wedding day when I have to pretend to be someone I'm not." She sighed onto his shoulder. "I just wanted everything to be perfect!"

Zander's face warmed again. His smile beamed like the sun as he squeezed her hand in his. "You're really ready to do this. Have a bairn with me? I mean, I know we went for tests, but I kind of thought you were just humoring me."

"Yes, but this shit with Leif is stressing me."

Zander pulled her close, kissing her temple. "I know, darling. These guys are among the USA's most dangerous MCs, and we need their alliance."

"What do they want with us?"

"That's unclear. He says he wants us to do business and wants us to front the money to make his business work, but I dinnae trust that. I dinnae want to upset Tyr. He looked terrified in their company today. I need you to agree to this meeting, darling."

B shot off the bed like a rocket. "No chance, good boy. Our path is leading us back to white. We're done with black, and that twisted asshole can fuck right off. He's done enough damage to Tyr."

Zander growled. "We cannae make an enemy of them. They will wipe us out. They have contacts across the states. We just need to hear them out. I'll assess the situation on Monday and go from there."

"And I have to become a bunny slut, seen and not heard."

"No, woman! Just be my loyal old lady who doesnae act like she owns everything."

B huffed toward the balcony, opening the doors, allowing the fresh air to flood her lungs. "But I do own everything!"

"I know, Welsh Cake. Please?" Exasperated, Zander gripped the bed sheets. "If Leif realizes the truth about the club, they'll seize everything, just as they did to other MCs nationwide. They consume club's darling. I must show them we're a traditional one-percenter MC that's no' to be trifled with. If they see that, whatever I say will keep them at bay and in our pockets."

B stood with her hands gripping her hips, her disdain for the situation crystal clear through her pouting face. "I don't like this."

"You and me both. That smart mouth and hot-tempered ass of yours could land us in trouble. Now you need to trust me on this, please?"

B huffed, rolling her eyes at him.

Zander approached with caution, placing a stray hair behind her ear. "Please, just be my good little old lady, so I can seal this before we get married. If I do this right, they might not even attend our wedding."

B glared at him with her fiery dragon eyes.

"Please? I'll make it up to you," he said, pulling her into him.

B's eyes became inquisitive under Zander's seductive gaze.

"I'll do that thing you like?" he said with a smile.

B raised her eyebrows, her salacious grin decorating her face. "Every day for a month!"

"A month. No' fucking fair! What do I get?"

"A wife you get to impregnate. Take it or leave it, big guy."

Zander shook his head. "I'd forgotten how much of a ball-buster you are when it comes to business."

"Then maybe I should be the one sorting Leif."

"No' fucking funny!"

B threw her hands in the air, breaking away from him. "Fine, whatever asshole. Have it your way. I'll take my month of pleasure," she said, entering the bathroom and slamming the door.

CHAPTER THIRTEEN
The Rus Reapers (Carnage)

The volatile roar of motorcycles rattled through the parking lot like a storm during hurricane season. Leif had brought a small but vicious looking pack to the morning meeting, including Leif, his son Ragnar, Carmichael, his SGT of arms, Nuclear, his roadie and Chad, his enforcer. Their cuts bore a patch with a Viking grim reaper riding motorcycle and a top and bottom rocker with "The Rus Reapers, San Diego," stitched in a blazing orange color. The standard one-percenter embroidery stood bold from the leather to avoid any confusion as to their stature within the motorcycle communities.

The Rus Reapers were armed and with a reputation not to be messed with. Caution ripped through the Sunnyville chapter as eerie eyes glared at the menacing MC tribe stepping off their motorcycles.

B had just returned from having her implant removed and was sitting at the bar with Mack, conversing on her mobile with the real estate agent about her recent purchase of the building behind the club. They agreed to purchase the building and transform it into a nightclub. B brimmed with excitement, showing Mack and Frankie around the premises, leaving Frankie, who was taking the lead as the new nightclub manager, to discuss renovating with the contractor.

The mayor rushed the planning permission for approval, eager to restore wealth to the town the Mauler had destroyed.

B had just finished her call when Leif and his entourage entered the bar, escorted by an anxious-looking Jimmy. Abrupt and angered, he ordered the remaining bunnies to fetch some drinks and entertain the guests before he went to fetch Zander from the bistro, following Zander's instruction to keep Leif waiting to show he wasn't fazed by the Viking's reputation.

Leif and his men made themselves at home in the center of the bar, fondling bunnies. Ragnar, who seemed disinterested in what was on offer, caught a glimpse of B leaving the bar, rushing over to block her path.

"And where are you going, hot momma? I choose you to come and play at the big boy's table."

"You couldn't handle me, sunshine!" B snapped with irritability in her voice, trying to pass him.

Ragnar gripped her wrist. "Oh, but I can, and I will. Ragnar takes what he wants!"

B ripped her wrist from his grasp. "No! Ragnar can play with what's been offered."

"Oh, I'll play," he sneered, grabbing her between her legs and pinching her labia between his fingers.

B saw red. Her fiery dragon eye's seared into him with rage a split-second before she punched him in the face, following through with her elbow, creating an almighty crack to his jaw.

Zander and Jimmy entered with astonished gasps as Ragnar bellowed, demanding the attention of the room. "You bitch! I will gut you like I gut my fish!"

B kicked him in the ribs in disgust. "Don't ever bloody touch me, asshole!"

A sharp pain screamed through her hair follicles. Her eyes scanned the bar at astonished eyes staring back at her, witnessing their Prez manhandle the love of his life.

B turned in horror to be met with the back of his hand colliding with her cheek, the force sending her flying until she hit the floor with a thud. "How dare you strike my guests. Know your place, woman!" he bellowed in a furious wrath.

Mack stepped forward in anger, only to run into Zander's fist, the impact breaking his nose. "She may be family, but this is my house, Irish. How I treat my woman is my business."

B glanced up at Zander, unable to recognize the man standing above her, his eyes no longer beautiful but filled with madness. Gripping her sleeve and wiping the blood from her nose, she clambered to her feet to stand before the gnarly Prez.

"Maybe your guests should know their place before grabbing your old lady's pussy?"

Zander's chest heaved, whipping his head in a menacing stare to growl at Ragnar, who had sat to revel in the entertainment.

"Is this true?" Zander snapped.

Ragnar shrugged. "I helped myself to what I wanted. So, what!"

Before he could blink, Zander darted across the bar, grabbing the scrawny bag of flesh by the throat, shaking him like a rag doll. "Nobody touches my old lady but me, asshole. You just signed your own death warrant." He squeezed his windpipe.

Leif's men drew their weapons, pointing them at Zander, while the gray wolves drew theirs.

Leif was the first to speak, standing to address him. "Zander, forgive my idiot son, he wasn't aware this fine woman was your old lady. The boy thinks with his dick..."

"He knew alright. I warned him never to look at her the night he arrived at my club uninvited."

Leif's demeanor shifted from amused to desperation as Ragnar struggled for breath. "Celtic Warrior, please release him."

Zander tightened his grip, allowing the bar to bear witness to his display of dominance. "He had the audacity to enter my house, disrespect me by declining what was offered, and assault my old lady. No, he dies!"

B recognized the fear in Leif's eyes as he pleaded. "Zander, I'm asking you as a friend, please kick the shit out of him. Teach him a lesson, but don't kill him for my failings as a father and not teaching the boy. I've already lost one son this year besides losing Tyr." His voice trembled. "I beg you not to make me lose another."

Zander's eyes and grasp didn't budge as Ragnar turned purple. His final breaths were imminent.

B stepped forward, placing one hand on his chest, and turning his head to meet her gaze with the other. "Hey," she said in an innocent tone, "perhaps you teach the boy a lesson and Leif can owe the club a debt? I may just be an old lady, but I'm also a parent. Please leave the petulant child alone as a wedding gift for your old lady?"

Zander snapped out of his trance, long enough to release his grip. His sadistic gaze softened as he stared at B with desperate eyes. Despite her anger, she empathized with his hurt after hitting her, though she had to suppress her emotions for the club's sake.

"Get her out of here!" he barked.

B felt Mack pull her by the arm, dragging her out of the club with haste.

Ragnar's agonizing cries rang out from the club house like bells, along with angry cracks and thuds.

Stepping outside, B pulled her arm away. The sun shone down on her bus beaten face: the swelling was already slowing.

"Shit, Dragon, let me see," Mack said, forgetting about his own injury.

Fury built up in B, bellowing like smoke in a smoldering forest fire. She had never felt so belittled, much less expected her fiancé to ever lay a hand on her.

"Asshole!" she cursed.

"Hey, hey, let me see," Mack pleaded, grabbing her head to examine her. "Shite, Dragon. That took some resolve. How did you stop yourself from unleashing your inner dragon and killing them?"

B pursed her lips, her temper boiling. "I never thought that bastard would ever hit me."

Mack gave her a sympathetic stare. "He's under a lot of pressure. If he hadn't hit you, they would have killed you."

B shrugged away, trembling in anger. "So, you're condoning that shit? Jesus, he didn't even bother to ask what happened. He worries more about his bloody reputation than me. Well, fuck him. Tell that prick I'm done and not to bother coming to Uskiville. The wedding is off. In fact, if he ever comes near me again. I'll fucking end him!" she screamed before turning on her heels toward her truck. Tyr appeared from the gym just as she was about to climb inside, catching sight of her face.

Dropping his protein shaker, he sprinted toward her, stopping inside her personal space to examine her injuries.

His face flurried into a fit of rage. "What happened?"

B shook her head. "A misunderstanding. Please don't worry about it, my lovely. I'm heading to Uskiville, so I'll see you later."

"Please tell me," he whispered.

B shook her head. "Let's just say I despise your brother as much as you. He caused some shit between Prez and I," she said, unable to stop the hurt from escaping her throat.

Tyr studied her. "Prez did this?"

B turned away. "It doesn't matter Tyr."

"It does to me. What did Ragnar do?"

"He grabbed me where a man shouldn't touch a woman without permission."

Tyr snarled, embracing her. "I'm sorry, Móðir, I will make this right."

B clasped a hand to his cheek. "I'm all good, lovely boy, and he's not worth it. Now, keep your head down and we'll chat later, okay?"

Tyr kissed her forehead. "Ice that face."

CHAPTER FOURTEEN
Rage and Restitution

Enraged, Mack returned to the bar, entering as Leif and Zander shook hands. His fury rose, seeing the pair laughing and joking while Hyde patched Ragnar up by the bar. He slid towards them, whispering into Ragnar's ear. "The Prez may have let you live, fuckwit, but you better sleep with one eye open after what you did to my best friend. And don't bother telling daddy because I'll gut that fecker like you threatened to gut my friend," he said, gripping Ragnar's damaged hand.

Ragnar winced as Hyde continued to dress Ragnar's ribs.

"Do you understand?" Mack snarled, crushing his fingers.

"Y-Yes,"

"Yes, what?"

"Yes Prez," Ragnar grimaced.

"Better. Now sit by daddy and keep your mouth shut unless you want to lose your tongue."

Ragnar gulped, removing himself from the bar, dragging his battered body toward the window seating where his father conversed with Zander.

Zander growled at him as Leif spoke. "Go wait by the bikes. You're an embarrassment!"

Mack followed him with his eyes, watching him leave.

That's right dickwad, keep walking. The first chance I get, I'm crushing your windpipe.

Mack sat for the next twenty minutes, watching Zander make small talk and smoke a cigar with Leif.

Fecking prick! Having the time of his life while Dragon is raging. If she has any sense, she'll stick to her guns and dump his ass.

Moments later, Leif handed Zander a binder before Zander and Jimmy escorted Leif and his men outside.

Frankie entered the bar, nodding curtly as the others departed. "So, how'd it go?" Frankie asked. "By the look of it, you've almost broken him."

"Not me. Dragon first and then Zander almost killed him."

"What?" Frankie's puzzled expression required answers.

"The little prick grabbed B's pussy. She was flooring him as Zander walked in." He crushed his soda can. "Prez fucking hit her, Frankie! Cracked her right across the face, then me, before all hell broke loose."

Frankie's jaw tightened and a familiar darkness filled his eyes. He became like the Grim Reaper, ready to collect his prey when his hackles went up.

Mack flipped a beer mat. "Dragon's gone. She's told me to tell him that the wedding's off and she'll kill him if he goes near her again."

Frankie cracked his knuckles as if he was readying himself for war. "She won't have to. Prez or not, he's gonna fucking die!" he said, turning on his heels in temper and bounding to the door in haste. Hyde, Eddie, and Top Shelf appeared from nowhere, restraining him.

"The deal's almost done. Just leave it Frankie," Hyde said.

Mack watched in amusement, knowing what was about to unfold.

3, 2, 1

Frankie launched himself into a crazed frenzy, throwing punches, connecting with anyone in his path. Picking up Hyde like he weighed nothing, Frankie threw him across the bar.

CHAPTER FIFTEEN
Tyr's Revenge!

Tyr watched B back out of the parking lot before going back to collect his protein shaker he had thrown away earlier. Retrieving it from the concrete, he walked around the parked cars towards the clubhouse as his brother emerged from the bar.

Tyr snapped, throwing the shaker at Ragnar's head before hurdling toward him and tackling him to the ground. The pair scuffled as Tyr overpowered his older brother, striking him in the face.

"I'll kill you! You fucking bully!" he shouted, gripping his brother by his cut to punch him again.

Ragnar pushed him off, finding his fight he'd lost in his two previous battles that day, hitting Tyr across the head with a stray rock.

Blood trickled from Tyr's head; his strawberry blond hair colored in a deeper shade of red.

"Oh, little brother has grown a pair!" Ragnar teased, collecting himself by wiping blood from his lip.

"You hurt my family. You'll pay for that." Tyr said.

"Ha, family. You don't know the meaning of the word. You're a disgrace to The Rus Reapers!"

Tyr lunged at him, his war cry loud and clear, gripping his brother, throwing him against the club wall, and knocking the wind from his sales. Tyr didn't hesitate in continuing his violent onslaught, kneeing his brother between the legs and delivering blows to his stomach.

Ragnar groaned in despair, glancing up at his younger brother in shock.

"You've bullied for the last time. You sick son of a bitch," he said, dragging Ragnar into the middle of the parking lot. He kicked him in Ragnars' already damaged ribs, forcing a squeal from his pained throat as he dropped to his knees to straddle him.

"Brother, stop!" Ragnar pleaded, struggling for breath.

"Years of abuse were bad enough, but you hurt my Móðir and insulted my club. Payback's a bitch!" he growled, punching him and gripping his head to crush it.

Ragnar's piercing screams ripped across the parking lot like a gusty wind until Tyr was tackled from behind, pushing him away from his brother.

Tyr scrambled to his feet to meet his next attacker. Confusion spread through him like an untreated disease, forcing him to catch his breath.

"He's had enough," Zander growled, "and as angry as you are, I dinnae think you want to kill him, son."

Tyr shoved him. "He hurt her like he hurt me, and instead of seeking justice, you hurt her, too! You're supposed to protect her. Where is your honor?"

"Tyr, I know you're angry, son, but some things are bigger than you and my old lady."

Tyr shoved him again. "Not to me! She took me in as her own when everyone else cast me aside like I didn't matter. Now Ragnar is mine to finish. He doesn't get away with his crimes. You taught me to stand up for myself and that's what I'm doing," he roared in pain, attempting to push past Zander again.

Zander gripped him, receiving angry blows from Tyr's throbbing fists.

"You've proved your point, laddie. Now stop before you hurt yasel'."

Tyr screamed. "Fight back or let me pass."

A crowd of Reapers, Wolves and customers gathered outside to witness the commotion, with Leif watching the scenario unfold. Hyde stood by, refusing to provide medical attention to a bloodied Ragnar until ordered to do so by his Prez.

Tyr's fists continued to slap Zander's back as Zander cradled him until he burst into frustrated tears.

Zander gripped him hard, placing a firm hand at the back of his head. "I got you, son. You're alright. He cannae hurt you anymore."

Tyr wailed in anger, gripping onto his Jarl. The unbearable pain proving too much as he released his stored trauma in a tormented bellow.

Tiny pushed through the crowd to aid his upset brother, wrapping his arms around the pair of them. He whispered into Tyr's ear. "Tyr, I'm proud of you, man. It took courage standing up to that piece of shit."

Zander peeled Tyr away from him, grabbing his head with both hands and placing his forehead to his. "I'm proud of you, laddie, and I fucking love you. Dinnae ever forget it!"

Tyr stifled his tears, sucking in a deep breath.

"We good now?" Zander smiled.

Tyr nodded. His speech betrayed him as his emotions continued to overwhelm him.

Zander released him into Tiny's embrace. His protective arm provided comfort to him.

"Get him inside for a drink. A few shots will sort him."

Tyr and Tiny walked toward the club.

"You hold your head fucking high now, brother. Walk past that pathetic excuse of a father like you fucking own the place and don't give him a second look!" Tiny said, pushing him forward with encouragement.

Tyr inhaled a nervous breath, puffing out his chest and wiping his tears as he stepped closer to his father.

"Tyr," Leif tried, extending his hand, watching Tyr push his hand away and continue into the bar.

"What are you all fucking gawking at? Move the fuck on!" Zander snapped, forcing the crowd to disburse. "Hyde, clean that piece of shit up, he's making the place look untidy," he said, pointing to Ragnar laying in a pool of his own blood next to him. He stopped before Leif, staring him down. "That was your doing, and I dinnae know what happened to Erik, but I suspect you had a hand in his disappearance!"

Leif glared at him.

"Tyr stays here unchallenged. He's celebrated as a wolf and loved by all. Can you provide that for him back home?"

Leif ripped his eyes away from the strong Scot.

"I dinnae fucking think so! Let's be clear. I'll look at your proposal. You can come to my wedding if you're seen and not heard but if I get a whiff of you being up to no good, I'll slice your fucking throat in your sleep and my Wolves will tear out the heart of every member of your sadistic fucking MC." He stepped forward to whisper in his ear, grinning at the other Reapers. "You picked the wrong MC to fuck with Viking. Tread very fucking carefully!"

CHAPTER SIXTEEN
Round Three

The Rus Reapers left in haste after Leif instructed them to move out as an eagle-eyed Zander stood in his power, watching them leave.

In the bar, Frankie continued to seethe, waiting for Zander's arrival. Despite the pack's efforts to calm him earlier, he still had business to address with Zander after Tyr's brawl with Ragnar distracted him.

No sooner had Zander walked through the bar door, than Frankie almost hit him back through it again, astounding the club members.

Zander stumbled into the wall and Frankie punched him again, waiting for Zander to retaliate.

"I'll no' fight you, brother," Zander said in defeat.

"But you'll lay a hand on my sister, you pathetic prick! You better fucking fight back because I have a lot of fucking rage to release."

Zander pushed past him, collecting a bottle of whiskey, and wandering into church, slamming the door behind him.

Frankie's blood boiled, following him with angry strides.

Flinging the door open, he growled at Zander, who sat in his Prez chair. "I'm not done with you, Prez!"

The other senior members lingered in the doorway as Zander poured himself a drink. "I'm ashamed of myself, brother. I was so scared they were gonnae kill her, I felt compelled to react. Better me slap her than them kill her," he sulked. Shaking his head, he continued. "The way she looked at me after I hit her damn near killed me. You dinnae need to be a big brother by reiterating the consequences for my actions."

Frankie lowered his fists, catching his breath and digesting the situation as Mack entered the room, pressing his palms into the table opposite an unfazed Zander.

"Come on then, Irish," Zander spoke in defeat. "You owe me a beat down, too. I'm sorry I hit you, pal. I had to-"

Mack hissed at him like an angry snake. "'You didn't have to do shite. A real man would have assessed the situation and asked questions before smacking their fiancée about. You don't deserve my Dragon and she sure as hell doesn't want you anymore. She left for Uskiville. She said to tell you the wedding is off and if you ever go near her again, she'll end you." Mack spat on the floor next to him, "You fecking disgust me. Now I'm heading home and I'm warning you to steer clear," he said, walking out of church with Frankie following him.

CHAPTER SEVENTEEN
Unwavering Shock

Tears streamed down B's face like mascara-colored waterfalls, staining her cheeks in thick, black streaks. Her heart was breaking in disbelief. She had been hit a thousand times before, but never imagined Zander would ever lay a finger on her with such vicious intent.

Speeding down the open road, determined to get away from the man she loved, her ugly cries compromised her vision, forcing her to pull into the side of the road.

Angry at her tears, she exited her truck. Slamming it shut, B stumbled down onto a grassy verge. Taking a deep breath, she wiped her tears using her bloodied sleeve and peered down at the blood droplets, forcing a flashback of the pain Zander inflicted upon her in his outrageous attack.

The demonic expression in her lovers' eyes when he ripped out her hair follicles with his firm grasp. The backhander that stunned her into a shocked silence left her with a heart full of hurt.

Weakened by the images propelling into her frontal lobe, she sat on the grass near a small lake, hugging her knees.

She buried her head in her Gillet; the collar rubbing against her swollen cheek. Only it wasn't the physical pain causing her tears. It was seeing a side to Zander she had never seen before. Overwhelmed and unable to process her trauma, she coiled herself into the fetal position, allowing herself to cry unobserved until she fell asleep. The man who she was going to marry in just a day had completely shattered her world.

B woke to Mack carrying her to her truck. Her weary eyes resisted the sun setting in the distance.

"Easy Dragon. Let's get you back home to Uskiville," he said.

Exhaustion collapsed in on her: her eyelids were too heavy to pry open as she slept in the comfort of her best friend's arms.

CHAPTER EIGHTEEN
You're Prez, For Fuck's Sake!

Zander sat on the floor, banging his head against the church walls. His anxiety had reared its ugly head, and the cold wall provided the short circuit he needed to collect himself. He had already thrown up twice, disgusted with himself for hurting B.

Zander had killed hundreds of people with his bare hands, and despite his temper, he never imagined ever showing B the dark side of himself that he'd unleashed upon her this morning.

Frankie and Mack had long since left for Uskiville, leaving Hyde and Jimmy to patch him up.

Jimmy entered the room, holding two cups of coffee and a cigarette, before closing the door.

"I've lost her Jimmy. She'll no' talk to me after this."

Jimmy handed him a coffee, taking a seat on the floor next to him. He lit the cigarette using a lighter from his pocket, inhaling a drag and relishing in the nicotine hit before handing the cigarette to Zander. "Here, get this in your system."

Zander waved his hand. "I cannae. I feel sick as a pig; besides I'm off the fags, remember? It's bad enough I had to choke down a cigar with that Viking prick earlier. A fat lot of good that did. Fuck knows what the future holds now."

"Are you shitting me? What you pulled off today was fucking brilliant. You oozed class and dominance, Zand. Leif literally shit himself. You're ten times the man he is, and he fucking knows it," he said, nudging him. "And as for Welsh Cake, you don't know crap! And we shouldn't disregard Mack's position in this. You know nothing until you hear it from the horse's mouth."

Zander brought the coffee to his lips, taking a sip. "She'll hate me now, Jimmy, and you need to reprimand me, take it to church. I broke the rules and struck a lassie. My fucking lassie!"

"Yeah, to save her fucking life! The charter is explicit: never strike a woman unless her life depends on it, and it fucking did!"

Zander shrugged. "It doesnae matter."

"Listen, she loves you, man, and you two have come through far worse."

Zander nodded. "Yeah together. This isn't even on the same page. I saw her face, Jimmy. Her eyes told me everything. I destroyed our whole fucking world in one moment of madness," he said, finishing his coffee and launching the cup at the door.

"Call her!"

"I cannae! My words cannae undo what I did. I am an animal! Who was I kidding, thinking I could have it all? That woman gave me everything and all I've done is let her down."

"Yet she still wanted to marry you," Jimmy said, dropping his cigarette into his coffee dregs and reaching up to the table to grab the bottle of whiskey and two glasses left from earlier. Pouring them each a glass, he stared at Zander. "I reiterate. She still wanted to marry you, Zand, didn't she?"

Zander dropped his head onto his chin. "No' anymore."

Jimmy chucked his whiskey in Zander's face, waking him from his sulking slumber.

"What the fuck?" Zander bellowed.

"Man, the fuck up and stop feeling sorry for yourself. So, you gave the woman a slap to protect her and while I don't condone woman beating unless absolutely necessary, this was fucking justified! The alternative would have seen you planning her funeral and serving life!"

Zander glared at him with his whiskey-washed face, his jaw clenched shut.

Jimmy kicked his foot. "You're the fucking Prez, for fuck's sake! At times, you must do what nobody else can. Certain decisions inevitably result in trouble, regardless of your actions. Now it's time to get off your ass and choose your hard."

Zander narrowed his eyes to him, forcing another boot from Jimmy.

"You either let Welsh Cake think you're a monster and continue down the self-pitying route or choose a better hard and go up there and pour your fucking heart out to the woman you love and save your relationship before it's too late." He pulled him up onto his feet. "The very fact you haven't left her a million messages demonstrates your shame because a weaker man would be different, begging for another chance until it happens again. That's not who you are, and we both know it."

"It'll no' happen again Jimmy."

"Don't fucking tell me that. I'm not the one who needs to hear it. Now stop feeling sorry for yourself, like a pathetic son of a bitch. It doesn't help or suit you, Dragon, or the club."

Zander stared him down. "You practice that speech?"

"Fuck off!" Jimmy raged.

Zander reached out his hand, smiling at his best friend. "It was good, like."

"Not too much?" Jimmy teased, clasping his back with his hand.

"I mean, the whiskey in the face was a wee bit too far. That's twice you thrown shit in my face now, pal."

"Woke you the fuck up from your pity party, though."

Zander smirked. "Aye. You think she'll forgive me, pal?"

"Grab your brain bucket and find out."

CHAPTER NINETEEN
Awake

B returned to consciousness amid a storm of bellows coming from the kitchen. Gathering her senses and casting her eyes around the room, she realized she was in her bed in her cabin in Uskiville.

Sitting herself up, she heard Zander's wrath. "I swear to God, Irish. If you dinnae stand aside, I'll rip your wee head right off your bastard shoulders!"

"You've done enough, asshole! You know where I found her? Sleeping next to a lake off the fecking highway. She abandoned her fecking truck because she was so broken and exhausted. Out for the fecking count, she was. She could have had a concussion; anything could have happened to her! I never expected to see my dragon with a tear-stained face, but you have a talent for causing it."

B climbed out of bed, thankful she was clothed, and listened by the door.

"Tell me something, did it empower you, make you fecking hard, showing everyone how big your cock is by breaking the woman you're supposed to protect?"

B opened the bedroom door, stopping in her tracks at Zander's rugged growls. "Tread fucking lightly, Irish. My patience has all but left me."

The agonizing hurt compressed B's chest, constricting her airways.

Her best friend and the man she loved were about to lock horns if she didn't intervene.

Storming into the kitchen barefoot, embarrassment, humiliation and anger filled her broken heart, her tears and mascara-stained face and bedhead evidence of the trauma she'd experienced today.

Zander's face appeared to shatter into a guilt-ridden expression, taking her back a little until her pained face recalled her anger. "I've got nothing to say to you, Scottie. I warned you about Tyr's family and you refused to listen. Now fuck off and don't come back! I'll decide what I'm doing with the business when I'm ready, but I promise it won't involve you or those bastard Reapers!"

Zander tried to push past Mack, only for Frankie to emerge from the bathroom to block his path too.

"Welsh Cake, I'm sorry. Allow me to explain, please? I was petrified, darling, and I know hitting you was a despicable act of violence, but they would have killed you if I hadn't. Please believe me."

"The thick lump of hurt forming in B's throat threatened to choke her as she battled away her tears in a rage, making a three-sixty toward her bedroom.

"Darling, wait, please?" Zander tried. "Just ask Mack and Frankie what they would have done in my position. Truthfully!"

Halting, B turned to her best friends to gage their response.

Mack was the first to speak. His snide and venomous tone was proof of the contempt he held toward Zander.

"I would have asked questions before slapping my old lady around."

"No, you wouldn't have, and you God damn know it!" Frankie said in a calm tone. As Zander and Mack watched, he crossed the room, taking B's hand. B met his gaze with uncertainty as he spoke. "B, I despise what he's done. Controlling the urge to kill him earlier was difficult; however, we all would have acted the same in his position."

B stepped away, her eyes bulging in disbelief, and Frankie continued.

"B it may not seem like it, but Prez saved your life today. Ragnar is a little prick who hides behind his daddy's power, but Leif will do anything for his precious son since he lost his first born. He would have watched Ragnar put a bullet in you, and I'm glad you're not on a cold slab somewhere because of that today."

B allowed her tired eyes to wash over Zander: the cuts and bruises on his face couldn't hide the sorrow in his eyes.

She cast her eyes back to Frankie. "Your handiwork?"

Frankie shrugged. "Yeah, and that stupid Scottish prick was so darn disgusted with himself, he let me. B, I rained blows down on him like it rains in Wales and he didn't stop me." Frankie gestured toward Zander. "Look at the sad bastard. He's broken and full of remorse. I know he never meant to hurt you, sweetheart. His anger and fear mirrored yours. Hear him out, and if you still want him to leave, I'll kick him out, so you never have to see him again."

B raised her eyebrows, wincing through the sharp pain in her jaw. "Five minutes!" she said, turning back to her room.

CHAPTER TWENTY
Getting Even!

Zander hesitated before turning the handle on B's bedroom door. Closing his eyes, he dragged in a deep breath and steadied his shaking hand before gripping the handle tight. Just as he wrapped his palm around the handle, Frankie appeared from the bathroom to whisper in his ear.

"You get one chance at this, Prez. Don't blow it!"

Zander nodded, closing his eyes as if he was praying for a miracle. "Her face Frankie, the bruising..."

"It's not the physical damage you should be worrying about. It's this right here," he said, tapping on his sternum. "Look, I don't know if it's too late but pour your fucking heart out. B will appreciate that. A broken and hurt B is very dangerous. Fix this," he said, grabbing his neck in encouragement.

Zander nodded before knocking on the door and entering the bedroom in a slow shuffle of his feet.

B remained sitting cross-legged, like a kindergarten pupil, on her bed. Her stern yet frightened face didn't look at him as he closed the door. He stood numb, his words escaping him as he faced the true extent of his actions.

B remained mute as Zander took a slow step forward, making her flinch and forcing him to step back.

She's frightened of me!

His heart broke and his legs buckled beneath him, forcing his back against the bedroom wall as he slid down onto the hardwood floor. "I'm so sorry, Welsh Cake," he managed, cradling his head in his hands to hide his face while a gut-wrenching, distraught cry vibrated from the depths of his soul. He couldn't compose himself, allowing himself to feel his guilt and letting everything out. Knowing he was his own worst enemy, placing the world on his shoulders and trying to fix everything, Zander struggled with the reality of the situation. His cries reverberated around the room, unnatural to him, as his body took control.

B moved toward him, hesitating; her fear clear as she reached out to him. Her hesitant stare resembled a terrified child as tears rolled down her cheek, dropping onto her blood-stained shirt.

"Darling, I apologize. I never wanted to hurt you; I swear!"

Her shallow breaths tickled his hands as she removed them from his face. No doubt to examine whether there was any truth in his eyes.

His trembling fingers hovered over her bruised cheek as he watched her chest rise and fall in quick succession.

Delicately caressing her face, he wiped her tears away. "Oh, darling. What have I done to your beautiful face?"

B broke down, sobbing, and Zander hugged her hard to his chest, holding her tight and stroking her head. His own tears leapt from his eyes, flooding his face until they became lost in his low hanging beard.

"Please, please, forgive me. I know I'm a monster, darling, but please dinnae leave me. I love you!"

B's body convulsed, her hands gripping onto his chest as she released her hurt.

Zander held her, scared to let go, their synchronized cries were the only sound coming from the cabin that night.

It was the early hours of the morning when Zander woke with B still cradled into his chest. Removing a stray hair from her face, he peered down to examine the yellow and purple bruises covering her left cheek. The bedside light highlighted the depth of color on her skin, instilling anger in his bone-tired body. Aware of his actions, remorse consumed him, and anxiety reared its ugly head, knowing B hadn't forgiven him yet. He hoped she would, despite his unforgiving self.

Zander's rigid body remained fixed to the wall, careful not to disturb her, allowing him time to digest the events of the day. B woke an hour later, interrupting his chaotic mind, peeling herself from his chest to meet his remorseful eyes.

He stroked her bruised cheek. "Does it hurt?"

B averted her eyes, shrugging away from him. "A little."

Zander shook his head, disgusted at himself. "Welsh Cake, I'm sorry!"

"Stop with the apologies!"

He took her hand. "Tell me how to fix this? I'll do anything."

B snatched her hand away. "I'm not sure you can."

Zander cupped the back of her head, bringing her forehead to his lips. "Dinnae say that, please."

B's bottom lip trembled. Shaking her head as if she was trying to shake the last sixteen hours from her existence. "You hurt me. Physically fucking struck me while shattering my bloody heart!" Every word shook from her mouth as she spoke.

Zander hyperventilated. "I know, beautiful, and I fucking hate myself for it. Please allow me to fix this; head, and heart."

"Scottie, we're supposed to be getting married in twelve hours! We were supposed to have everything perfect for our wedding." She shrugged in a soft murmur. "Perhaps the universe is encouraging us to take a step back: see the wood from the trees."

Zander snapped his head towards her; his gravelly tone was thick with hurt as he spoke. "No. This isn't what I want. You're my entire world. The reason I live and breathe. Please let me make this right. Christ! Please?"

"How can I guarantee this shit won't happen again? The first time you lost your rag; you tanned my ass. Kinky shit, I can get with, but getting smashed in the fucking face, good boy, is a brand-new bag!"

Pain engulfed Zander as if someone had stabbed him in the heart. "Blethen, no!" his words shook. "I promise I will never lay a hand on you ever again. Fear took hold of me. In a moment of insanity, I feared the worst. Please believe me; I would never put you in harm's way."

She averted her gaze. "Was it worth it?"

"What?" he said, screwing up his face in confusion.

"Was it worth it? Did you get the outcome you wanted with Leif?"

Zander closed his eyes and shook his head. "Nothing is worth hurting you, Welsh Cake."

B glared at him. "Is he gone for good?"

"He's arriving in Uskiville later to see what I think of his business proposal."

B stood, creating distance between them. Her eyes were wired and raging. "So, let me get this bloody straight. The man who sexually assaulted me and his psycho father are coming to our wedding to discuss business after I took a backhander from my fiancé?"

Zander tried to speak until B snapped.

"Fuck you, Scottie! Fuck you, the wedding and the club. How fucking dare you?" she spat. "How fucking insulting is that?"

Zander stood to calm her, reaching out his hands and B slapped them away with vicious intent. "He wants to apologize and to thank you for stopping me from killing the wee prick who grabbed you. Darling, he's trying to mend bridges and, to be honest, I would have agreed to anything just to make him leave. You were on my mind throughout."

B scoffed. "Yeah, right, then? That's just guilt talking, and as for that red-headed prick, he just wants my money," B said, storming off into the bathroom. Whipping her head over her shoulder, she spat her words like toxic venom. "Find another bloody cash cow, good boy, and find another fiancée."

Zander clenched his fists. Conniption rallied through his soul as he followed her, flinging the bathroom door open. His nostrils flared as he lost his cool. "You think that was fucking easy for me? Walking into a bar to discover my old lady beating the crap out of The Rus Reapers' VP?"

B glared back at him. He could see she'd called the Dragon out of her slumber to deal with what her fragile mind couldn't.

He continued, refusing her a chance to answer his rhetorical question. "My only fucking thoughts were, 'she's gonnae die and I'm gonnae lose the love of my life',"

"Oh, I'm sorry defending myself from a sexual assault caused an inconvenience to you. Should I have allowed him to take me while your brothers watched?"

"No! Christ! You could have screamed for help, anything but no, you had to let that fucking fiery dragon rear her ugly head and show everyone how tough you are!"

"Well, I ain't no dam-"

"Damsel. Oh, and dinnae I know it! You've rammed it down my throat enough times."

"Fuck you!" she hissed, turning on the shower.

He palmed the wall. "No, fuck you, Welsh Cake! Like you, I reverted to what I'm programmed to do."

"What? Hit women?" she shrieked, throwing her shirt at him.

"Argh, no! God, you're so damn impossible sometimes. I meant finding solutions to keeping you alive and out of harm's way!"

B's eyes screamed blue murder as Zander raised a palm like a stop sign. Calming, he took a steady step toward her, noticing her heaving chest. "All I'm saying is I found myself in an impossible position. My primary instincts were to keep you alive and despite the disgust I feel after hurting you, you're still breathing and that's more important to me."

B shook her head, dragging down her jeans. "So, I should forgive you, seen as your actions were so justified?"

Zander took another step forward. "I'd like you to try, darling."

B clenched her fist before throwing a right hook, clattering him in the eye in a rampant rage, sending him stumbling backward. Panting in anger, her eyes were ablaze, boring into his.

Pressing his fingers to his eyebrow, the wetness covered them as blood trickled down his face. "You fucking hit me!"

"Not fucking nice, is it, good boy?" she snarled.

Zander gritted his teeth. Knowing the dragon had come out to play made his blood boil. Shaking his head and providing his menacing glare, he could see B wasn't frightened anymore. The shock of the incident, a distant memory as her fiery dragon eyes glowered at him.

He stood a breath away from her, his chest heaving in anger just as hers did. "Make you feel better, darling?" he growled. "Restore some Dragon pride? Allow you to regain some fucking control, did it?" he said, edging her into the shower.

"I'm levelling the bloody playing field, good boy. I'm sorry your club has brought so much disrepute into my life that you felt it was your duty to save my ass. But Newsflash! I'm done. You don't need to put yourself out anymore!"

Zander gritted his teeth. Seething, he stepped closer, forcing her under the shower spray, watching the water crash onto her head, forming a waterfall down her back. "Well, I'm certainly no' done, Dragon. You're my property, remember? I own your beautiful ass. It belongs to me!"

B raised her hand to strike him again. Only Zander caught her wrist, pinning it to the cold-tiled wall. She raised the other hand for Zander to catch it, pinning both hands above her head and pressing himself against her. He growled, knowing Dragon only responded to bold assertiveness. "You can be pissed for however long you need. I'm good with that because I know deep beyond the shock you know how much I love you, but this drama ends now!"

His bloodied eye dripped down her chest as she tried to push him away until he crashed his lips into hers with force, feeling her anger diminish beneath him with every stroke of his tongue.

"Let me go!" she snapped, coming up for air and gathering her senses.

"Is that really what you want, Blethen?" he asked seductively, tracing her neckline with his lips and feeling her melt beneath him.

B moaned.

"Dinnae fucking think so!" he said, picking her up and pinning her against the wall.

B raked through his hair with frantic hands, pulling him and forcing her tongue down his throat with her dragon anger.

He loved how passionate she became when he turned her on, awakening his arousal through his soaked denim jeans.

He tugged on her nipple with his teeth just hard enough to make her whimper.

"Good girl. Now let me release your rage like you know I can, beautiful," he said, releasing himself from his jeans and positioning himself at her entrance.

She froze in his arms as he watched her panic-stricken face crumble. "No, Scottie, stop, please?"

"Welsh Cake, you know it calms you, darling. Dinnae fight this. Allow me to make things right," he whispered into her ear.

"Black. Black!" she screamed, cutting through him like a hot knife through butter.

Panic washed over him, and his heart pounded in confusion. Releasing her, he stepped away from her; hands raised in a state of shock. "You dinnae want me?" he whispered.

B stepped closer. "I'm so fucking mad at you and God knows how long it'll take me to forgive you, but I do want you."

Zander fell into a defense mode of his own. "Dinnae lie to me. I saw the fear in your eyes when you screamed black."

B placed her hand on his cheek. "I'm not lying, Scottie. I froze because I don't want this moment to be how I remember us conceiving our first child. This was supposed to be different. I want it to be special, not a relief fuck."

Zander's panic transpired into compassion. "That seems to be the story of our lives," he said, reaching his hands around her waist.

"I'm sorry," she said, softening. "For stopping you from fucking the rage out of me, that is. Not for hitting you. You deserved that."

Zander smiled, running his hand through her soaking wet hair. "You know you hit like a bloke? I was seeing stars for a second there."

B flushed with embarrassment, checking his injured eye. "If it's any consolation, my knuckles are killing me. Your head is like stone, good boy."

Zander grabbed her hand, kissing her knuckles better. "I'm sorry, Welsh Cake. For everything." He kissed her bruised cheek. "Tell me how to make this better. I'm desperate to marry you. You're the love of my life."

B bit her lip. A telltale sign she was choosing her words wisely. "You still want to get married?"

Zander laughed at her. "Of course, I do!"

He watched her sigh, making him nervous as she continued. "Then you need to call Leif and explain he's welcome at our wedding, but you're not doing business until after our honeymoon. Tell him what you want about me but give me our wedding day and keep that wanker son of him away from me and Tyr."

Relief washed over him. "Whatever you want, beautiful, and dinnae worry about Ragnar. Tyr battered him after I give him a pasting."

B's jaw dropped. "What?"

Zander grabbed a towel from the towel rack, wrapping it around her. "Aye, he faced his demons, darling, and I was so fucking proud of him."

"Is he alright?" B asked with concern in her tone.

Zander rubbed her back. "He's fine. Tiny's looking after him. Now, is there anything else you need to get off your angry dragon chest before I get out of these wet clothes?"

B stared at him with serious eyes. "Yeah. You ever lay a bloody hand on me other than spanking me in the bedroom, I'll kill you!"

Zander swallowed his anxiety. "I dinnae doubt it, darling, but it'll no' happen again. But I will say, you're hot as fuck when you're angry. I had to hold back from drilling you to the wall after you hit me,"

B laughed, "Yeah," she said, dropping her towel and pushing him into the shower.

Ripping off his shirt in a flash, Zander kissed her lips, brimming with excitement.

"Mm, Scottie. You are smoking hot. Let me give you what you need."

Zander closed his eyes as B reached down to grasp his bulging cock from his unbuttoned jeans, before yanking on the cold shower and running away in hysterical laughter.

"Oh, Jesus. That's cold!" he hissed. The icy water shocked his every synapse.

Zander loved seeing her eyes dance as she laughed. Her naughty smile teased him as she looked so pleased with herself. He switched off the shower, diving out after her, sliding across the floor into her grasp and grabbing her. Picking her up and throwing her over his shoulders, he carried her to her bed, laying her down and climbing on top of her, devouring her mouth with his. "I cannae wait to marry you, Blethen."

"Right back at you, handsome."

He studied her face. "Promise me we're okay now?"

"We're okay, Scottie," she said with a sincere smile.

CHAPTER TWENTY-ONE
Mateo and Greyhound: Messing with Nature.

Mateo strolled into the Greyhound MC with his minders, as if he owned the place.

"How is he today?" he asked the tubby VP.

"Same as usual. Miserable as sin."

"Don't worry. He's about to be on top of the world," Mateo laughed, handing him a document with details pertaining to the latest shipment of fentanyl and methamphetamine. "Tonight's shipment. It's a big one. I want it packaged and ready for distribution in forty-eight hours, prior to my departure this weekend. I'm entertaining, so I require a kilo of each ready for collection tomorrow evening."

"Sound. I'll get everyone on it as soon as it docks."

Mateo gestured to his minder. "Pay him."

The curly-headed minder handed the VP a manila package containing several bricks of cash.

"Sound. This will keep the club going for a short while."

Mateo strutted to the beaten-down club dorms, sneering at club members. He despised how his older brother lived, especially when Mateo offered to house him in more comfortable surroundings.

He walked through his brother's open bedroom door to see him smoking in his chair.

Swiping the cigarette from his hand, he dabbed it out on a nearby plate.

"Cut it out," Anton snapped.

"Come on, man. What's the matter with you? Get your mask back on!" Mateo said, wheeling the oxygen tank within Anton's reach and handing him the mask.

Anton slapped the mask from his hand. "What's the point? I'm practically dead, anyway."

Mateo sighed, retrieving the dangling mask and handing it back to him. "Cover your face and I'll share something to make you feel better."

Anton's gray and decaying face stared at him with inquisitive eyes.

"Put the mask on, big bro. You need to build your strength."

Anton placed the mask over his face, drawing in the fresh supply of oxygen and coughing as if he was choking on it.

"Take it easy," Mateo said, wiping down a chair and sitting opposite him. Making himself comfortable, he grinned at Anton. "We found him. You're getting your pound of flesh."

Anton's dead eyes sprang to life as if his body had been jump-started. Removing his mask, he leant his creaking body forward. "Are you certain you have the correct Irishman this time?"

"Oh, come on! It was an easy mistake to make. The guy looked just like him. And yes, I got the right guy. He lives a few hours west of here. We're leaving shortly to collect him." Mateo scoffed.

"I'm coming with you," Anton said, trying to shift his frail body. His condition saw him presenting like an eighty-year-old rather than a sixty-five-year-old.

Mateo leapt from his chair. "Hold your horses. You're staying here where it's safe. Besides, I'm using him as my champion first. He can pay off what I lost when he took you all out and halted distribution. My current champion has slowed down; the side effects of the Gen Force. I'm not sure he'll see the next tournament through."

Anton growled, provoking an uncontrollable coughing fit as he worked himself up.

"Easy. You'll wind up back at the hospital if you're not careful."

Anton slowed his troubling breaths. "I want payback!" he stammered.

Mateo stood, placing a hand on his shoulder. "And you'll get it! There's thirty million riding on this, and let's face it, the guy can fight. He can win the tournament, then after the final, I'll drag his ass here and you can have at it in front of the entire MC."

"How long is this campaign?"

"Ten weeks! Our Cuban cousins demanded we extend it, boasting they would have won the last tournament if my guy had to endure two more fights. As if," he cussed, admiring himself in the mirror hanging on the nicotine-stained walls above his brother's head. Adjusting his suit, he continued. "Ten weeks, then you can have your revenge. Take what he took from you."

Anton removed his mask again. "And what if he dies prematurely?"

Mateo kicked his head back in a fit of laughter. "I only bet on winners. He's a decent fighter, and he'll last. My super drug will jack him up. He's the last test patient I need before I can take my proposal to the military. Can you imagine the United States Army with an infantry of super soldiers? I'll be printing my own money."

"What about its longevity? You said yourself it has side effects."

Mateo picked up an old newspaper. "Old news. My company has modified it. Its compound is more durable, placing less stress on the cardiovascular system. The drawback is needing another drug to counteract the comedown." He sighed into his page turn. "You can only take it short-term, which is why I need a new champion."

Anton took another hit of oxygen, shaking his head. "You're messing with nature, Mateo. You're ambitious, I get it, but the military won't sign off on something so unstable. Go through the proper channels,"

"Impossible. My research failed ethical approval. No. I have a contact who's informed me they'll overlook the ethical clearance if my drug shows promise. They'll have documented research and they'll be stupid to turn it down."

"Documented research of unsanctioned human testing. You'll get a life sentence."

Mateo chuckled. "Don't be such a square. Who do you think comes to bet on my champion? I have government officials, millionaires and foreign representatives witnessing history unfold. After your nemesis pays his dues, I'll have what I need to change the face of military operations, and I'll sell it to the highest bidder. We might even find you a new set of lungs." He kissed his brother's forehead. "I'll call you when I have him. Don't go dying on me yet, bro. I'll see you in a week or two."

Anton grabbed his sleeve. "Don't underestimate that Irishman. The fearlessness in his eyes is undeniable. He has a fucking screw loose!"

Mateo placed his hand on his brothers. "The only look he'll have is one of desperation when you rip out his heart. Rest easy, bro," he said, leaving the room.

CHAPTER TWENTY-TWO
Wedding Ready

B had just finished getting ready and was waiting for Mack and Frankie to walk her down the aisle. Excitement and nervousness swept through her as she sat waiting to marry the man of her dreams.

The door knocked, making her jump, and Mack popped his head into the room, beaming at her.

"Dragon," he gasped, entering and closing the door behind him.

B stood to greet him. "Do I look alright?"

"Incredible," he said, stepping toward her and taking her hands.

B smiled. "You scrub up pretty well yourself, sunshine."

"B," he said, catching her off guard. He had never called her by her name before.

He cleared his throat. "Are you sure you want to marry that Scottish prick?"

B narrowed her eyes in distaste. "What the bloody hell is that supposed to mean? Of course, I do. I wouldn't bloody be here if I didn't."

Mack pursed his lips. "Really? You don't feel coerced, pressured, or anything?"

B ripped her hands away, stepping away from him. "No! Now what the fuck is going on? Why are you trying to ruin my wedding day, Mackie? You're supposed to be supporting me like a best friend should."

Mack stepped closer to her. "Maybe because I know you have feelings for me. You may not want to admit it, Dragon, but I saw it written all over your face when you arrived here wanting my help."

"So, you chose my wedding day to fuck my life up? What the fuck is wrong with you? I love Scottie. I want to marry him! What do you not understand about that?"

"But you don't deny having feelings for me?"

B turned away from him and Mack pressed his chest to her back, tilting his head and whispering into her ear. "Please, Dragon. Just be honest with me. This is fecking torture. I need to know how you feel, once and for all."

B raised her head to the ceiling. The hurt in her heart, rattling old trauma loose from the depths of her soul. "Okay, Mackie. Let's get everything out in the open," she said, wandering over to her vanity table to sit.

Mack followed, kneeling before her. She couldn't help but study his attractive face as he stared into her eyes. Taking his hand, she pursed her lips. The pain she was bringing to the surface threatened her with floods of tears. "You're right. I was in love with you. I fell in love with you the day I met you, and part of me will always love you."

Mack gasped, "Dragon!"

She raised her free hand, curbing his excitement.

"I fell in love with you when I was so broken by the world. I didn't want to confess my feelings to you because I was scared that my brokenness would eventually poison our relationship and ruin our friendship, as I was living in fear. Mackie, I suppressed every feeling for you, not knowing how you felt and convinced myself I wasn't good enough for you."

Mack knelt up to caress her face. "Dragon, yo—"

"Please let me finish," she whispered.

Mack sat back on his heels, giving her a nod to continue.

"By the time you confessed your love for me, I'd surpassed everything. You witnessed my promiscuity at the Sultry Slalom, making me doubt your respect for me as a partner. I assumed you thought I was a fuck up and I told myself you were just lonely. Mackie, I told myself you didn't love me. You just wanted me for convenience."

Mack's face crumbled; his glacier eyes full of sorrow. "Dragon, I've loved you at your worst. What made you think I wouldn't love you at your best? You've grown into the most beautiful woman on the planet, and my love for you has continued to grow." He caressed her cheek. "You are my forever, woman."

B's voice wobbled. "Mackie," she said, standing to hide her tears. "I wanted to find Junior for you, hoping it would prove my worthiness as your life partner. But then Ari appeared, and we know what happened next."

Mack rose to his feet, circling to face her. His distraught countenance reflected anguished tears. "I wish you'd have said something. If I knew I had a fraction of a shot with you, I'd never have given her a second glance, Dragon. I swear!"

B pursed her lips, wiping her tears with the pads of her index fingers.

Mack placed his hands on her hips. "Choose me now, Dragon, please? And I'll swear I'll make up for lost time. I'll worship you for the rest of my life."

B shook her head, breaking free from his embrace. "Not this time, lovely boy. I've grown through all the trauma and worked through the emotions that kept me bound and hurting by you."

"Please, Dragon!"

"No, Mackie. I don't love you like that anymore, and I choose Zander. He loves me like a woman should be loved. I chose him for throwing his life on the line to protect me. I choose him for his lack of ego and for not endangering my life." She sighed. "Sometimes, Mackie, love just isn't enough."

Mack stared at her as if he was searching her soul for more of an explanation as B continued.

"He worships me as much as I worship him. There's no imbalance between us. He wears his heart on his sleeve and couldn't care less about materialism or status. Like me, he just wants peace. I will always love you, Mackie, but Zander is the man I live and breathe for," she cried.

Mack pulled her into his embrace. "Don't cry beautiful. I understand, but the moment that changes, the moment he lets you down, and he will, Dragon, you run to me so I can welcome you home with open arms."

"Oh, Mackie."

Mack grasped her shoulders, holding her to examine her. "Dragon, no man will match my love for you. Zander taught you how to feel again, making you more beautiful than ever. I get that, but we're twin flames, Dragon. I see you in all your glory, baby. I see you shine in the darkest places when he struggles with that side of you. My torch for you will burn always."

B choked down her tears, allowing a sob to escape. She had never revealed her feelings about Mack to anyone, not even herself, until today.

He stroked her face, inching closer.

"Please respect my decision, Mackie," she whispered.

Tears fell from his eyes as he placed his head on hers. Finding her lips, he kissed her. An unexpected B found her lips entwined with his, and his tongue exploring her mouth, before pulling away and just as Frankie entered the room.

Her head remained in place, undistracted by the shock in Frankie's wide eyes. "Mackie. Please? Say the words and let me go."

Mack trembled in an agonizing cry. "Best friends never quit."

B held him steady, the pain in her face crippling her as her tears threatened to ruin her make-up.

Frankie closed the door in a hurry, stopping dead and staring dumbstruck as tears rained from Mack's face.

Mack pulled away, turning to compose himself as B stood in desolation.

"What the fuck's going on?" Frankie growled.

Mack bowed his head. "That's just it, Frankie, nothing is going on."

"Glad to fucking hear it. Now go wash your face while I talk to B," Frankie snapped. His tone was as harsh as frostbite on icy skin.

Mack turned, casting a last glance at the bride who wasn't his. Nodding, he squeezed her hand again. "It's my honor to walk you down the aisle with Frankie, beautiful."

B smiled. "Thank you, Mackie. That means the world to me."

Mack gave her a cheeky wink and B watched him leave the room.

Anguish ripped through her, crippling her into a sob.

Frankie rushed to her side as she steadied herself on the back of the vanity chair.

"Jeez, B, what's he done now? Upsetting you on your wedding day. I'll kill him."

B shook her head, pained by it all. "No, it's okay. All those words left unsaid needed to be spoken today. I couldn't marry Zander until everything was out in the open."

Frankie helped her to her chair, collecting the bottom of her dress, allowing her to sit.

"Talk to me," he said, leaning against the wall.

B chuckled in disbelief, grabbing a cotton pad to fix her make-up. "He told me he loved me, and I was honest about my feelings."

Frankie bit down on his bottom lip. "Shit!"

"No, I told him I've always loved him, but I was so broken back then, I was too scared to admit it. Then he met Ari." Her voice wobbled, "and it broke my heart all over again. I never told him how I felt until today, and I'm glad I cleared the air."

Frankie retrieved the spare chair from the room's corner to sit next to her. "B,"

"No," she interrupted. "The first time he told me; I was vulnerable and distrusting from my divorce. We were growing Frankie, but Ari fucked all that, then Mackie turned into a fucking lunatic."

Frankie retrieved his spare handkerchief, dabbing her new tears. "B, if you want to cancel the wedding…"

"No, no, she panicked. That's not what I'm saying."

Frankie furrowed his brow.

"I was hurting. Then Scottie appeared like a beacon of hope. The instant attraction, the rush of love I felt knocked any feelings for Mackie out of the park." She clutched her chest. "More real than any feeling I've ever felt. I may have been in love with Mackie, but Scottie stole my heart. Every fiber, every synapse in my body called out to him, Frankie. There's no other man I'd rather be marrying today. I just needed to free myself from my past and get everything out of my system, and what you saw was me asking Mackie to let me go."

Frankie glared at her.

"Look. He kissed me goodbye and agreed to walk me down the aisle. He'll always be my best friend and part of me will always love him, but I'm not in love with him. Zander owns all of me and I love him more than life itself."

Frankie clasped his hand to his chin, rubbing it.

"Say something," she pleaded with desperate eyes.

"I'm gob smacked by the revelation. You kept all this bottled up until your wedding day?"

"Mackie brought it up, and I let everything out. Frankie, it's taken me so long to come to terms with everything. I'm so much stronger than the woman you met all those years ago."

Frankie tilted his head in a sympathetic gaze, whispering to her. "But that kiss, B. It didn't look like nothing to me."

"It took me by surprise, yeah, but Frankie, it was a goodbye kiss. I promise. I'm gonna tell Scottie, just not today. We need some positivity amidst all the negativity we've endured. Frankie, we need to win, and so does the MC."

"B, if you tell Prez, it'll ruin the club."

B's eyes shot open. "I'm not keeping this from him. We have no secrets between us!"

"I'm simply saying that some words should remain unspoken for everyone's benefit."

B faced the mirror, fixing her make-up. "No Frankie, we can't build a relationship on lies. Transparency is what we need. Look how the cascade of lies damaged us. I'll explain to Prez, he'll listen to me."

Frankie raised his head to the ceiling as B fixed her make up and powdered her nose.

"He'll still want to kill Mackie, and you'll be stuck between them again."

B paused; her make-up brush still pressed to her cheek. "I'll sort it. Scottie will be relieved of the closure. Mackie gets the picture now."

Frankie laughed. "B, you just confirmed what he's known in his heart for years. If nothing else, Mackie boy is relentless. All you've done is empower him."

"Stop it, Frankie."

"B, he loves you, and even though you are besotted with Zander, it won't ever prevent Mackie from wanting you."

B shrugged. "Well, he'll have to accept it, because I don't want him. I've made myself clear and closed that cycle out."

Frankie smirked, handing her lipstick. "Spoken like a true old lady. Listen, let the dust settle before you tell him and give me a head's up so we can prepare for his almighty wrath."

B stood, pulling her dress into place. "Well, how do I look?"

Frankie stood to meet her gaze. "Like my sister, adorable and about to marry her dreamboat, Prez."

B dived into his arms. "Thank you, Frankie. You're my rock and I love you so much."

"Oof," he said, hugging her back. "I love you too, sis. Now let's get you hitched before more drama finds us."

CHAPTER TWENTY-THREE
Confession

Zander sprayed himself with his best aftershave, knowing the strong undertones of pepper and bergamot made B's heart flutter as he readied himself for his big day. He was adjusting his suit blazer when a knock at the door interrupted him.

Jimmy gave him a puzzling glance.

"Come in," he bellowed, his nerves echoing in his tone.

Mack entered the room, with Zander scanning the desolate look on his face.

"Hey, Irish, how's my beautiful bride? Shouldn't you be getting ready to walk her down the aisle?" he asked.

Mack pinched his lip between his thumb and index finger, making Zander's fight-or-flight kick in.

"What?" he asked in exasperated defeat. "Please tell me she's no' panicked and stood me up?"

Mack shook his head. "Nah, brother, she'd never do that. She loves you."

Jimmy cast Zander another confusing glance.

"Then what the fuck is it?" Zander said with faltering patience.

"I need to be honest with you."

Zander raised an eyebrow while pulling out a chair to take a seat. He crossed his legs and straightened his tie. "And this cannae wait until after my wedding?"

"No! I told her I loved her again today, got some truths out of her."

Zander tore his tie from his shirt.

"Hold up," Mack said, raising his palm. "Let me finish."

Zander growled. His white knuckles showing his restrained anger.

Mack puffed out his chest. "I knew Dragon had feelings for me and today she told me she had. I kissed her Prez, confessed my love, hoping she would pick me."

Zander tapped his knee, trying to contain his rage as Mack continued.

"Selfish I know. It was my last feeble attempt to win her back. Only, she doesn't love me, brother. She fecking worships you!" His voice shook with hurt. "I'm telling you this because I know she'll feel guilty. She didn't kiss me back, Prez. She made me let her go. And while I'm not sorry I tried, I'm sorry I hurt you both on your wedding day."

Zander ran his hand through his fixed hair, tussling it into a hot mess, and Mack didn't give him a chance to speak.

"All I'm saying is, don't punish her for my actions when she tells you because she did nothing wrong. She's not my Dragon anymore, she's yours," he said, fighting against his tears.

Zander stood in disbelief and Jimmy's trembling body turned away from them, no doubt predicting his Prez's actions.

Zander nodded. Approaching Mack and placing a hand on his shoulder, he smiled at the broken man. "Thank you for your honesty, brother. That must have been a hard pill to swallow."

Mack stared up at Zander now, pursing his lips.

"I'm sorry," he cowered, as if he knew his fate.

Zander tilted his head, acknowledging him, patting his back before stepping away.

Mack released a sigh of relief until Zander turned on his heels, upper-cutting him, sending him flying.

Mack crashed onto the floor in a thud as Zander foamed at the mouth, spitting through his teeth.

"You dinnae know when to quit, do you Irish?" he wailed to a sprawled-out Mack, watching the blood pump from his nose, and his cheek swell before his eyes. "What did you expect? She would run off into the sunset with you," he said, kicking his feet like he was blasting a soccer ball into the back of the net.

Fury tore through his bones, waiting for Mack to answer. His evil eyes staring him down like a predator sneering at his prey.

"No." he muttered. "I knew she wouldn't pick me, but I had to be sure Dragon no longer had feelings for me."

Zander grabbed the chair, straddling it and resting his arms on the wooden frame. "So, tell me, Irish. Did you get what you needed? The confirmation she dinnae love you."

Mack sat cross-legged like a naughty schoolboy, sniffling. "She loved me once, a long time ago, just not anymore."

Zander growled. "And that's my fucking point! You think I dinnae know she had feelings for you?" His sarcastic laugh unnerved Mack, who jumped at his bellowing tone. "Everyone and their fucking cat could see it, but she keeps telling you no, pal, and you dinnae listen. I made her mine and yer still trying to fuck her!" He grimaced. "Christ. She's finally in a good place and you cannae let her be happy. What the fuck is wrong with you?"

Mack pinched the bridge of his nose, trying to ensure the blood didn't drip onto his suit.

"I can't help being in love with her. I try so fecking hard, yet it consumes me."

"Aye, I understand, but be a fucking man and show some restraint."

"You're right. I apologize," he said, catching his blood in the palm of his hand.

Jimmy handed him a box of tissues as Zander scratched his head. "No means no, asshole!" Zander's temper flared again. "If you cannae leave my lassie be, there's no place for you in the Gray Wolves. Dinnae undermine me again." He sighed in frustration, peering down at his broken brother. "Christ, if you dinnae mean so much to her, I'd slit your fucking throat here and now, but I cannae be mad knowing how much you must be hurting. You dropped the ball, Irish, and I was lucky enough to find it. Christ, you must be crazy if you think I'll ever give it back."

Mack hung his head in shame. Soft tissue dangled from his blocked nostrils, making him speak funny. "I know. I'm an asshole."

The anger dwelling in the pit of Zander's stomach compelled him to further reiterate to the already devastated Mack. "Welsh Cake is my old lady. I love her beyond fucking measure, and I'll never let her go. You did, and the question is brother, can you live with that?"

Mack sniffled. "You're right! I must, for all our sakes. So, what now?"

Zander stood from his chair, placing it aside. Extending an arm to Mack, helping him to his feet. "Now, you clean yourself up and walk my old lady down the aisle and if you cannae keep your shit together, you need to drop the cut and fuck off to Alaska. Honestly brother, the next time you try it on with her, I'll no' be so fucking hospitable. Now fuck off!"

Mack gave a sympathetic nod, dragging himself out of the cabin.

Zander bent over, gripping the corners of the dining table, heaving in disgust.

"You alright, man?" Jimmy asked, approaching him, and clasping his back.

Zander dragged in a breath, trying to calm himself. His nerve-endings continued to flare in satanic rage as he tried to suppress the irritation in his lungs. "Do you think she still has feelings for him, Jimmy?"

"Not for a fucking second. Look, you can't change their history, but if Welsh Cake wanted him, she wouldn't be preparing to marry you." He grabbed Zander by the scruff of his neck. "She is a strong-minded, take no BS woman who knows her own mind and won't let anyone sway her. You've been through wars to get here, and let's face it, she isn't marrying you for your fucking money. Now get Mack's mindfuck out of your head. She wants you!"

"Aye?"

"Yeah, fucking, 'aye.' Think about it. The woman who fucked and ran is donning a fucking sexy wedding dress for you, you big bastard. Taking vows with you. This was just Mack's desperate attempt to fuck with her. She wants you Prez, don't let Mack ruin that with his feeble attempt to win her back."

Zander stood, expelling every carbon dioxide particle into the air from his overworked lungs. "I dinnae know what to do with him, pal."

Jimmy clasped a palm to his cheek. His stern gaze fixed upon Zander's hurting eyes. "Look, after the wedding, Sunnyville keeps its distance from Uskiville. The businesses are separate, and Welsh Cake is gonna be busy growing your pack. Do you think she's gonna even glance at him when you plant your fucking seed inside her? Nah brother, her head's gonna go mushy as fuck with baby shit and her love for you is gonna grow beyond anything you've ever felt before."

Zander's sorrow transmuted into glee. "I cannae fucking wait to see her big old pregnant belly."

"There we are, so get your fucking tie back on and sort your fucking sporran. Now marry that woman, for fuck's sake."

CHAPTER TWENTY-FOUR

B and Frankie were about to leave her cabin when Zander's number flashed across her phone. She glanced at Frankie and froze.

"Mackie!" he said.

B's heart sank upon answering the phone, placing it on speakerphone.

"Hey, shouldn't you be at the altar?" she asked, trying to hide her nerves.

"Dinnae worry darling, I'm here, ready and waiting. I just wanted to tell you, I know, and I dinnae care."

B gulped. "Know what."

"Mack came to me. Told me he kissed you and I know you dinnae kiss him back, darling. I know you sent him packing sweetheart, I guess I just need to hear you say you want me beyond all reasonable doubt."

B welled up, fighting back her tears.

"Blethen, I fucking love you. I dinnae care that you had feelings for him. Christ, woman, I saw the hurt in your eyes when you talked to him, but I need reassurance that you picked me. I need to hear that I'm the one you wanna grow old with," his tired voice trembled.

The torment in B's face transformed into floods of tears. "Of course, I bloody do. Listen. I don't want Mackie. I want you. I love you, good boy. If I wanted Mackie, I'd be with him and not in a bloody dress, ready to marry you. You own my heart, Zander, please believe me when I say that."

Zander's rugged voice wobbled. "Thank you, darling. I really needed to fucking hear that."

B broke down, unable to contain herself, and Frankie placed a loving arm around her.

"Aww darling, dinnae cry. I love you and I cannae wait to marry you."

Relief washed through her. "Sorry, you'll have to wait a bit longer. My make-up is ruined."

Zander chuckled. "Darling, I dinnae give two fucks about your make-up. You can walk down the aisle in a trash bag as long as you say, 'I do.' Now go on, get sorted. I cannae wait to take your hand and walk into the next adventure of our lives."

"I love you, Scottie."

"Love you darling, see you soon."

Frankie held her. "Jeez B, there's never a dull moment with you, is there?"

B laughed. "Life would be boring without my crazy."

"How about we chill the fuck out for the rest of the day?" He stepped back to study her. "You fix your make-up for the fifteenth time, then we'll have a stunning wedding day. No more drama?"

"Fuck, does that exist? I mean, I'd really like that," she said, blowing air from her cheeks.

CHAPTER TWENTY-FIVE
The Red Wedding!

The wedding and the reception took place in the retreat's gardens, in a mesmerizing marquee, at the foot of the valley. B even requested to have her wedding photographs at her favorite spot at the top of the valley. Everything was perfect!

B's family and friends, including Madoc, Rhys, Spencer, David and the Uskiville pack, filled the handcrafted chairs to the left, while the Sunnyville pack and the Rus Reapers sat to the right.

The guests waited in their seats as Zander and Jimmy stood at the altar waiting for the bride.

"I'm digging these kilts man, talk about easy access. No fucking around with my zipper," Jimmy joked, adjusting his sporran.

Zander belly laughed. "Trust you."

"Come on, you must have taken a woman wearing your kilt."

Zander grinned, raising his eyebrow, "just dinnae forget to move your sporran, that fucker will get right in the way."

"So, you have fucked in a kilt. I knew it."

"Aye..." Zander trailed off; his attention diverted to B. He swallowed against the lump in his throat, glimpsing her in the distance.

Her white dress clung to her fabulous curves as Frankie helped her out of her truck. He watched as she linked arms with both Frankie and

Mack as they continued down the aisle to the sound of a harp playing a beautiful melody.

Nerves tore through him like a riptide as B edged closer.

She looks breathtaking.

Zander was ready to marry his dream woman from his bucket list.

Luna sprinkled flower petals like a princess leading B down the aisle and Zander gave her a smile before fixing his gaze at his future wife.

As B approached, her eyes glistened as her beaming smile decorated her face. The tiara she wore sparkled, matching her crystal blue eyes, as she tugged on his heartstrings. Overwrought with emotion, Zander reached for her as Mack took her hand, placing it in his. "She's yours now brother. Take good care of her."

Zander nodded; his words trapped in his trembling throat.

B locked eyes with him, smiling brightly as tears built in Zander's eyes.

Friends and family sat in awe of the happy couple in their stunning surroundings, as Eddie the club chaplain conducted the ceremony.

Overwhelmed, Zander squeezed B's hands as they exchanged their vows, promising their love and devotion to one another. He still couldn't quite believe he was marrying the woman he had fought so hard to be with. They had been through death, lies, deceit in a bundle of what B called a *Cascade of Lies*. Despite enduring storms that often destroy relationships, they were about to be married.

Happy tears filled the reception as Eddie continued with the ceremony.

"If anyone present knows of any reason, this couple should not be joined in holy matrimony. Speak now or forever hold your peace."

Zander grinned at B. His nerves now filled with exciting bliss. He was moments from being married to her, and he could not wait to scoop her up into his arms.

Silence loomed in the room full of smiling faces, waiting for Eddie to continue with the ceremony and just as he opened his mouth, a voice called out.

"I have something to say!"

Gasps echoed around the reception as a tanned man wearing a designer suit strutted down the aisle toward them, escorted by four brutish agents. At least thirty more emerged, surrounding the reception, holding everyone at gunpoint.

Gasps ricocheted around the marquee. "Hello Mr. Kelly, nice set up you got here," the man spoke. His firm tone demanded everyone's attention.

CHAPTER TWENTY-SIX
Your Ass is Mine!

B stood next to Zander watching Mack step forward to face the tall, slim, black-haired Cuban-looking man interrupting her special day.

"And who the feck are you?" Mack hissed with Irish venom. "This is a wedding and you're not on the guest list."

"Oh, this won't take long, Mr. Kelly. I've simply come to collect you as my next champion."

Mack threw a puzzled expression at him.

"Oh, forgive me and allow me to explain. You met my brother a while back. Stepped onto his property at his club in the dead of night and beat him in an unprovoked attack. You left my brother with life-altering disabilities. Now, he can't even take a piss without requiring oxygen."

Mack scratched his head, grinning. "Jog my memory. I've taken out a few people."

"Funny guy! He is the Prez of the Greyhound MC,"

Ari gasped and B glowered at Mack, nodding in agreement with the suited stranger. "Yeah, I remember the sick son of a bitch. He attacked my woman. He's lucky he's still breathing!"

Mateo pinched his chin between his thumb and forefinger, smiling sadistically and stepping towards him, "And which woman is that? The bride or your old lady who's fucking your marriage counsellor?"

Mack's face exploded into a ball of fire.

"Oh, you didn't know." Matteo shrugged, leaning into Mack's personal space. "She's been fucking him since the second meeting, but it's not like you care, right?" he slapped Mack's back, turning to the angry reception as if he was entertaining them. "Everyone knows she's the one you want." He said, pointing to B.

B watched Mack cast his eyes on her as Zander placed a firm hand around her waist, pulling her into his side before staring at a crying Ari, making her blood boil.

"Mack," she cried as Junior stepped away from her.

"Save it!" he growled.

"Are you sure you don't want to talk it over with her? This may be your last chance," Matteo said, retrieving his gun.

Mack sneered. "If you wanted to kill me, I'd be dead right now. So cut the shite and tell me what the feck you want?"

Matteo laughed, tapping a tiny handgun on Mack's temple. "You're not as stupid as I thought, and you're right! You've practically killed my brother and cost me way too much money to comprehend. So, you're going to pay me back with interest."

"And if I don't?"

"I'll wipe everyone out, here and now!" Matteo waved his gun around, encouraging his entourage to cock their weapons.

Mack gritted his teeth. "I'm listening!"

Matteo placed his gun arm around his shoulder. "Like I said, Mackie-Boy. You're going to be my new champion."

"No chance, sunshine!" B snapped. "This is my fucking wedding day, asshole!" she said, breaking free from Zander to punch Matteo in the face, forcing him onto one knee.

Mateo bellowed, licking the blood from his curling lips. "Oh, Mr. Kelly, you've been holding out on me. I planned to select you as my champion, but this one is quite feisty." He turned to B. "Congratulations, momma. You get to take his place!"

Three agents tried to grab B, who kicked the first between the legs, and punched another in the face before the third agent placed a gun at her chest, stopping her in her tracks.

"Dragon," Mack said, charging forward.

The swift agent at Mateo's side struck him in the head with one swift blow, the butt of his gun colliding with Mack's face.

Mateo stood over him with a salacious grin. "I'm going to watch your house burn, Mackie-boy. Once this fishwife is done being my champion, you'll serve your purpose and die by my brother's hands."

Mack wiped his mouth on his sleeve. "You'll die first!"

Mateo kicked him in the face, knocking him unconscious as Leif ran toward Mateo to confront him.

Mateo embraced him, surprising the pack of wolves. "Good work Leif!"

The reception gasped once more as The Gray wolves stood in outrage.

"Where's my son?"

"Serving his time."

Leif lost his temper, gripping Mateo by his suit lapels. "We had a deal, you bastard."

"Cry me a river, Viking. Your son was a traitor. He cost me millions of dollars. Did you honestly believe this would make us even?" Mateo laughed at him.

"You scrawny piece of-"

"Your son's life belongs to me," Mateo sneered as one of his agents placed a gun at Leif's head.

"Leave them," Mateo said. "I've found my new champion. I'll be back for Mackie boy when this one's served her purpose."

"Over my dead body," Zander bellowed, rushing towards B.

"Oh, I can make that happen," Mateo said, and proceeded to shoot Zander in the chest.

B screamed as a guttural rasp ripped from Zander's vocal cords before he dropped to the floor. She tried to reach Zander, who was struggling to breathe, but the guards dragged her away.

Tyr charged forward only to be shot in the thigh while Hyde and Frankie rushed to pack Zanders wound with cotton chair covers.

"Stay back Viking boy. Daddy has already lost one son. Let's not make it another," Mateo teased.

Tiny rushed to Tyr's side as David and Spencer held onto Madoc and Rhys, and Junior and Remy helped a tear-ridden Ari with an unconscious Mack.

The rest of the reception sat in stunned silence as both the Sunnyville and Uskiville packs stood helplessly, witnessing B's abduction.

CHAPTER TWENTY-SEVEN

The emergency services arrived in miraculous time aiding a blood-soaked Jimmy and Frankie. Wasting no time and fearing the worst, they requested emergency helicopter transportation for Zander, who appeared to be hanging on for his life.

Frankie stepped clear, assessing the situation as another EMT rushed to Tyr's aid who had also lost a lot of blood following his gunshot wound to the thigh.

"You'll be alright, Tyr. You're strong." Leif said, sitting by his son's side.

"You're a traitor. This is your doing!" Tyr screamed.

Leif stepped back, stumbling into Frankie, who planted a fist to his face, followed by a knee to his groin before tossing him on the ground.

A crazed Frankie kicked him in the stomach as the Rus Reapers stood by in fear.

"You stitched us up, you worthless piece of shit," he spat, kicking him in the face. "Spill your fucking guts about that asshole! Tell me everything, now!" he snapped, picking Leif off the ground with his bare hands.

"It won't help. She's gone. You won't see her again. Mateo is untraceable."

Frankie head-butted him, dropping him once more. "Nobody is

THE RED WEDDING

untraceable, asshole!" He turned to a trio from the Uskiville pack. "Get him to church and keep him there. If his pack comes near, shoot them in the fucking head."

The trio grabbed him, escorting him past the police officers, questioning the wedding guests.

Frankie approached Mack, who was being jostled awake by Junior in floods of tears, while Spencer and David tried to console Madoc and Rhys.

The Uskiville retreat looked far from idyllic as he watched the drama unfold.

Collecting his bearings, Frankie barked his orders.

"Those not assisting with the investigation can head to the marquee. Get some food in you. It's going to be a long night. That includes you, Reapers," he bellowed before addressing his wolves. "Wolves, muster here, now!"

All the uninjured wolves rushed to Frankie's side. The panic on their faces as they watched a paramedic place the defibrillator paddles on Zander's chest unnerved them.

"Pay attention. This is an active fucking war zone. So, shape up. Prez is in expert hands and with Mackie, Jimmy and Tiny busy, I'm taking the reins."

The wolves displayed unwavering devotion, acknowledging Frankie's role in running the retreat in Mack's absence. Their loyalty stood tall as they focused.

"We need to diffuse this situation as fast as possible. Uskiville pack except for Gnarler. This is your backyard. I need you to keep the peace and watch the Reapers. They don't leave until we get answers. The guests are terrified, and all require questioning by the police. It's your job to assist and ensure that goes smoothly."

He faced the remnants of the Sunnyville pack. Marshall, Eddie, a blood-soaked Hyde and a few prospects remained, standing next to Gnarler, formerly of Sunnyville. "Our mission is to discover the identity and motives of the prick who abducted B. Gnarler, find everything you can from the Reapers, starting with that little prick, Ragnar. Remove his

God damn teeth if you must. I'll start with Leif. We gather intel and meet in church in an hour. Now roll out."

The pack dispersed, and Frankie rushed to Mack who had since sat up to receive treatment from another EMT.

"Mackie, you alright brother?"

Mack tried to rise but tumbled back down. "I got to find her, Frankie."

Frankie steadied him. "Not in that state, brother. Let the medic check you over," he said, placing a hand on his shoulder. "Mackie, I need to know their identity."

Mack winced as the EMT cleaned up his bloodied face. "The guy. Never seen him. The MC. It's the one you rescued me from. Frankie, you know as much as me."

"Why now, though?"

Mack shrugged. "I don't know. Frankie, we should be searching for my Dragon."

"Patience Mackie boy. First, let's uncover the facts. Sort yourself out and come find me."

Frankie stepped away and Mack called him. "Frankie. How's Zander?"

Frankie gave him a bleak stare. "They're doing everything they can, Mackie, but that prick slugged him right in the chest. The blood..." he drifted off before collecting himself. "I'll keep you posted. I'm going to find out what Leif knows."

Frankie walked toward Zander, who was being placed on a gurney. Jimmy shook his head, approaching him. "They're taking him to Rush Mount Hospital. The helicopter is on his way, but he's already flatlined twice. It doesn't look good, man," Jimmy cried.

Frankie gripped his brother, consoling him. "He's a tough bastard. He won't go down without a fight. Listen, I got things here. Tiny is joining Tyr and Mack in the ambulance. Go with Prez and keep me informed. He needs you, man."

Jimmy wiped his tears onto his bloodied shirt. "Yeah, thanks. You sure you got this?"

Zander shrugged. "I used to run an entire company of soldiers. This is a piece of piss. Now go on and give Prez my love."

CHAPTER TWENTY-EIGHT
Slipping Away

Zander choked on the blood rising from his throat. He didn't feel pain as his brothers tried to pack his wounds and keep him conscious. His only thoughts were on B and how he was helpless to save her from Mateo.

He slipped in and out of consciousness as his brothers called out to him; his brain unable to distinguish between the conscious and unconscious.

Fuck, I'm dying. I cannae die like this. I need to save her!

Jimmy's words brought him back to consciousness. "Hang in there, man. There's a helicopter ready to land and fix you up. Don't you dare fucking die on me. You hear?"

The taste of his own blood brought reality to the situation as he tried to breathe. He felt like he was choking on the blood and feared his time on earth would soon end.

Unable to speak, tears rolled from his cheeks.

I dinnae want to go like this. Please, God, let me live so I can save my lassie. She doesnae deserve this.

He blacked out, waking temporarily in the helicopter. The noise of the propellers frightening him awake.

"We got him back." An EMT shouted, holding the defibrillator pads.

Zander's eyes shifted to find Jimmy's white face staring back at him.

He appeared gaunt and paralyzed by the sight of his brother lying near death.

"Hang on in there, Zander. You're almost at the hospital," another EMT said, pushing medicine through his cannula.

Zander slipped out of consciousness as the cardiovascular surgeon whisked him from the helipad to surgery. With urgency in his tone, he barked orders to his team, vaguely registering in Zander's awareness.

"GSW to the chest. Substantial blood loss and he's going into shock. Let's do what we can, people."

CHAPTER TWENTY-NINE
Captured

B, bound, with a bag over her head, realized she was up north from the helicopter ride, long drive and sudden temperature change.

"Where are we?" she snapped as the agent manhandling her, pulled her along by the rope binding her wrists.

"We're near Lake Whatcom in Bellingham. Not that such matters concern you," Mateo said to her left.

"Why cover my head if you intended to inform me?"

"The stops we made earlier. That's a need-to-know basis."

"And let me guess. I don't need to know?"

"Bingo! She's smart, Carter, don't you think?" Mateo said to the agent, bundling her along.

"Sir!"

"Now, you're about to enter my home and den of champions. Dragon, so many have come before you. You should feel honored I selected you for this."

"Oh, I'm bloody charmed, sunshine. I tell you what, untie me and I'll show you how pleased I am that you chose me for your sadistic games."

"Ha! I like you, Dragon. You're going to help me make history. Now watch your step," he said, removing the black cotton bag from her head so she could walk up the steps to his ancient mansion.

Glancing over her shoulder and squinting at the low hanging sun in the distance, B glimpsed the river beyond the acres of green grass at the front of the building, and to her right, trees lined the river that stretched for miles.

"Eyes forward." The agent snapped, pushing her into the building.

Rustic décor with solid wooden beams propping up the ceiling boasted a man's touch with the hunting armor and an array of creepy taxidermy mounted on the walls. Transforming a historic building into a hunting establishment disgusted B.

The open hallway had a cold eeriness to it as B scanned her surroundings. Solid oak, double hand-crafted doors opened into an enormous hall, much like a ballroom on her right, and the left boasted a long corridor leading to what she assumed was the kitchen with the mouth-watering aromas beckoning her tastebuds.

"I'll let you get settled in, and once I know you're calm, we'll talk. We have much to discuss," he said, ushering Carter to escort B down the long corridor.

B attempted to take in her surroundings, creating a mental map of the building and searching for windows and exits. These attempts seemed futile as B's guide directed her past the kitchen and down a cold, narrow service corridor, causing her bones to chill. The poor lighting and the incoming stench of death made her hairs stand on end as she stepped from the corridor to a dreary and poorly lit space akin to a Victorian dungeon.

B gulped at the blood-stained stone, grateful for a distraction from a familiar-looking tall male in his thirties. Dressed in a butler's outfit and turning a narrow corner, he clattered into her, knocking her into Carter.

"My apologies!" he said staring at her with disbelief.

"Watch it, traitor. Or we'll lock you up with her!" Carter snapped.

The strawberry-blonde haired and crystal blue-eyed man gave her a last sympathetic glance before hurrying down the service corridor.

Uneasiness swept through her as Carter continued to edge her further down the dungeon-like cavern until he reached a steel door with a keypad. Punching in the numbers, he waited for the door to slide open, pushing B inside as soon as the door opened wide enough to fit her hour-glass frame.

"Enjoy your stay, Dragon," he said. "Oh, and get out of that ridiculous dress. I'll be back for you soon," he added, closing the door behind her with one press of the keypad.

B pressed her hands to the cold steel door, noticing a slight dent and some old claw marks. No doubt from the room's previous inhabitants. She wasn't keen on spaces without windows or at least a door that she could prop open. Even her Sunnyville office bedroom had windows after she insisted the builders fit them.

B checked for vents and escape routes, then noticed the room's cameras. She acknowledged being trapped and scanned the room. The décor confused her. From the outside, she was sure that they would force her into a cold, damp cell, but to her surprise, the room greeted her with bright, clinically clean surroundings. It had brilliant white walls, a solid hand-crafted double bed with fresh bedding, a built-in closet, bedside table, and an ensuite bathroom.

B couldn't help but chuckle at the irony of the closet.

Because all abducted people carry luggage, just in case the day comes and they're like, oh yes, my abduction attire.'

Opening the closet out of sheer nosiness, her mouth dropped into an angry 'O,' sound.

What the fuck?

Clothing filled the closet. On one side, jeans, T-shirts, shirts, suits, all with the name 'Mack,' handstitched to the front like a name tag. The other side boasted attire for B's taste. Jeans, vests, sneakers, heeled boots, hoodies and scantily clad clothing, all with Dragon, handstitched into the left-side of each item, like Mack's.

B dragged open the drawers, each set of boasted underwear for both a male and female. All designer wear, just like the clothing hanging in the closet.

This is bloody mental!

B followed Carter's advice, slipping out of her ripped wedding dress and folding it before placing it at the bottom of the closet.

You can't escape in a wedding dress, B.

She raked through the closet, grabbing a pair of jeans, a white vest, a light gray hoodie, white socks, and a pair of sneakers. She had just finished dressing herself when Mateo entered the room.

"I hope you find the clothing to your liking. My assistant had to rush out following my last-minute alteration to the champion selection," Mateo said. His arrogance exuded through his rich, Cuban accent.

B slammed the closet shut. "What the fuck is this?"

Mateo smiled like he was enjoying her vexation. "Well, as you can see from the closet, I intended on capturing your dearest Mackie, only I saw showmanship in your flare for the dramatics. The way you tried to defend him was..." he kissed his pinched thumb and forefinger, "chef's kiss!"

B lunged at him, forcing the agents to react. Hudson caught her wrist while Carter, another agent, punched her in the stomach, knocking the wind out of her.

B tried to catch her breath as Carter grabbed her by her hair.

"Enough," Mateo said. "I want her vexed. Nobody touches her. You don't breathe near her, and you certainly don't fuck her. Dragon extracts fuel from her sexual prey. It's like power to her. Displaying dominance calms her frantic mind and I want her agitated, volatile, and ready to kill."

The agent released her as B shoved him away.

B glared at Mateo. "What the fuck do you want from me?"

Mateo grinned, resting his clasped hands in front of his body. "I told you. We're making history and you're my next champion. You could, in fact, be my last."

B narrowed her eyes at him and if looks could kill, Mateo would have died a thousand times over.

"Please?" he said, gesturing to her to sit on the bed. "Let's not act like uncivilized animals. In my house we talk like adults."

B scoffed. "Tell me, what's civilized about abducting a woman on her wedding day?"

Mateo placed his right glute on the bed, sitting half on and half off with a weariness about him that suggested he knew how unpredictable B was, and ensuring his readiness to retreat from her presence at a moment's notice if needed. "Regrettable but necessary, I'm afraid. You see, I'm an opportunist, Dragon; a businessman and while my family has a score to settle, with well, yours," he pointed to her. "Seeing you presented an opportunity for me to become the most powerful person on the planet."

B laughed. "Great, another whack job. Tell me, did your high school yearbook predict you to be the next psychopath? You may wear a fancy suit, but you scream lunatic," she laughed. "I got to hand it to you. I've met my fair share of crazy men going through a midlife crisis, but yours, sunshine, takes the biscuit."

Mateo's smile vanished. "Rude. Didn't they teach you manners in England?"

B punched him as hard as she could in the face, sending him flying from the bed and onto the hard floor. "I'm Welsh, asshole. If you're gonna ruin my wedding and abduct me, at least have the decency to know where I'm from!"

Mateo raised his hand, stopping the agents from attacking B, who puffed like a dragon, ready to breathe fire on her enemies.

He stood, dabbing his bloodied mouth with his suit handkerchief. "If that's how you want it," he said, nodding at Hudson.

B directed her war face to Hudson, who removed a set of LVAD wires and a hospital wrist band from the inside pocket of his suit blazer. Grinning, he tossed them at her as she stared him down.

Catching the items, B peered down at the bloodied wires. Trembling, her fingers ran along the wristband, unearthing the news her mind didn't want to discover.

Mr. Alexander McGovan D.O.B 03/25/82

B studied the items, trying to catch her breath. The unbearable pain shredding her heart into pieces and threatening her to collapse her lungs.

Mateo stood a whisker away. "I see I now have your attention. Yes, your almost husband is on a cold slab in the morgue. I figured you may need a little convincing to do my bidding. Now, if you don't want to see your son's heads mounted on my wall, I suggest you follow my instructions."

B screamed in temper, grabbing Mateo, and slamming him into the

THE RED WEDDING

closet; her piercing shriek almost deafening the agents racing to drag her away. She clawed down Mateo's face like a lioness, maiming its prey. "I'll kill you!"

Hudson threw her on the bed, pinning her chest with one hand and slapping her face with the other while Carter checked over Mateo's injuries.

"I'm fine!" he snapped, brushing him off. "Get her on her knees!"

Hudson and the other agent grabbed a rabid-like B from the bed, kicking the back of her legs and forcing them to buckle.

Anguish, anger, guilt, and sorrow competed for dominance in her mind as tears ran down her cheeks, meeting her baring teeth.

Mateo's eyes beamed, smiling down at her. "Oh, you'll do just fine, Dragon. You are going to fight for me," he said, stroking her face. "Pretty and a killing machine. My buyers will lap you up like the delicious treat you are."

"Buyers?" she spat, as her blood pressure threatened her straining heart.

"Yes buyers. Dragon, the moment I set eyes on you, I knew you were the perfect last candidate for my clinical trials. I told you; I am a businessman, and nobody has come close to creating what I'm selling."

B turned her head away from his slick piano fingers.

"I've created a wonder drug that enhances senses and physical performance. I call it Gen Force, but I may call it DragonX after this," he teased. "Their faces when they see a woman tear their champion apart." He pressed his hands together, bringing them to his grinning lips.

B slowed her breathing to ensure she was assimilating the information Mateo provided.

"Every Friday for the next ten weeks, my buyers will arrive, bringing their fiercest competitors and you will destroy them as if you were destroying me." He gripped her throat, squeezing her windpipe with enough force to catch her breath. "Use me as your fuel Dragon. The man who murdered your true love and wields the power to slaughter your family in a push of a button. Imagine you're slaying me, Dragon. You want to keep your family breathing, you fight!"

B's face turned purple as he held her throat for another second before releasing her. She fought to drag air into her lungs, choking down the oxygen with haste on her hands and knees.

"The research clinician will be ready in due course to administer your first dose and explain the side effects. You have three days' grace to get used to the medication. You will not resist Dragon, and you will listen to your trainer. He will assist you, answer questions and ensure you comply with my demands. You can expect his introduction in the gym today. He will assist you throughout the trial until you no longer need him. He will bring your meals, and Dragon, you will eat."

B glared at him. "You'll die by my hands, Mateo. You can't cage me forever."

"On the contrary, Dragon, I can. Once my team has administered my drug, you will become priceless, just like the only surviving champion before you."

He shrugged, scoffing. "There are no guarantees with research trials," he kneeled, cupping her cheek. "But boy, do I have such high hopes for you, Dragon. You'll be my best accomplishment yet. Militaries across the world will use a drug tested by you. Doesn't that make you feel special?"

B spat in his face. "Fuck you, good boy! I'm already special!"

Mateo blinked away the saliva from his eyes, standing to leave. "Yes, you are!"

CHAPTER THIRTY
Hospital Blues

Jimmy sat in the hospital's corridor in a fresh set of scrubs given to him by the hospital staff after the police took his clothing as evidence. He sat distraught in the rigid plastic fold-down seats for over an hour, waiting for news of Zander's surgery with each minute passing tormenting him.

Jimmy kept replaying the scenario in his head. The ordeal was surreal to him as he shook his head in contempt for Mack.

Mack, you son of a bitch! You keep causing shit and we're living with the consequences. How many others are involved in your cascade of lies?

After texting Frankie, he heard Clarabelle call out to him from the nearby opening elevator. Rushing toward her, he embraced her.

"Belle. What are you doing here?"

"I'm here to check on you, silly," she said, rubbing his arm.

Jimmy went quiet.

"Oh, my God. Is he?"

Jimmy raised his hands, startled by her question. "No, no. He's still in surgery. He's in pretty terrible shape."

"Hey, come on now, he'll be alright," she said, directing him to his seat. "He's tougher than a new pair of cowboy boots. He'll pull through, you'll see."

Jimmy sat. "Thanks Belle, for coming here, I mean."

"Just checking if you're okay. Today was well, er, tough," she said. "I can't stop thinking of B and what she's going through, and those poor boys, watching their momma get dragged away and their step daddy..." she wiped a stray tear from her eye.

"Dang it! Sorry, I'm supposed to be helping."

Jimmy took her hand in his. "You are, Doll face. Just being here is enough."

She smiled at him, "good."

"Come here," he said, placing his arm around the top of her chair and pulling her close.

They sat in silence with heavy eyes, waiting for news as Jimmy's heart raced at a rate of knots.

I can't lose another brother... another best friend. Please Zand, pull through for me, man. I fucking need you!

The surgeon arrived two hours later, waking the pair who slept in each other's arms. Embarrassment flushed their faces, realizing how entwined they were with one another.

Jimmy shirked away, adjusting his scrubs, before standing to greet the surgeon.

"Mr. Creak. Your friend is out of surgery in a stable but critical condition. We've had to place him in an induced coma to allow him a fighting chance. The bullet ricocheted off his sternum, embedding itself in one of his ribs and almost penetrating the intercostal wall. He's extremely fortunate that he was shot with a small caliber handgun; anything else would have been catastrophic."

"But he's alive?"

The surgeon gave him an optimistic smile. "He is. However, the next twenty-four hours are critical. Your friend flatlined many times and went into shock. It's up to him to fight for his survival now. At present, we remain optimistic."

Jimmy dropped his head, trying his best to keep his composure. "Thank you, Doctor."

Clarabelle wrapped her arm around him, addressing the surgeon, who kept a stiff upper lip as Jimmy struggled. "Can we see him?" she asked.

The doctor nodded. "He's on his way to the ICU. A nurse will come to escort you once he is settled. Don't be alarmed by the machines. They are there to aid his breathing while he's in an induced coma. We'll endeavor to remove these once we bring him around in about thirty-six hours. Depending on his stats, we may try after twenty-four hours, but like I said, we'll see what he's like once we get him through tonight."

"Thank you," she said, rubbing Jimmy's back.

Jimmy watched the doctor walk away before sitting back in his seat. He dragged his hands down his face before ripping them through his hair in despair. His eyes became evil as he wailed at the ceiling in anger. "When will this shit end? You've already taken one of my brothers. Wasn't that enough for you? Our family is living through hell, and you keep hurling more at us!"

Clarabelle sat next to him in silence, placing a hand on his knee until he calmed.

"Sorry. It's just. We've all been through so much. It's taking its toll, you know."

"I know, she whispered, but Zander's alive. Anyone else would have died on the spot."

"Not him. He'll never leave Welsh Cake."

"Exactly. He's survived, against the odds, and he'll come through this. Once he awakens, he will need a considerable amount of support. Please ensure you keep your strength up in order to help him."

Jimmy nodded.

"Hey, I'll help you. Don't you worry that pretty head of yours. Right now, you just hang in there."

Jimmy stared at her; his heart was full of gratitude and in an emotional moment, he leaned in and kissed her cheek, stunning her. Pulling away in embarrassment, he quickly apologized.

"Sorry, Belle. I'm just so grateful you're here."

Belle smiled into her rosy cheeks. "Don't apologize. Call it a moment of grief or whatever you like. I'm flattered."

Jimmy sat up straight. His eyes bulged, surprised by her response. "You are?"

"Yeah, silly. You're an attractive man, Jimmy. Truth be told, I was excited to meet you. A real man who can cook? That doesn't happen often where I'm from."

Jimmy grinned. "I'm just sorry I ruined our first meeting."

Clarabelle waved a dismissive hand. "Oh, water under the bridge."

He leaned closer. "What you said about the bunnies? The truth is, I've never believed I was good enough to have an honest woman on my arm, then T broke my heart, and I just became, well, er…" he scratched his chin.

"An angry lion with a splinter in his paw?"

Jimmy chuckled. "Yes!"

Clarabelle gazed into his eyes, captivated by their mesmerizing beauty. The dazzling speckles of hazel and green seducing her as she spoke.

"Lucky for you, I'm great with splinters."

Jimmy swallowed into his grin, stuttering into his next sentence until the nurse arrived to show them to the ICU.

The loud beeps bred fear into Jimmy's thought pattern upon entering the room.

"You won't have long, I'm afraid. He requires continuous monitoring and plenty of rest. It's best if you go home and rest while he's recovering. He'll be out for a while. You can come back in tomorrow and sit with him after we've got him settled in properly."

"Right," Jimmy muttered, stepping closer to the bed.

Zander lay still with a breathing apparatus attached to him. The noisy machines inflated his chest as he remained unconscious.

"Hours ago, he was the happiest guy on the planet. His face, as Welsh Cake walked down that aisle, had been something special. I'd never seen him look so happy. Now my brother has to fight a battle he didn't see coming," Jimmy said, trying to stem his tears.

Clarabelle held his hand. "He's your Prez. He'll pull through, Jimmy."

"And what if he doesn't? He's the closest family I have left."

Clarabelle's stern voice snapped him out of his whimper. "Now don't you dare! You stop thinking like that, Jimmy, or you'll have me to deal with. You got that?"

He swept his tears away. "Yes, ma'am."

"Good. Now say goodnight and let him sleep. He'll have me to deal with if he doesn't pull through and rescue my friend from that God awful man who's taken her."

Jimmy took Zander's hand, surprised by the warmth he felt from his incapacitated brother. "Zand, I swear to God, I'll kick your sorry ass if you bail on me. You don't get to do that! I fucking need you, brother. I get you miss Noah, but he can wait a little longer. Your family needs you. Welsh Cake needs you!" His voice wobbled as he kissed Zander's head. Emotion overwhelmed him as he struggled to function.

Clarabelle tugged on his hand as the nurse waited in the doorway.

"I'm sorry. I have more tests to run. He's in excellent hands and we'll notify you of any changes in his condition," the nurse said.

"Shall we go back to the cabin, handsome? I'll rustle you up with something special. Rest up and you'll be back in the morning before he wakes."

"Sorry Doll face. I'll be staying outside the ICU tonight. Prez is vulnerable, and I don't want anyone taking another shot at him."

"Then I'm staying too!"

Jimmy escorted her from the ICU. "Belle, I appreciate this, but I can't protect Zander if I'm worried about you, too. Please, head back to B's and cook something special for the club. You're needed there."

Belle pursed her lips. "You'll be alright while I'm gone?"

Jimmy smiled. "I'll be fine."

Clarabelle hugged him. "Well, I'll bring you some warm clothes and some good, wholesome food." She reached into her handbag, pulling out a bundle of notes and pressing them into his hand. "Here, take this for coffee and snacks."

Her kindness took Jimmy back. Her endearing eyes burnt into his, pleading with him to accept her help. "Thank you. You know, you're a beautiful soul, Belle."

Clarabelle flushed a thousand shades of red and before she responded, Jimmy rushed in to peck her lips like a nervous teenager.

He studied her expression, shuffling backward. She smiled before stepping into his personal space; his nervousness shone like a bright light as she tip-toed to kiss him, pushing her tongue inside his mouth.

Jimmy's nerves fell away. Closing his eyes, he caressed the back of her neck, reciprocating by massaging her tongue with his, lost in a moment of peace.

CHAPTER THIRTY-ONE
Beat Down

Blood dripped from Leif's swollen mouth, following a myriad of venting blows from Frankie.

He sat in the Uskiville church, a broken man, as Frankie landed another brain-shattering strike to his throat, almost strangling the life out of him.

"I can go all night mother fucker! Now tell me everything or you'll be begging for death," he said, dropping him to the floor in a heap.

Leif coughed, encouraging the excess blood and vomit to exit his fragile throat, trying to compose himself until Frankie gripped his jaw. His grimacing whine showed evidence of the pain Frankie had already inflicted on him. "Let's try this again. You got into bed with the devil and brought my family into it, correct?"

Leif nodded, exhausted by Frankie's merciless brutality.

Frankie transferred his grip from Leif's jaw to his cut, throwing him onto a nearby chair. "You sold us out, for what? To get your son back? Your first mistake! You never make a deal with the devil unless you know how to destroy hell. Now, why did he take your son?"

Agonizing screams from the bar penetrated their ears. "That's right dickwad, Ragnar's having the time of his life with Gnarler. You want to lose another son? One of you will talk or you and your entire MC die tonight."

"Alright! I'll talk. Please leave Ragnar alone."

Frankie crouched down to get up close to him. "I'll leave him alone after you squeal, little pig. Spill your fucking guts before Gnarler spills Ragnar's all over the fucking floor. Tick Tock mother fucker!"

Leif began explaining his history with Mateo.

"I am a lifelong friend of Antons. Mateo's brother. He started out as my prospect a long time ago until he quit running his own pack and working for his brother. He returned a year later with a business deal. His brother is a big-time businessman. He ships in illegal drugs, hiding them with legal pharmaceuticals, to our shipping port in Tacoma. He offered us a deal to collect the shipments and distribute fentanyl and methamphetamine. We supply it on our side and the Greyhounds do the same in Tacoma. Mateo has someone else as distro in Seattle. I do not know who."

Another gut-wrenching screech rattled the church walls.

"Please," Leif begged, pressing his palms together. "Please stop hurting Ragnar. I'll tell you everything."

Frankie gauged the fear in his eyes before banging on the adjoining wall.

Gnarler entered with a drill in hand, its attachment caked in flesh.

"Drag his ass in here," Frankie instructed.

Moments later, Gnarler threw Ragnar's broken body at his father's feet, closing the door behind them.

"Ragnar my boy," Leif cried.

"There'll be time for a reunion later, providing you keep talking," Frankie said, gripping Ragnar by his hair and dragging him across the room. "Now where were we?"

Leif gulped, unable to take his eyes off his son. "Mateo's demands were becoming unrealistic. Our town became overrun with addicts. Fentanyl is an awful, awful drug."

"No shit!"

"I tried to free us, but Mateo showed up as he did today and threatened my club. We did our research, thought we could outsmart him, and he wiped out half of my club."

"So, what did Erik do?"

Leif shook his head. "Silly boy. Unbeknown to me, he tipped off RICO. They seized a shipment, but it was clean. He took Erik to punish me. Calls him his champion. I do not know why, and Anton refused to help me. He will not cross his younger brother."

"And you tried to broker a deal to get him back?" Frankie asked.

"Correct. Mateo contacted me a few weeks ago. Offered to return Erik in return for your Mack. I was unaware of his plans. Mateo asked me to gather intelligence. That is all."

Frankie smirked at the naivety of Leif. "And let me guess. He promised to return Erik at the wedding?"

Leif nodded. "I had no choice. I want my son back and if I refused," he shook his head. "Well, you see the result of refusal."

Frankie jammed his hands into his hips. "Well, where's he taken them?"

"No idea. He has a home in Seattle, but nothing happens there. He has agents guarding him twenty-four-seven and Erik is not there. Wherever his lab is, you will find your Prez's old lady? Rumor is, he conducts disgusting human testing for his pharmaceutical company somewhere up north. We have yet to find it. I do not know whether my son is still alive."

Frankie felt sick to his stomach, thinking of his next move. The thought of B being used as a human guinea pig riled him beyond vexation.

Leif dragged himself to his feet, standing before him. "I am sorry Frankie. I did not mean to harm your kin. The Rus Reapers shall help you on your quest to finding your Dragon."

Frankie gripped his shirt. "That Dragon. The Prez's old lady," he said, glaring at them both. "She is my sister, and you both better hope we find her alive or I will unalive every one of you!"

Horror cast across their already disheveled faces before Leif added. "We will find our people together. Let us work together please! It is our only hope."

Frankie pursed his lips. "Fine, but you cross me, and Mateo will be the least of your worries." He turned to Gnarler. "Get Hyde to clean these bastards up. The Rus Reapers don't leave this retreat. Assign them cabins and gather everyone in the bar for a meeting once the police finish questioning everyone."

The police didn't bring any new information to light, patronizing Frankie with their standard response to the heinous crime. Their attitudes posed as no surprise to him, reminding him of his own views before he found his MC family. Criminals shooting criminals had become the norm to them and they were no further forward in tracking down Mateo with no hits in AFIS.

Frankie had Marshall conduct a thorough investigation of his own, discovering Mateo's only known address in Seattle was impenetrable, requiring facial recognition to enter. With no paper trail to follow, and Mateo's no doubt, air-tight alibi for the time of the abduction. Leif's words rang true. Mateo was, in fact, a ghost.

He bellowed across the bar, demanding attention as the angry Uskiville and Sunnyville wolves intimidated the Rus Reapers, who lined the bar wall.

"Enough! God Damn it. Now listen in. The Rus Reapers are now aiding us. I understand you're all pissed, but remember, B needs us, and when Prez comes around, he'll want an update on what we've done to find her."

"Yeah, but where do we start? Everything is a dead end," Eddie said.

"You're right. That bastard is squeaky clean with no paper trail to lead us elsewhere. There are no subsidiary properties or people of interest to investigate. We're on our own on this. I reached out to old friends about the dock's case. Maybe we'll find something. We're on lockdown until further notice. I also know my sister, so don't write her off on this. If she sees a chance to communicate or escape, she'll take it. I've briefed her plenty on scenarios like this."

"What about her necklace from Mack? Can you track it again?" Hyde asked.

Frankie shook his head. "It's still in evidence. She never got it back."

Groans spread across the bar.

"What about the club we rescued Mack from? Why don't we ride up and take his brother? An eye for an eye. Force him to return Dragon," Bamfa snapped.

Marshal interfered. "We know nothing about them. They could be expecting that. I'm gathering all the intel I can on them and their Tacoma distribution business."

Frankie called order to the conversing club. "Onto other business. Zander's out of surgery but still critical, while Tyr is lucky to get away with a flesh wound, despite the amount of blood he lost. Mack had been told to remain in hospital overnight; he was all over the shop earlier. Tiny will keep an eye, but I need volunteers for their protection. I want two patches with Jimmy at the hospital on Prez, and two on Mackie. Mateo came for him first, so we can't guarantee he won't come back."

"Hyde and I will protect Prez," Eddie said.

"Tiny and I will protect Mack and check on Tyr, unless I'm needed here tonight." Gnarler asked, growling at Ragnar.

"Go and stay safe. I want hourly updates. The Uskiville chapter will watch the perimeter tonight, with Bamfa leading the team. You'll switch in the morning."

"And what about us?" Leif asked.

"Find out everything your club can remember about your dealings with Mateo. That goes for old ladies who may have seen or overheard anything. Reach out to anyone who may have information about that son of a bitch. The more we know, the better we can help our families."

Frankie ordered the MCs to disperse, calling on Bamfa before he left.

"Frankie. It's nice to see you, brother. I just wish it was under better circumstances."

Frankie embraced his old friend. They had worked together before Frankie revealed his true identity as an FBI agent.

"Hey, man. Listen, I need you to make sure the Rus is under constant surveillance. Double man the gates, too. All wolves need to be connected to the grapevine. I'll keep my radio on at B's. I'm needed there tonight."

Bamfa scratched his head. "Shit, yeah, man. Of course. How are Madoc and Rhys taking it?"

"I haven't seen them yet. With the hierarchy down, I've been delegating. I'll head over after I've cleaned up. I don't want to traumatize them any more than they already are."

Bamfa nodded. "Right. Yeah. Well, I got you, brother. Anything you need just holler, alright?"

Frankie slapped his hand in a handshake. "I appreciate it. Safe night tonight. Don't take any chances. If there is any suspicion, communicate via radio."

"Yeah, respect brother. Get some rest, yeah?"

CHAPTER THIRTY-TWO
Mack

Mack swiped away the doctor's torch. "I told you I'm fine, God damn it."

"Mr. Kelly. You've suffered head trauma. Now, if you'll please allow me to do my job."

Mack sat sulking. His pouting face showed his impatience with the young doctor.

"Your CT scan is clear, but you may have a concussion. I would recommend you stay in overnight for observation."

Mack dived from the gurney. "Not a fecking chance! I got places to be."

"Mr. Kelly-"

"Mack!" Ari and the doctor shouted in tandem.

Mack sneered at Ari, who had returned from purchasing herself a coffee outside of the A&E department. "Can it! I'm leaving. And you," he pointed at her, scaring her to her spot. "Frankie was right about you. You're nothing but a fecking harlot! After all I've done for you, and you repay me by screwing our marriage counsellor?"

The doctor slipped out as Mack flapped around in frustration. "People have fecking died because of us, Ari. My Dragon, your BFF could die because of our cascade of lies."

Ari remained mute as he gripped the gurney cover. "You're dead to me, Ari, and so is that prick who abused his duty, and just as soon as I find my Dragon, I'm gonna slit his slippery throat. And let me tell you, you better burn that property of tat from your adulterous skin because if it's there when I return, God help you!" he spat, grabbing his suit jacket and storming out of the cubicle.

CHAPTER THIRTY-THREE
Teen Tears!

Frankie relieved himself of a loud sigh, and his face filled with dread as he headed towards B's cabin to check on Madoc and Rhys. Frankie lacked the expertise to console them after their mother's abduction. He had just returned from showering in his cabin, not wanting to show up covered in Zander's and Leif's blood. As he stepped into B's cabin, an icy chill ripped through him, making him just as nervous as when B was taken. The goose pimples rippled across his muscular frame despite the heat blazing from the roaring log fire.

Madoc and Rhys sat on the large couch between David and Spencer, while Junior and Remy sat on the opposing couch, with Alex sleeping across their laps. David and Spencer's caring arms wrapped around Madoc and Rhys like a warm hug until the teenage boys clasped sight of Frankie, leaping from the couch to question him.

"Have you found her, Uncle Frankie?" Rhys asked in desperation. His red eyes were a direct correlation to his suffering.

Frankie shook his head, grabbing them, and dragging the strapping teenagers into his chest. He kissed their heads before placing his hands on their cheeks. Stooping his broad figure to meet their gaze, he stared at them with all the confidence he could muster.

"Boys, I'll find her! I promise!"

Their terrified faces shook into tears, clinging to Frankie in a vise grip hug.

Frankie glanced at Spencer, who was being consoled by David. The cabin was far from the content home, it usually reflected.

"Is Zander okay?" Madoc asked. His muffled tone was almost incomprehensible from burying his head in Frankie's shirt.

"He's out of surgery. He'll be alright. Jimmy will ring with another update as soon as he can."

"Can we see him? My mum would want us to look after him," Rhys said, stepping away to compose himself.

"We'll head to the hospital as soon as Jimmy sends word."

"Rhys, we can't!" Madoc said. "Dad is on his way to collect us."

"Do you want to go to your dad's boys?"

"No, he insisted. Dad says it's too dangerous to stay here," Madoc said.

Frankie's face filled with frustration. "You're safe here. I'll allow nothing to happen to either of you. Now, if you want to stay, I'll handle your dad."

"We do. We want to stay for Mum coming home and to support Zander," Rhys said, with Madoc agreeing.

"That's settled then. Now pull up the takeout app on your phone. If you want to help, you need to keep your strength up. I'll stay in the guestroom next to yours tonight," Frankie said, walking into the kitchen and giving Spencer a nod to join him.

"Hey boys. Tell me what's the best takeout in Uskiville? Spencer never allows me to have takeout, so I want the works," David said, distracting them.

Frankie retrieved a bottle of whiskey from the kitchen counter. The already opened bottle reminded him of B's nervousness this morning. He had poured her a shot just before they headed to the wedding reception. Pouring a glass now, he waited for Spencer to join him, offering him a shot.

"Not for me, thanks. I'm a Prosecco man."

"There's plenty in the marquee. Should I have some brought over?"

"No thanks," Spencer said, blowing air from his cheeks. "What the hell happened, Frankie? B's gone, Zander's fighting for his life, Tyr shot in the leg. It's like something straight from cable tv."

"Mackie pissed off a lot of people avenging Ari and just when we think we're alright, the Cascade of Lies comes back to fuck us in the ass." He raised his whiskey hand. "Pardon the expression."

"Don't worry about it. I'm used to B's colorful vocabulary, remember? So, what are the police saying?"

"About what you'd expect. Nobody knows anything, no leads. We're on our own."

"Do you have a name? I can do some digging?"

Frankie poured himself another shot. "Mateo Torres. A pharmaceutical conglomerate from Seattle."

"Wait! Wasn't that the guy who tried to sue an ethics committee?" Spencer whipped his phone from his pocket. Tapping the screen, he thrusted it in Frankie's face. "Yeah, see. That's our guy! The ethics committee rejected his research proposal. They almost charged him with a string of offenses, including reckless endangerment. He denied conducting unregulated human trials."

"What? We didn't find that in our database."

"Come on man. Don't you watch the news? He lost a massive court case last year."

Frankie stared at him blankly.

"He wanted to create a drug to weaponize the military's infantry. Promising he could produce a more effective adrenaline shot that not only aided injured soldiers but made them feel invincible during combat situations. He believed he could create super soldiers." Spencer chuckled into his drink. "Of course, they rejected him. Telling him it would be like giving their infantry crack. The guy's a whack job. He was spouting nonsense to the press. Something about working with adrenaline and the patients' inhibition to control their actions. He lost a fortune on that lawsuit. I knew I recognized that bastard."

Frankie retrieved his phone from his pocket and hit the call button. "Dad, do another check, cross reference human trials from last year. See what you can find."

"Did I help?" Spencer asked.

"Yeah, Spence. This is great intel. Now what to do with the boys? Nothing can cheer them up at the moment."

The front door flew open, making Frankie jump. He was about to rip his gun from its holster when Sigrun bolted through the door, jumping on Rhys. Tyr hobbled in on crutches, with Tiny following.

"Tyr!" The boys screeched, rushing toward him.

"Hey," Tyr said, hugging them with one arm.

"You're alright?" Madoc asked.

"Here, sit and I'll get mum's footrest for you," Rhys said, ushering him to the couch.

"Thanks boys. I'm alright."

Madoc and Rhys rushed around; pampering Tyr as Frankie stepped in to converse with him.

"Shouldn't you be at the hospital?"

Tyr made himself comfortable. "Nah, I'm fine. I'm here for the boys. Bamfa briefed us. I'm going to take the couch tonight if that's cool?"

"Of course! Glad to have you."

Tiny, butted in. His abrupt interruption caused alarm. "Frankie a word."

Frankie narrowed his eyes to Tiny. "Alright man, let's step onto the back porch."

He led them outside, sliding the door shut behind them. "Problem?"

Tiny rubbed the back of his head. "Maybe. Mack took off an hour ago. Ari found me as Tyr was discharging himself. She was in a right state!"

Frankie shrugged. "I couldn't give a flying fuck about that skank. Do you know where Mackie's gone?"

"I assumed he'd come straight here. Nobody has seen him, and his bike's gone! Bamfa has left his post too."

Frankie punched the porch pillar, re-opening the cuts on his knuckles he'd obtained from the beatdown he gave Leif earlier. "Hasn't he caused enough crap? The last thing we need is Prez going rogue again. You track their phones?"

"Yeah, they're an hour from San Diego."

Frankie stepped down the porch steps with his hands on his hips, releasing a rip-roaring bellow. "Fuuuckk! Mackie-boy, you stupid bastard!"

Panic spread across Tiny's face as he raced down the steps to confront him. "You know where they are going?"

Frankie hunched over, gripping his knees and dragging in an angry breath. "Mackie's gone rogue again! They're heading to Mateos brothers MC. That fuckwit barely made it out alive last time. We had to rescue him. The stupid son of a bitch has gone on a suicide mission and they're both gonna get us all killed."

"We'll take a team to catch him."

"What? And leave all the boys and MC families vulnerable. No! Mateo may have eyes on us."

"We can't just fucking leave him to die."

Frankie straightened himself up. "Why do you think he's taken Bamfa?"

Tiny's bewildered expression showed his cluelessness until a penny-drop moment widened Frankie's gaze into a fear crazed expression.

"Bamfa is an explosives expert. They're going to blow up the club."

"Shit! Shit! Fucking Shit!" Tiny stamped his feet before kicking a garden chair into the pool.

"Fuck! We'll have to go, Tiny. We'll bring Gnarler, that's it. We can't risk anyone else."

"No, brother. You need to stay. With Prez, Jimmy and now Mack awol, you're the only one who knows what the fuck you're doing around here."

"Then my dad's going with you. Trust me, he is more skilled than any of us. You'll need him. You find Mackie, drag his ass out of there."

"Understood. Look after Tyr for me, will ya? He's suppressing the shit out of everything. Acting like nothing's happened."

Frankie embraced him. "I got him, man. Make sure you all come back alive. We've lost enough wolves of late."

Frankie headed inside to discover Spencer arguing with B's ex-husband, Callum, at the front door, who insisted Madoc and Rhys fetch their overnight bags.

Tyr was trying to pull himself to his feet when Frankie placed his hand on his shoulder. "Settle down, man. I'll handle this. Keep the boys inside and away from the window."

Callum shuddered at Frankie's presence, stumbling back down the front porch steps as Frankie paced toward him, grimacing and closing the front door behind him.

"I just want my boys. Their mother has gone and I'm their legal guardian," he stuttered.

"They're staying put."

"They're my son's. I'm taking them!" he cried.

Frankie continued marching forward. "Wrong, asshole. B appointed me as legal guardian in her absence. Your lawyer was sent the paperwork to inform you weeks ago, and right now, they're waiting to see their stepfather. They're worried and want to stay. They are safe. We have an army here. If I allow them to leave with you, they become vulnerable, and I qualify as a better caregiver than you in B's absence."

Callum backed into his clapped-out blue estate. "You think you can bully me? I'll have the cops down here in a flash and have you arrested."

Frankie chuckled, grabbing him by his hoodie and throwing him over the car's hood, threatening the skinny man. "You realize I'm former FBI, jerkoff, and acquainted with every police officer and agent in this region? I'll have you up on bogus charges before you could make the fucking call. You leave them here until they see Zander. After a few days, you all fly to the UK and you'll remain there until I am certain it's safe for the boys to return."

Callum stood in the road, a good eight feet from Frankie's grasp.

"You think my sons are in danger?"

"I'm uncertain of anything right now, but I'm not taking any chances. The boys mean everything to B. I want to make sure they're safe."

Callum scoffed. "They can't mean that much to her; she went into business with criminals. This is her fault. She put them at risk. I'll be contacting social services and I'll be filing for full custody."

Frankie's vexed expression had Callum racing to his car door to escape his wrath. Frankie dived over the hood, sliding across it like a movie scene to dive on a terrified Callum.

"You never learn, do you?" Frankie said, dragging him to his feet. Checking back at the house to ensure the boys weren't watching, he punched him in the stomach and held him against the car.

"I may need to contact my friends about your assault with a deadly weapon. You attempted to attack me with a knife in front of a lawyer, a former CIA agent, and several witnesses at the retreat." Frankie stepped to within an inch of Callum's face. "You know the court allocated your visitation after your last slip with cocaine, and what would the boys think if I told them you tried to attack their uncle with a knife?"

Callum trembled, paralyzed by Frankie's frenetic demeanor. "I don't have a knife."

Frankie ripped his blade from its holster, forcing it into Callum's hands, laughing as Callum stared in disbelief. Frankie ripped the blade back out of his hands, slamming it onto the hood. "You took mine from my back pocket as I walked away from you. Prints don't lie, mother fucker! Now, choose your next move fucking carefully, dickwad."

"Fine, fine. I'll do what you want, but I'll need B's credit card. I'm brassic!"

Frankie sneered at him. "Do I look fucking stupid? I'm not giving you money to get off your nut. I'll book the flights if it comes to it and put money in the boys' account. They decide what they need, and you even think about bullying them. I'll snap your druggie neck. Got it?"

"And what about my upheaval?"

Frankie punched him again. "You don't even work, asshole. Be grateful I've allowed you to live this long and no fucking funny business. I have agents around the world who will slit your wrists and make it look like suicide, so don't fucking test me." Frankie snatched his blade, placing it back in its holder, leaving Callum to gasp for breath as he walked toward the cabin.

"So, I'll wait for your call?"

Frankie glanced over his shoulder with a growl, eyeballing Callum who dived into his car and sped off.

CHAPTER THIRTY-FOUR
Mack's Mission

Mack and Bamfa raced off the highway along the narrow roads to the MC. Mack hadn't been near there since the night Frankie and his pack rescued him from the Greyhound MC, although his photographic memory remembered each detail as if it was yesterday.

The MC sat on the outskirts of downtown, almost hidden from the road. Anton had chosen the location to stay out of sight, enabling his criminal activity to remain unnoticed.

Mack cut his engine around the corner, concealing his motorcycle behind the club's perimeter wall.

Bamfa parked too, placing his bag on the ground.

"What's the estimated assembly time?" Mack asked.

"Adding the finishing touches now. It's remote access, so we can plant this baby and watch it blow from our bikes."

"No chance!" Mack said. "I'm walking in there and ramming it down that asshole's throat."

"Prez, that's suicide!"

"Mateo took something precious from me, now I'm taking something from him. Don't worry. I'll be out in no time. Just watch my six."

Bamfa worked with urgency, completing final checks on the homemade explosive device. "You sure about this, Prez?"

"Bamfa, I'm sending a message and making it clear."

"And what's stopping him from killing Dragon in retaliation?"

"He won't. Mateo needs her for something and for whatever reason, she fits the bill instead of me. He wouldn't have taken her if he hadn't intended on using her. I want to flush him out."

Bamfa handed him the bomb. "And what if he sends an army to wipe us out?"

"I'm counting on it. I just need one of his agents to give up his location. God knows his brother won't. He's a greasy fecker. We won't get anything from him. There will be one less sick and twisted MC in the country when I blow the joint. Bamfa, he deserved to die the first time around. He's on borrowed time and I'm taking it back."

"With you all the way, boss. What's the plan?"

"We're walking through the front door. It looks dead. You'll have your piece ready to blow anyone away from behind, and I'll handle what's in front of us."

"What if it's an entire MC?"

Mack grinned. "That's what this baby is for," he said, holding the bomb.

"Careful with that Prez. There's enough there to flatten the building. We're gonna have to be fast. Don't step too far inside. Make your point and then we leave."

Mack made tracks toward the club. It appeared quiet as they approached with the safety off their weapons. They marched up the steps and opened the bar door, ready for battle. Six pairs of eyes stared back at them as they stepped inside, and Mack recognized two men from his revenge days. The club president sat just ten feet away attached to his oxygen mask and his Sergeant of Arms sat to his right; Mack remembered head-butting him and breaking his nose on his last altercation with the club.

"Hello, feckers! Remember me?" Mack asked, pointing his automatic weapon at them.

One man reached for his gun, and Mack fired a round into his chest showing no concern for the oxygen tank attached to Anton. "Uh, uh! Weapons down boys."

Anton, the club President, now with a greying face and hair, removed his oxygen mask.

"Let me guess. You met my baby brother?"

"Yeah, and he has something of mine."

"You mean your whore. Not the same one I groped before. Get bored, did we? You're more of an idiot than I thought." He coughed, placing his mask back onto his disheveled face.

"Oh, and why's that?"

"Because you dare come to my club when your card has been marked. You think your bitch is still alive? Oh, I bet my brother has allowed all his agents to tear through her before he conducts his human trials. She's a fucking guinea pig now, fuck face. You fucked with me and now you and your pet Dragon are paying the price."

Anger smashed through Mack's soul like a wrecking ball, making him laugh maniacally while retrieving the bomb from his jacket. "Interesting! From where I'm standing, you're the one who's paying the price. Now you have five seconds to tell me where they've taken her, or you go bye-bye."

The men retreated from their chairs in fear, leaving their Prez at the table on his own. Mack opened fire on the men, his automatic unleashing a deadly round to all and catching Anton in his arm, tearing his flesh from its bone.

Mack rushed over while Bamfa remained on watch. "Where's the rest of your MC?"

Anton conceded. "At the port. There's a shipment due. They'll be back any minute and don't bother searching for evidence. You'll find nothing. My brother isn't stupid."

Bamfa fired a shot past them, shooting the sergeant of arms in the head as he coughed up blood and struggled for his gun.

Mack gave him a nod and turned his attention back to Anton. "Oh, he's stupid alright. Nobody fucks with me and my dragon!"

Anton grimaced. "Mateo will kill you for this."

"Let him fecking try!" Mack said, ripping off Anton's cut and kicking him to the ground. He snapped the oxygen mask from his face, laughing at him, struggling to breathe. "You won't be needing this. Try breathing in hell fecker!" Mack said, filling his chest with bullets.

He placed the bomb on the table before exiting in haste with Bamfa. They ran to their bikes where they donned their helmets and Bamfa waited for him to press the trigger. "What are you waiting for? Press the damn thing!"

Mack laughed. "What's the rush?"

"The rush? You heard him. Their entire club will be back any minute."

"Exactly. I'll pull the trigger when they step inside. I'm taking no survivors and sending a message to Mateo. With a bit of luck, they'll have his shipment, too."

Bamfa ripped off his helmet. "Are you crazy? These dudes get one whiff of us and we're dead."

Mack nodded towards a black van with fake plates and four bikers turning the corner into the club. He jumped back off his bike and hid at the perimeter wall's edge, waiting for the men carrying duffle bags to go inside.

Angry shrieks came from the MC as Mack waited for the last man to enter the building. He sneered at their panic, striking the trigger switch before diving behind the wall for cover. The explosion rocked the concrete beneath them like an earthquake as Bamfa revved his engine.

"Let's fucking go!" he shouted as the building collapsed in on itself and fire breathed from the gas mains.

Mack jumped onto his bike, revving his engine as it roared to life and the pair sped off into the dusty night.

Smoke billowed for miles as they headed for Uskiville. They were thirty minutes down the highway when Tiny, Gnarler, and Marshall flashed them in the opposing traffic.

"Keep going. They'll catch us at the next junction," Mack said to Bamfa.

They were another twenty minutes down the road when Tiny caught up with Mack. Calling his cell, Mack answered.

"Yeah!"

"What the fuck did you do, Prez?"

"What I do best. Get fecking even!"

"With respect, Prez, you're a fucking idiot. We're fragile as it is. What happens if Mateo turns up to wipe us out tomorrow like he did with the Rus Reapers?"

"I'll kill him before he gets the chance."

"What about him and his army? Get real, Prez, and you can kiss Dragon goodbye now. If you've done what I think you've done, she's dead and we're next!"

"Not on my watch, brother!"

"You're a dick. I've lost all respect for you tonight." He hung up the phone and signaled Gnarler and Marshall to follow as they sped off into the distance.

CHAPTER THIRTY-FIVE
Needle

B lay on the bed clutching the LVAD wires and Zander's wrist band to her chest, allowing her guilt to crush her.

I've killed him! I've killed him!

Unable to process her emotions, her body stilled. She hadn't shed a single tear. The day's shock overwhelmed her, numbing her to her core. B used to be an expert at locking her emotions away until Zander forced her to face them, only this time she knew she needed to shut them off to survive.

If I open the floodgates, I'll drown, unable to cope with what I've done.

She couldn't rest or take time to fathom her next steps as her mind ping-ponged from Zander's shooting to the fear in her boys' eyes while she was being dragged away. There was no rest bite or time to fathom her next steps, although she tried to think of an escape.

She bolted upright, hearing footsteps outside the door and a muffled conversation. She placed Zander's belongings under her pillow with haste and stood upright to snarl at the door.

Hudson entered the room with three other agents, all pointing their handguns at her.

"Time for your medicine, Dragon," Hudson teased, slapping a set of handcuffs on her wrists.

"Move," he said, pressing the gun into her back.

He directed her to a medical suite to the right of her cell where a team of clinicians waited.

"Get her in the chair!" The tiny doctor said without making eye contact. His averting eyes and impatience suggesting to B he didn't approve of her as the next candidate in his trial.

Hudson and Carter dragged her into the chair, removing the handcuffs to secure her wrists to the arm rests and secured her ankles.

"State your full name and age," the doctor said with a robotic undertone.

B giggled, his voice amusing her as she watched his patience wear away.

"Name and age," he repeated.

B giggled again, tickled by his voice, making him snap.

The disturbing doctor gripped her throat. "Test my patience again and I'll make your stay here very difficult." He ripped his hand away.

B caught her breath. "And how will I fight if you fuck with me? Let's not corrupt your data, doctor. It might ruin your study," she teased. "Besides, I thought human-testing had to be consensual."

"Not for this. Now state your name," he growled.

"Screw you, Boyoh! I don't take orders, I give them!"

"Fine. Have it your way. Taser," he said to his female colleague, whose eyes widened at the request.

"That's unnecessary, Michael. I know you don't approve of Dragon as your next candidate, but I assure you, she is the best fit." Mateo said from the doorway.

"She won't survive the first dose."

"Well, lesson learnt if she doesn't. Now, I have her details. Just inject her with the drug already."

B's natural instincts kicked in, trying to resist the long needle directed at her neck.

The doctor attached a series of monitors to an aggressive B as Mateo beamed with glee.

"Hold her head," the doctor said as he plunged the needle into her, releasing the toxic green medication into her system.

B's body shook and her veins bulged in her hands and forehead. The heat ripped through her like molten lava, burning her insides. Screams ripped from her throat; she'd never experienced pain like it. It felt like her heart was ready to explode and her head was fit to burst with pressure.

She could just about make out the doctor relaying her blood pressure figures and cardiac output before she shrieked in pain. Rage fueled her. She had never felt so consumed by anger. It felt as if someone injected her with liquid evil. She spat through her menacing stare, foaming at the mouth. "I'll kill you all!"

"No Dragon. You'll kill who I tell you to kill, and if you're good, I'll bring you some of that whiskey you like, after you've done my bidding of course."

The very mention of whiskey brought clarity to her fragile mind as she tried to resist the drug.

Frankie! Yes! He'll look for a needle in a haystack. He can track the whiskey, and he'll find me if that prick orders it.

"Blood pressure is stabilizing," the doctor said.

If you are ever taken hostage, ask for something obscure. Something I can track, like whiskey and Welsh cakes together. It'll allow them to find a paper trail.

Frankie's words ruminated in her head through the insufferable pain. Her head kept replaying a discussion they had from yester-year. After watching an old abduction blockbuster, B's curiosity was piqued, and she began asking about methods of escape if someone was to be abducted.

"Welsh cakes," she spat. "I want bloody Welsh cakes, too."

Mateo laughed. "Is crazy talk a side effect, doctor?"

"You altered the sample. I need her medical file so I can map out the rest of the trial. My research is all based on male anatomy and physiology. We're playing a totally different game now."

"Good, Erik was exceptional, but I expect more from Dragon. I'll have my team gather the information you require and who knows, Dragon's feral temperament may benefit us, too."

The name rang familiar with B, only she didn't know why.

"Right, she's stable. Get her to the gym. I'm unsure of the shot's duration or impact. Better to get straight to the first round of physical testing," the doctor demanded.

B struggled with the changes in her body. Her heart raced while her head pounded. She experienced immense irritability and almost unbearable pain throughout her body. All she could do was scream through her trauma. She figured she must have blacked out when she realized she was no longer in the clinic, discovering she was lying on gym mats. Opening her eyes, the pain still threatened to stop her heart. She sat up, grabbing at her throbbing head.

"You want that pain to stop, Dragon? You need to exercise. Calm yourself and release endorphins. Erik is there to direct you," Mateo said from behind the reinforced glass.

B knelt up; her vision took a minute to come back to her as she steadied herself. Collecting her bearings, she saw whom she thought was Ragnar, making the fire within her burn her insides. Her temper flared as if an unknown force was controlling her actions when she lunged, grappling him to the floor.

"Dragon, no! I'm here to help you!" Erik said, raising his arms in defense.

B rained down on him with her fists in a vengeful frenzy, forcing Erik to defend himself. He pushed her off, standing to attract Mateo's attention, who laughed when she tackled him to the ground again, scrapping with him like children in a playground fight.

B's inner dragon had to illuminate the threat, punching, scramming, elbowing him before grabbing his hair and dragging him toward the dumbbells. "Let's workout asshole," she teased, aware she wasn't in control of herself.

She released her hands to pick up a thirty-kilo dumbbell like it was fresh air, launching it at him, missing him by a whisker.

"Are you going to stop this before she kills me?" Erik bellowed toward the mirrored glass, once again trying to defend himself from B by jumping to his feet and backing away.

B screamed from her diaphragm, determined to kill him, swinging her fists to connect with his jaw. Blood sprayed on the mats as he dropped to the floor, unconscious. She dived at him, raising her fists to finish the job, when she realized she wasn't fighting Ragnar. She was fighting the butler from the corridor.

B stared in confusion at the unconscious man and then at the mirrored glass. Standing, she walked across the gym mats to the dumbbell wracking, retrieving a forty-kilo dumbbell this time around.

"That's right, Dragon. He's your enemy. Finish him!" Mateo encouraged from behind the glass.

B's brain could not comprehend her reality. She wanted to fight; her anger told her so by ripping through her body in uncontrollable urges, only something in her told her fight wasn't with the familiar man lying unconscious. It was with the man behind the mirrored glass and with the weight firmly in her grasp, her feet stomped in a three hundred sixty-degree rotation at speed, and she threw the dumbbell in the air like a javelin, smashing the unbreakable glass.

The adrenaline coursed through her as her eagle eyes waited for Mateo to appear. She knew she hadn't killed him yet. She could feel it in her bones, and as soon as she caught sight of him standing again, she sprinted towards the window.

"Tranq dart, now!!" he bellowed as B was almost upon him.

The desire to kill him flooded through her veins.

"No! It'll kill her!" the doctor bellowed.

"Fucking do it now!" Mateo wailed.

B was mid-dive through the window when Hudson took her out with a tranquilizer dart, putting her down like she was a savage beast.

CHAPTER THIRTY-SIX
Reckless

Mack waltzed into a packed bar, ready to celebrate his small win to be confronted with Frankie's fist, knocking him on his backside.

"What the feck, Frankie? Who do you think you are?"

Frankie bent over, gripping onto Mack's shirt, punching him until Tiny dragged him away.

"You've sentenced her to death, dickwad! If anything happens to her, that's on you!" Frankie said, seething as Marshall helped restrain him.

"Calm the feck down. He needs Dragon alive," Mack said, standing to catch his breath. "And he called her his champion. Frankie, it's clear he wants her for his gain and if he's testing on her, he's not about to let her die. We need to determine his agenda. With the Greyhound MC gone and his drugs destroyed, we will get his attention."

Frankie lunged at Mack as he grabbed a beer from the bar fridge. "What the fuck? Do you hear yourself?"

Mack's washed puzzled expression away with his beer as Frankie roared.

"The entire nation of America turned him down for his inhumane antics, Mackie. He didn't get ethical clearance, and now he's testing on my fucking sister with God knows what, like a fucking mad scientist!"

Mack went pale.

"Dawning on you now, is it? You stupid prick! B's right! You'll never change. You're responsible for all of this," Frankie said, picking up a bar stool and throwing it at him.

Mack dodged it in a stunned silence as Frankie's wrath continued. "All this is because of you. Instead of taking responsibility like a man, you create more trouble. We're supposed to be a team. What the hell is wrong with you?"

"There's nothing wrong with me, Frankie. I'm trying to get my Dragon back and if burning down an MC flushes that son of a bitch out, I'll burn down plenty."

Frankie launched a small, circular bar table at him, sending drinks hurdling toward him as the club members ducked for cover. "And what if he wipes us out, like he did the Rus Reapers when they pissed him off?"

Mack's puzzled expression infuriated Frankie further. "See, while you were out making flames, we did some digging. Marshall, Gnarler and Spencer have discovered damming shit, and Leif and his MC have been filling in the blanks. Mateo, the asshole who abducted B, is far more than a flash bastard in a suit. He is dealing along the west coast and has an affinity for pharmaceutical science."

"Science?" Mack questioned.

Frankie dragged his hand down his jaw before ushering Gnarler to hand him a beer. "We think he's conducting human trials to create a drug that might weaponize the military infantry."

"What, like super soldiers?"

"Fuck knows. What we know is you've just confirmed he's testing that drug on B as we speak and has probably tested it on Leif's son Erik already. The likelihood is, Erik didn't survive the testing, and he was coming for you next."

Mack slumped into the seats lining the back wall of the bar. "What. No," he whispered.

"Mackie, Gnarler, has been listening to the chatter on the dark web. He's taken plenty of folk and they haven't returned. Calls them his champion. He injects them and if they survive, they fight in a fucked up weekly tournament. He's been showing off his potential candidates to some dangerous people across the globe, and I'm guessing you've just killed his brother?"

Mack nodded. "I killed them all, Frankie. They had to die. They took my Dragon."

Frankie slid next to him while a full bar witnessed Mack realizing the magnitude of his actions. "Mackie Boy, the cowboy stupidity must stop. B doesn't need a maverick right now. She needs her best friends, her fucking family."

Mack's face hardened as he whispered. "I'm telling you, Frankie, he needs her. She's still alive. We need to save her."

Frankie gripped the back of his neck, pulling him into his embrace. "If I know B, she'll be doing what she can to save herself."

"And what if she can't? What if she's drugged up and helpless somewhere?"

Frankie laughed, causing Mack to flinch. "Come now, Mackie boy, B may be a lot of things, but she's never helpless. She only needs to survive until we reach her."

"Do we have any idea where she is? This is killing me. It should have been me, not her."

"Like she would have let you leave. Look, what's done is done. Now, get your ass in church so we can bring you up to speed."

CHAPTER THIRTY-SEVEN
Pain and Suffering

Zander's eyes flickered at the light, his consciousness returning to him with each passing second. He tried to focus on the surrounding voices, aware of Jimmy's presence as he battled to stay awake, and his dry throat throbbed from the breathing apparatus that was removed before he returned to consciousness. His chest stung with increasing discomfort as he returned to himself.

He growled in pain as he felt the warmth of a hand in his. "Welsh Cake," he murmured.

"It's Jimmy, man. I'm right here."

Zander's eyes sprang open, recalling his ordeal; his last vision of B being dragged away filling him with fear. "Welsh Cake!" he said, waking.

The sutures in his chest threatened to tear as he winced in pain. "Ah, Christ!"

He began hyperventilating in pain, as the doctor entered, placing an oxygen mask over his mouth.

"Breathe Mr. McGovan. You're recovering from a gunshot wound to the chest."

"No shit!" he spat. The agony in his chest made him grit his teeth.

"You were incredibly lucky. The small caliber round glided off your sternum, embedding itself in your rib. There's a lot of damage and you're at risk of infection. You're still fragile. Rest. Unless you want to be back in that operating room."

Zander nodded through painful breaths, watching the doctor leave. Once he was certain he had left, he ripped his mask off, clambering to his feet and staggering until Jimmy caught him, forcing him back into bed. "What the fuck are you doing? Get your ass back in that bed before I shoot you myself."

"I need to find her, Jimmy. How long have I been out?"

"Eighteen hours! It should have been longer, but the doc figured you were turning a corner and brought you round earlier than expected."

"WHAT!!" Panic spread across his anguished face. "Jimmy, that's too long. I need to get out of here."

Jimmy placed the covers back over his fragile friend. "And do what? Keel over by the time you reach the elevator. You want to help? Get better. We need you at your best."

Zander winced through every shallow breath. His body trembled in immense pain that he refused to acknowledge. "Where is she, Jimmy?" he breathed.

Jimmy leant against the bed next to him, taking his hand.

"You're making me nervous, pal. Where's Welsh Cake?"

Jimmy jerked his head back into an emotional sigh. "We don't know. Zand. Mack picked the wrong person to fuck with this time. This guy..."

"Yeah?"

Jimmy shook his head. "He's not someone to be trifled with. I don't know all the details because my concern has been you, but from what Frankie has told me, he's trying to play God."

Zander wasn't sure if it was the pain or drugs that confused him. Jimmy appeared to be talking in code. He pulled his mask off again. "Jimmy, talk and make sense. I'm too drugged up for riddles, pal."

Jimmy stared him straight in the eye. "A drug dealer whose primary business is in pharmaceuticals. The military rejected his request for human trials. Word is, he may have gone ahead with the trials, anyway. Frankie believes it may be why he wanted Mack."

"To test on him?"

Jimmy lowered his voice into a solemn whisper. "Yeah, only weaponizing a woman seemed more appealing."

Zander's eyes filled with tears. "No, Jimmy. This ain't happening, pal. Tell me you're lying?"

"This is just speculation, Zand, but I can't lie to you. Marshall and Gnarler haven't found one survivor from the hundreds of people Mateo has abducted. Even Leif's son is still awol."

Zander's wrathful eyes burned. "That wee prick set us up. I'll kill him!"

"Frankie is handling him. I'll get the lowdown later. There's a more pressing matter for your attention now."

"Jimmy, the only pressing matter is finding Welsh Cake. I demand a church meeting now!"

"I'll set up a morning meeting. But right now, you should make a call?"

"And who the fuck do I need to talk to?"

"Madoc and Rhys. I've had a billion missed calls. I think it'll do them good to hear your voice. Tyr is with them, desperate to hear you're okay. He took a bullet to the thigh, trying to help Dragon, too. He's alright though. Just a flesh wound."

Zander's face softened, clasping a trembling hand to catch his jaw. "Christ. How are they doing, Jimmy?"

"I dunno, man. Here, call them please?"

Zander's trembling hand took the cell phone and hit the call button. The phone rang three times before Rhys answered it.

"Jimmy, is Zander, okay?"

A boulder-like lump formed in Zander's throat as he tried to speak. "Hey Wee Man, I'm alright. Are you ok-"

A shriek of relief exited Rhys's mouth. "Zander. You're alive. Madoc, it's Zander. He's awake!" he said to his brother.

Unknown emotions whirled through Zander's struggling mind. Hearing the elation in Rhys's voice made him realize just how fortunate he had been to survive. It took him aback, knowing how much the boys cared. He loved the boys as his own, unaware of their feelings until now.

His eyes welled up with tears, staring up at Jimmy, who gave him a reassuring smile before he reverted to his strong masculinity.

"How are you and your brother holding up?"

"We're okay. We just want you and mum back. You'll get her back, right? Just like you did last time."

"Dinnae worry, laddie. I'll be with my wolves to bring your mother home as soon as I'm discharged."

"Can we come and see you?"

Zander's heart strings almost broke. "Of course you can. I wanna see you both too. Tell Frankie to bring you by tomorrow. I should know when I'm getting out then."

"Okay. Do you need us to bring you anything, like? PJ's and slippers?"

Zander couldn't help but smile. "That would be awesome. Thanks, pal. Please put Tyr on the phone for me."

"Okay, bye," Rhys said, handing Tyr the phone.

"Prez!" Tyr vocalized in relief.

"You alright son? I heard you took a bullet trying to help Welsh Cake. Thank you for trying to save her."

"I failed you, again, Prez. I'm sorry," Tyr sniffled.

"Dinnae do that to yourself. We were blindsided and outgunned. I'm just grateful you're still breathing."

"No, this is all my fault. My father betrayed us. I should have seen it coming. I thought he was after me."

Zander reached for the bed adjustment buttons, sitting himself up and wincing as he did so.

"We all did. Look pal, Jimmy will update me, and your task is to guard those laddies with your life. I know you're hurting, son, but we must keep them safe. Where they go, you follow."

"Understood. What do we do now? How will we find her?"

"Dinnae worry pal. We'll sort it, and if I know Welsh Cake, she'll be doing everything she can, too."

CHAPTER THIRTY-EIGHT
Guilt

B woke up in her bed a few hours later. For a split second, she believed she'd been dreaming until she digested her surroundings. She was back in the room Hudson had placed her in when she'd arrived. Her blood-stained vest, a reminder of her attack on the innocent man in the gym.

Her windowless room lacked natural light, providing her with no indication of time. B surmised it was late evening as she became agitated by the flickering artificial light.

I should be enjoying my first dance as a married woman, right now, and where am I? Caged by some monster and my almost husband...

Her thoughts trailed off in a flurry of hurt. Her left hand glided beneath the pillow, reaching for the hospital items again as her right hand clutched her chest.

He can't be gone. He just can't! Please don't let this be true.

Her head pounded like a beating drum. The nausea was almost as troubling as her grief and her body twitched as if the liquid evil still corrupted it.

Tears threatened her face until she snapped herself out of it.

No! That asshole doesn't deserve your tears! This situation doesn't deserve your tears. Whatever is happening, deal with it! Nothing is permanent and they don't call you Dragon for nothing. You still have your family, despite losing your true love. There will be time to grieve later. Now get up, wash your face, and contemplate your escape plan.

B's pep talk forced her to sit up, pushing the hospital items back under the pillow. She had to focus. Dizziness compromised her vision as she dragged her pulsating body to the bathroom. The vertigo-like symptoms crippled her to her knees, forcing her to crawl to the toilet. Hanging onto the basin as if her life depended on it, involuntary spasms in her stomach coerced the contents from her body in a series of projectile vomits. Sweat poured from her pores as she rested her head against the cold, clinical-looking bathroom tiles until she fell asleep in exhaustion.

"Dragon, wake up!" the voice called, jostling her awake.

B's blurry eyes tried to make out who was kneeling before her as he shook her awake.

"Tyr?"

"No," Erik said, with a sympathetic smile just like Tyr's. "Close. We look alike, but he's my kid brother."

B's consciousness woke her like a freight train. "You!" she said, flinching and failing to scramble to her feet.

"Chill out! I'm not interested in round two," he said, easing her back to the floor. "Lady, you have one hell of a punch. You must have Viking blood running through your veins. I can see why my brother has so much respect for you."

B sat panting at him.

"Breathe. Your current anxiety and paranoia are side effects from the injection. The first dose is the worst. Listen, Dragon, I'm trying to help. You won't survive this treatment if you don't let me help you."

"You did!" she snapped, glaring at his black eye and swollen nose.

Erik's lips curled into a smugness that would make most women quiver. "Yes, but I wanted to die. Dragon, they're giving you a more concentrated dose of what I had and let me tell you. I should not have survived. This drug is an abomination. The addiction, the feeling like your heart is about to detonate in your chest, the irritability and all-consuming rage; that's going to get worse before it gets better."

"I'm listening," she said before retching into the nearby toilet.

Erik held her hair so she could eject the last of the bile from her stomach. "The things this drug makes you do." he bowed his head. "Dragon, this drug can make you forget who you are and prevent you from thinking for yourself. You gotta let me help you, for both our sakes."

B sat back, wiping her mouth on her wrist, taking in his every word. "How did you survive?"

"I fought, Dragon. Literally, fought and killed people to stay alive. The side effects had me climbing the walls. You noticed the claw marks on the door, right?"

B stared at him.

"Shit is about to get rough, and I can help if you allow me?"

B scowled at him. "Why should I trust you? You treated Tyr like crap; you and your family. Why should I trust someone who damaged my beautiful boy?"

Erik jerked his head back. "Because you helped him heal from my family and by that comment, I know you love him like he's one of your own."

B raised an eyebrow, scrunching up her nose and forehead.

"And you're right. I was an awful big brother. Dragon, I tried to reconcile before ending up here, but fate had different plans."

"I thought you didn't care about him. You and your asshole brother made his life hell at your father's command."

Erik sat back on his backside, turning away from her in disgust. "We had no choice. Like here, it's kill or be killed." He ran his fingers through his long Viking hair. "I made myself sick every time I did something cruel to Tyr. The truth is, I'm envious of him. He had the courage to do what Ragnar, or I couldn't do. Nobody leaves Leif the Viking. Not really. Just like nobody leaves this place, but at least I can try to save you some pain as a thank you for helping him." He offered her his hand and B hesitated before taking it and feeling him press a small circular object into her palm.

Erik stared into her eyes. "Cameras."

"What is it?" she asked, placing her hand in her lap, careful not to reveal it to the watching eyes.

"The final pills to end my reliance on Gen Force and regain normalcy."

"Don't you need them?"

"Not anymore. I received ten too many from the pharmacist. I can't risk addiction like before. Mateo brought me level to use me as his personal servant for crossing him. It's the only reason he didn't kill me. That and because my body is worth a lot of money to him. They test me like a human guinea pig to improve their drug," he said, pulling up his sleeve and showing her his track marks. "God knows what they've done to the one they've given you because you were like Satan himself when you woke in that gym."

"Shit, sorry. I thought you were your brother, and I went mental."

"Ragnar?"

B grimaced at his name.

Erik laughed. "I see he made an impression. Hmm..." He put a playful finger to his lip, reminding her of Tyr when he joked in her kitchen. "He grabbed your, you know?" he said, nodding to her privates.

Answering, her heart stung. Not for Ragnar, but for Tyr and her sons. "Yeah," she said, clearing her throat. "He soon learnt not to touch what doesn't belong to him."

"You hit him?"

"Me, the Prez, then Tyr beat the crap out of him."

Erik's smile beamed like a proud father. "At a boy little brother! I knew he had it in him. He'll make a fantastic Prez one day."

"Yeah, he will."

"Dragon, I'm going to stand now to conceal you from the cameras. Take the pill. It will combat the drug and lessen the side effects. Please trust me."

I have nothing to lose.

B nodded, watching him stand to cover her. B brought her hand to her mouth and took the pill. Swallowing it, the dry pill dragged down her throat as if it were trying to claw its way out of her mouth until she swallowed again to ensure it went down. She smiled, extending her hand, and Erik helped her to her feet.

B reached for the tap, turning on the hot water and pressing a blob of handwash into her hands to scrub them.

"There're exactly eleven tablets left in my room, enough for 1 per week. B you must accept you're here for the long hall; you get one after each fight. I'll slip it into your food somehow. It's all I got."

"Thank you, Erik. Tyr would be proud of you," she said, drying her hands in a white hand towel from the heated radiator.

Erik smiled, ushering her to her bed. "I've brought some food, although you probably don't have much of an appetite. Trust me when I say you'll regret it if you don't. I learned the hard way, so I'll help where possible."

"Thanks," B said, scanning the meal tray.

"It's safe, B. You're a priceless gem to him now. The chef's a bit of a douchebag, but his food is delicious. There's also a dessert and hot chocolate. You need thousands of calories."

B sat on the bed, picking at the food. She glanced at the boxes on the floor next to the closet. "What's with the boxes?"

"There's a case of both protein bars and shakes. Eat and drink as much as you can. It helps so much."

"Thank you," she said, placing a forkful of chicken pasta into her mouth. "God, I feel like shit!"

He sat on the bed next to her. "It'll pass with the tablet. It got to work on me quickly, and Dragon, Mateo expects you to train with me every day, like I'm your sparring partner."

B raised her eyebrows. "For the fights?"

"Yes. but your performance should mirror your first training session. Dragon, you're going to have to fake it and act like I haven't lessened the effects of your dose with the tablet."

"I'll do my best."

"Good. You'll get another shot before your fight."

"What's my opponent like?" she asked, taking another bite.

"I'm unsure who it is but, they'll be tough as nails. Prepare yourself for the biggest fight of your life. You'll face a psychopath in the upcoming fight. They won't receive the drug, but they'll all have something to prove to their masters, and they'll be baying for your blood."

"It won't be the first time I've fought a bloke."

"Good. You have some experience, at least."

"I knocked you out, good boy, or have you forgotten who gave you that shiner?"

Erik whipped his head back in roaring laughter. "True, true. You're alright, Dragon. I'm glad it's you I'm getting to help."

B smiled. "I appreciate it. Now, how do we get to escape?"

"We don't! We're miles from anything. Our closest exit is through water, but we lack a boat."

"Crap! There must be another way."

Erik's face crumpled into a depression. "B, I've tried everything. I'll do my best to assist you for as long as I can. Just don't hold on to hope too much. It'll destroy you."

B reached for her pudding, choosing to ignore his lack of confidence in her plans to escape. "Tell me all about Mateo and this facility? Knowledge is power, and I don't plan on staying long."

Erik gave her a sympathetic stare. "You're lucky this building's so old they couldn't add audio. Those cameras are basic. Mateo is eccentric. He has his people conduct everything he needs, only he fears electronics and technology. Mateo's a bit of a conspiracy freak or a paranoid prick. He thinks big brother is watching. For someone as bright as him, he believes in some weird shit. But seriously, we're not getting out."

"Watch me!"

"You'll die trying. I almost did."

"There must be a phone or internet connection, right? I need to get word to my family. Tell them where we are."

"No internet here. Agents are prohibited from having cell phones. Even Mateo leaves his phone in a safe outside of town. Like I said. He's a strange one. He's so paranoid that the government will discover his human trials. He keeps this place in the dark ages."

"Surely, there's a landline nearby."

Erik scratched his head. "The only outside line is in his office, and this place is heavily guarded. Hell, the nearest town is apparently an hour's drive, and you'd die of hyperthermia as soon as you dip a toe in the river. Hold on," he said, standing in realization. "Back up. You know where we are?"

B chugged her hot chocolate. "Near Lake Whatcom, Bellingham."

"How do you know?"

"Mateo told me."

Erik snarled. "I knew it looked familiar. Dragon, after each fight, Mateo leaves until the following week."

"Then the landline is our only shot. How do we get in?"

He paced, rubbing his shaven chin. "We don't. It can't be done."

"I don't believe in can't, good boy."

"Aren't you afraid of what he'll do to your family?"

The pain in B's body threatened to kill her. Zander was gone, and she'd caused that. Snapping herself from her pity party, she clenched her jaw. "My wolves will fight to the death for my family. Nothing will happen to them." Erik had provided her with enough of a lifeline to bring back her determination. "Besides, a caged Dragon is a bloody dangerous one."

Erik's face became broken.

"What is it?"

"I have a child B. My father doesn't know about him. I turned informant and slept with my handler. She got pregnant and had my kid. I don't know if Mateo knows about her. It's partly why I'm here. I'd stopped myself from having hope of seeing her again."

"You can't be a daddy in here, my lovely. It's time to put on your big boy pants."

Erik tapped his chin with his index finger. "Okay, but we do it my way. I've tried and tested everything here, Dragon. Access to that building section could take weeks. I have only just gained trust to roam the basement."

"I'll follow your lead, then."

B wasn't sure if she could trust him. Her heart wanted to believe she could. He didn't share the same demeanor as Leif or Ragnar. She saw Tyr when she stared into his eyes.

"Thank you, Dragon, for giving me hope and lighting a fire in me."

"Right back at you, good boy!"

CHAPTER THIRTY-NINE
Retaliation

Mateo sat in his lavish penthouse suite in downtown Seattle, sipping a margarita as if he was sunning himself on a Hawaiian beach. He hadn't long returned home from watching B in action after receiving her first dose of his wonder drug. In a celebratory mood, he had spent the evening with an escort until his cell phone disturbed him.

Answering the call, a stern voice met him.

"Mateo...."

"Yes. To whom am I speaking?"

"This is Sheriff Johnstone from the County Sheriff's Department. I'm afraid I have some unfortunate news to deliver."

"Oh?"

"I regret to inform you that there was an explosion at your brother's bar tonight, and there are no survivors. Formal identification will be difficult due to the charred remains. It could take a while, I'm afraid. The locals have informed me that your brother was almost bed-bound. I'm sorry to ask this. Can you confirm the likelihood of him being elsewhere tonight without his oxygen tank?"

Mateo's blood boiled. Pushing away the escort nestled into his crotch, he stood in temper.

"My brother never leaves that club, officer, and he can't breathe without that tank. Now what the hell happened?"

"The forensic team is still working on the evidence. However, I can confirm that a pipe-bomb caused the explosion. That, combined with your brother's oxygen tank, created one hell of a blast. If your brother was in that building, I'm afraid he's gone. Now, I understand how hard this is, but I have some questions. Would you mind coming to the station? We may have an update for you by the time you arrive."

"Of course. I'll have my driver leave immediately."

"Thank you. Again, I'm sorry for your loss."

Mateo's hand fell to his side, releasing his phone onto the marble floor.

"Are you alright, Mattie?"

"Leave!" he breathed.

The model-like escort stepped back in fear before grabbing her clothes and clutching them to her naked breasts. Knowing the ramifications if she stayed a minute longer hurried her to the exit.

"Problem sir?" Agent Carter Asked.

Mateo gripped onto his enlarged quad muscles, bowled over by grief. He roared in a temper before picking up his margarita and launching it at the wall.

The agent froze in fear. Few survived Mateo's wrath: it was common knowledge that Mateo took his anger out on the agents closest to him.

"My brother is dead!" He screamed. "A bomb exploded in the club. Find out everything you can. Get hold of someone, anyone. Just find out what happened."

"Y-Yes sir. Shall I call your mother?"

"No! I want everything confirmed before I call her. He may have escaped. This will kill her. And I need you to take me to the County Sheriff's department.

"Yes, sir." The agent hovered in the doorway, lingering like a foul smell.

"What?" Mateo hissed.

"Forgive me, sir, but you don't think the Wolves might be responsible? After all, we shot their Prez and abducted his wife?"

Mateo's tear-stained eyes narrowed into his snarl. "If they are involved, the death toll will rise exponentially. Investigate and meet me in the lobby in twenty minutes!"

Mateo insisted his driver put his foot on the gas upon leaving his apartment. He sank into the leather seats, crushed by the news of his brother. Mateo knew his brother hadn't survived the explosion. His health had deteriorated tenfold since Mack had unleashed his fury upon him, and his fragile breaths tormented his little brother. He also admired Anton, even when he fell into a life of crime. Mateo knew he had to help his brother, being family. After graduating, he took a loan to produce his own pharmaceuticals. He wanted to make his big brother proud of him after Anton became his biggest deterrent to MC life when university became challenging. Whenever Mateo felt down and lost self-belief, Anton was there to support him. He even deposited a weekly allowance into Mateo's bank to ensure that he didn't stray into crime because of financial hardship. No, Anton wanted better for his little brother, initially refusing Mateo's newfound wealth after Mateo asked him to become his biggest distributor of illegal drugs.

Mateo laughed to himself with a heavy heart, casting his mind's eye back to that day. Anton was furious with Mateo for even suggesting becoming a drug dealer. He wanted so much more for him. It was only after Mateo showed him the potential in his business, providing him with a structured business plan with guaranteed success, that Anton agreed. The sheer number of zeros on Mateo's forecast proved too tempting to him, and as the years passed and Mateo built his empire, Mateo adopted the big brother and caregiver role with no resentment toward Anton. He felt an overwhelming sense of gratitude as he returned the favor. Now that was to become a memory; another chapter in Mateos' life as he grieved the loss of his brother.

"We're here, sir!" his driver said, snapping Mateo out of the memories of days past.

Gathering himself, Mateo dragged his hands down his face, wiping away the tears he hadn't realized had fallen. He straightened his tie and stepped out into the night, steadying his breath before entering the police department.

CHAPTER FORTY
Preparing to fight!

The night had long since drawn in, and after discussing their options, Erik retrieved the food trays and headed for the kitchen to allow B a chance to shower and rest. She viewed Erik as her ticket out of the monster mansion, even though he didn't feel confident about their escape plan.

Feeling disgusting, she wandered into the bathroom to take a shower. Washing away the day's trauma made her feel normal. Wrapping herself in a bathrobe, she rifled through the wardrobe for some pajamas: her obliterated mind called for rest. To her disgust, the only pajamas she could find were bright pink and fluffy.

Fuck my life! What the bloody hell are these?

Crabbit, she heaved on her pajamas and threw her clothes into the washing basket in the bathroom. She was just about to climb into bed when she noticed her blood-stained wedding dress hanging from the wardrobe. Crouching down, she drew it close inhaling its smell, hoping for a waft of Zander's essence. The fine material caressed her skin as her own potent perfume found her nostrils. She searched through the blood-filled dress until she found what she was searching for. Dragging herself to her bed, she hugged the dress to her body, intoxicating herself with the last of Zander's scent. Tears streamed down her emotional face, thinking of him and how she might never see him again, never rest in his loving arms or kiss his perfect lips.

I keep living a bloody nightmare! I must have been an evil bitch in a previous life to deserve this karma.

B tried her best to sleep. Only the dull, pulsating ache at the base of her brain prohibited it. Her body jerked in sporadic fits, as if a puppeteer was controlling her body. Her mouth became dry like the desert despite her efforts to consume the electrolytes she discovered amongst the vast array of boxes of protein bars and drinks. When she wasn't tweaking, B found the constant urination frustrating.

Disoriented, she forced down a protein shake; her trembling hands could hardly bring the bottle to her lips.

This can't be good. My body is struggling. I'm presenting with diabetic symptoms at the very least, and at the rate I'm drinking, I'll either die of hyponatremia or dehydration. There's no middle ground. I'm going from one extreme to the other. Come on body, regulate yourself with this fucking death drug!

B cursed her anatomy and physiology background in that moment.

You're not teaching now B. Shut that shit off or you'll panic! Focus. Think of happy memories and sleep there, good girl. You wanna go home? You need to stay strong!

CHAPTER FORTY-ONE
Confirmation

The Sheriff kept Mateo waiting in an interrogation room for almost three hours. His patience had almost left him when the officer entered, handing him a cup of cheap coffee, a stirrer and some sugar packets.

"Sorry to keep you waiting Mr. Torres As you can understand, there is a lot to digest."

Mateo ripped two sugar packets open, adding them to his coffee before stirring it.

"Of course,"

"Now, the coroner has discovered fragments of certain club members. However, with a case of this magnitude, formal identification will take some time, I'm afraid. What we can confirm is your brother's oxygen tank contributed to the blast."

"Then my brother is dead?"

"I'm afraid it's highly likely."

Mateo placed his coffee down on the table and stood to button up his blazer. "I understand. Thank you for informing me. I better inform my mother of her loss."

The Sheriff stood in his path. "Can you help me with a couple of questions before you leave?"

"Of course. I'll assist however I can."

The Sheriff ushered him back to his seat. "A substantial amount of fentanyl and methamphetamine, among other narcotics, survived the blast. Practically a whole shipment blown through the window and the club entrance."

"I wasn't aware my brother was undertaking in illegal activity officer. He couldn't even tie his shoelaces because of his health."

A smugness washed over the Sheriff's face, creating an uneasiness within an already impatient Mateo.

"That maybe so, but he had a whole MC at his disposal. Maybe he delegated?"

"I wouldn't know about that, Sheriff. I deal with legitimate pharmaceuticals."

"That's right. You're big business here. The rising star in the industry. I can't turn around without seeing your face on a billboard or newspaper."

Mateo raised his hands, grinning. "What can I say? I guess people love a hard-working self-made millionaire,"

"Ha, who doesn't? Just one more question."

"Shoot."

The Sheriff leaned in. His stern gaze unnerving Mateo. "How does ten kilos of a legitimate businessman's branded pharmaceuticals end up blown up in his outlaw brothers' MC, along with eight kilos of cocaine?"

Mateo smiled. "Nice try, Sheriff, but I would never jeopardize my reputation or my pharmaceuticals business for anything. You must be mistaken."

"Then explain this?" he said, slamming an evidence bag containing a melted Fentanyl pharmaceuticals pill container onto the table. "These little gems littered the grounds of the MC. Your brother's MC. You expect me to believe you knew nothing about this?"

Mateo's expression of shock and guilt splashed over his nervous face. "Sheriff, I don't understand what's going on here, but I assure you, I store my pharmaceuticals under lock and key. There are guidelines to follow. I couldn't have released these to my brother even if I wanted to. Large transactions must be counter-signed by two other board members. Wait! Unless?"

"Unless what?" The Sheriff clipped.

"My shipment. It was due earlier this evening. Officer, I need to check my latest delivery. Only theft could explain drugs in my brother's possession. I receive a shipment on the first of every month. I can call now to check if you like?"

"Make the call. Place it on speaker phone."

Mateo clambered around, all fingers and thumbs, with his phone like a nervous Nelly, dialing Carter's number.

"Sir?"

"Hello, Carter, my dear friend. I need you to check the inventory of tonight's shipment. Can you check it's arrived and make sure it's all accounted for on the invoice? It appears my brother was in possession of large quantities of my pharmaceuticals. Tonight's shipment is the only plausible answer."

"Yes, sir. Do you need your attorney?"

"That won't be necessary. I'm doing all I can to aid the police department in their line of enquiry. That will be all."

"I'll return the call as soon as I can."

Mateo ended the call, shaking his head. "I can't believe. I won't believe my brother betrayed me like this."

The Sheriff softened. "He knew when your shipments arrived?"

Mateo shook his head. "I took him to the port last month. My aim was to remove him from the club. I was trying to convince him to come and live with me, and I offered him an apartment in my building with nurses to take care of him. I wanted him away from the life that ultimately killed him. My brother is presumed dead, and I discover he's been stealing from me."

Awkwardness etched over the Sheriff's face. His apparent reaction showing to his lack of experience of a grown man ugly crying.

"Uh. Families are tough. Listen, where would your brother purchase a huge amount of cocaine and where would he get the cash? We are not talking pennies here!"

"I-I don't know," he cried. "I feel so betrayed right now. I tried to help him."

"There, there, son. We'll sort this out," the Sheriff said, patting his shoulder. "I'll fetch a fresh coffee. You take a moment to pull yourself together."

Mateo continued to cry, resting his head onto the table as the Sheriff left the interrogation room. Concealing his phone, he sent a message under the table while jerking into sobs.

"Carter, our guy at the docks, needs to be found dead at the port. The rest of my shipment needs to disappear from our check-in system. A stolen shipment is required here. Call me in ten to confirm that the shipment has disappeared."

Mateo quickly placed his phone back into his pocket, allowing his sobs to turn into sniffles in time for the Sheriff's return.

"You alright, son. It's a lot to take in."

Mateo retrieved a handkerchief from his blazer pocket, blowing his nose, making the Sheriff uncomfortable.

"I'm sorry, Sheriff. What must you think? A grown man sobbing like that?"

"Grief and betrayal are powerful things. The shock will settle. Any word on your shipment yet?"

"Uh, where's' my phone?" he said, patting himself down before putting his hand into his trouser pocket. "Here, I'll check," he said, retrieving it. "Nothing yet. It shouldn't take long to check the inventory. The computer will show if the shipment has been accepted into the office," I'll leave my cell on the table for when he rings."

"Well, you might as well drink your coffee. I brought you a snack to go with it."

"I appreciate your hospitality. I'm sorry for all this."

"It's my job. Besides, we'll get answers soon enough."

They sat in silence until Mateo's cell rang. Placing it on loudspeaker, Mateo waited for the news.

"Sir. The shipment hasn't arrived. I called the port, and nobody is answering."

"Unacceptable!" Mateo said with certainty.

"What can I do, Sir?"

Mateo glimpsed the Sheriff for advice.

"I'll have my officers head to the port to investigate. You just sit tight."

Mateo nodded. "Thank you, Carter. That will be all,"

Carter hung up the phone, and the Sheriff stood from his seat. "Head home and get some rest Mr. Torres, we'll call you when we know more."

"Thank you, Sheriff. I don't quite know what I'm supposed to do here, but please let me know how I can assist you further. I would like some closure. The press discovering this would mean the end of my career."

"Don't worry. We'll deal with this swiftly," he said, shaking Mateo's hand and escorting him out. "Give my condolences to your mother."

Mateo dived into the car. "Fake cries did the trick. I've played the idiot card. Any news at your end?"

"Yeah! CCTV from the nearby food warehouse captured this." He handed Mateo his cell phone, presenting an image of two Gray Wolves on motorbikes, heading away from the Greyhound MC after the explosion.

"Find out their current location. We strike while the iron is hot."

"Uskiville is a no go. We had to bide our time until the wedding to get access last time. That place is an impenetrable fortress."

"Then we hit Sunnyville. Hard and fast, taking no survivors except for Mack. Gather a small elite squadron. I want them in my briefing room at midday tomorrow, and Carter, that dock man must die before the sheriff's men arrive."

CHAPTER FORTY-TWO
Struggling

It was early morning when Madoc and Rhys arrived at the hospital, rushing to embrace Zander with Tyr, hobbling on his crutches behind them.

A wave of emotion ran through him, watching the relief pour from their youthful faces as they ran into the room.

"Hey laddies, you alright?" he asked as an unfamiliar pang of pain and relief swept through him.

Reflecting on the shooting, moments before losing consciousness, he remembered fearing death and thinking of B and the boys. Zander had grown so close to them, treating them like his own flesh and blood. In recent months, he had defended them on occasions when he thought B was being a little harsh on them; their arrival brought him so much comfort in their time of sorrow.

They embraced him on both sides of the hospital bed, refusing to let go. Zander held them, placing his hands on their heads to comfort them with as much strength as he could muster.

"We're so glad you're okay, Zander," Rhys said.

"Thanks, me too. You both good?" he said, watching them peel away.

"We're okay. We just want Mum back," Madoc sighed.

A boulder-sized lump formed in Zander's dry throat, preventing him from speaking, making him reach for his glass of water on the bedside table.

"Here, I'll get it," Rhys said, handing him the glass.

"Thanks son," Zanders hands still shook as he took a sip.

Handing the glass back to Rhys, he cleared his throat with a gravelly rasp. "Hey, I promise I'll get her back. I won't stop until she's home. You have my word."

Smiles ripped through the room as Tyr spoke from the doorway. "See, what did I tell you? Prez is a fighter. He doesn't give up," he said, hobbling closer to lean in and embrace Zander with a firm handshake.

"Thanks for keeping an eye on them, Tyr. I'll be up and about soon enough. Just waiting for the doc to allow me home."

Tyr laughed. "You're not going anywhere until you're better. We need you strong, Prez. Wounded or not, I'll wrestle you to that bed if I must."

Zander pursed his lips. "I'm fine, son. I need to get out of here."

"No, you need to rest. The doctor said you're not even eating. They're concerned."

"That's because the food is revolting! I wouldn't feed a dog what they're serving up. Even the Jello is shit!"

"You're just spoilt with mum and Jimmy's cooking," Madoc teased. "But don't worry, Rhys made you some bridies, steak pies and shortbread this morning, and I brought your favorite soda."

Zander's eyes lit up like the midday sun. "Aww, thanks very much. I'm starving."

Rhys opened an array of Tupperware, revealing the homemade goods as Madoc placed some soda cans on the bedside table and Zander couldn't wait to delve in, munching on a bridie as if they were going out of fashion.

Rhys and Madoc's smiles warmed his heart, with Zander acknowledging how pleased they seemed with themselves to be helping him.

After filling his stomach, Zander's energy levels increased exponentially, despite how fragile he remained.

The doctor came around, explaining that his blood panel had returned to normal, along with his blood pressure, reiterating to Zander that despite his results he still required recuperation time. His stern gaze fixated on a fragile Zander.

"You were extremely lucky, Mr. McGovan. It's crucial you take care of yourself. The bullet created some damage to your soft tissue, and your sternum remains fragile despite the bullet deflecting off it and wedging itself close to your ribs."

"When can I leave, Doc?"

The doctor placed his stethoscope on Zander's chest. The cold stainless steel made him flinch.

"Easy Mr. McGovan. It'll take some time to heal. All being well, you'll be discharged in a day or two. I don't want you back here next week with a rupture."

"Oh, thanks Doc, for everything."

The doctor gave a curt nod. "I'll be back to brief you on your recovery plan upon your release. Meanwhile, the nurses and on-call doctors will care for you," he said, leaving the room with his group of interns.

Zander's smile beamed across his face. "See lads, I told yer. You cannae keep a Scot doon fir long."

"Yeah, but you still need your rest," Tyr insisted.

"Dinnae worry. I got this! Now update me, please?"

"Frankie and Jimmy are chasing leads," Tyr said, shooting Zander a serious stare and casting his eyes to Rhys and Madoc.

"Hey, can you laddies do me a favor and run to the cafeteria? I fancy a coffee and some candy. Get yourselves something nice, too. Tyr here will pay for it."

"No problem," Madoc said, getting up from his seat while Tyr handed Rhys a roll of notes.

"See you in a bit," Rhys said, ushering Madoc out of the room.

Tyr's gaze tracked them down the corridor before he sat on Zander's bed. "Honestly, Prez. It's been crazy. Mack lost his head and blew up the Greyhound's MC, wiping them all out. I know I shouldn't be telling you this in your condition, but you need to understand what's happening to our MC. It's the reason Jimmy didn't come to visit this morning. Him and Frankie are preparing for retaliation."

Zander gritted his teeth, frustrated that he was in no condition to lead. "For Fuck's sake! He's a fucking loose cannon. I'm sick and tired of us fighting for our lives because of his shit."

"I know, Prez, I'm sorry. Frankie and Jimmy thought it was best to keep you out of the loop. They need you to heal as quickly as possible, but I couldn't keep it from you."

Zander placed his hand on his shoulder. "Thank you, Tyr, I'm glad you told me. So, what's the play here?"

"Frankie has been epic. He's a born leader and took control of the situation as soon as shit unraveled. He delegated and gave my father a pasting. Gnarler went to town on Ragnar for stitching us up too. They've agreed to work with us, although Frankie has them on a tight leash."

"And you? How are you taking this?"

"Personal," Tyr snarled. "Prez, I'll never forgive my father for putting everyone in danger. I'm sorry. I feel responsible for my family's actions. I will make this right and I'll die trying to bring her home if that's my fate."

Zander squeezed his shoulder; Tyr couldn't bring himself to say B's name. "We'll bring her home together. Now, are there any leads to where they've taken her?"

Tyr's face crumbled into sadness. "Nothing. Prez, there's something else?"

Coldness filled Zander's eyes; his intuition forewarning him that Tyr's next sentence would be hard to digest. "Tell me," he whispered.

"The guy who took her," he said, stumbling over his words. "They denied his clearance for human testing for a messed-up drug. Rumor has it he was going to take Mack and use him as a lab rat for his new drug," Tyr gulped before continuing, fighting back his tears. "Anton, the Prez of the Greyhounds told Mack he's going to conduct those trials on her. They're going to use her as a fucking lab rat, and it's my fault. I thought my family was after me. I'm so sorry!"

Zander sat himself up. A toxic concoction of emotions ripped through him, spiking his blood pressure, and sending his observation machine into a panic. Zander ripped the pulse monitors and canula from his arm and dived out of bed, roaring in pain as he did so.

A nurse rushed in. "Get back into bed. You'll be back in surgery if you're not careful."

"Sorry sweetheart. I'm signing myself out. I'm done resting." He glared at an inconsolable Tyr. "Save your tears, laddie. This ain't on you. We're getting the fuck out of here and finding Welsh Cake. As long as I'm still breathing, there's hope."

Tyr wiped his face and stood up straight. "Yes, Prez!"

CHAPTER FORTY-THREE
Rise and Shine!

The research doctor woke B from her slumber with annoyance in his tone. "Rise and shine, sleeping brutality. Change of plans. Mateo has moved your first fight up to today, so I'm here to prep you for the day ahead."

B sat up, wiping the itchy sleep from her eyes. "Bloody hell, I've not even got over the first dose. I'm rattling worse than a fucking rattle snake. You hit me with another shot and my heart will give out!"

The strait-laced, emotionally crippled doctor shrugged. "Perhaps he'll bring me someone worthy of my research when you fail."

Contempt sent her hormones into overdrive with the remnants of her first dose reigniting within, numbing the back of her skull. The doctor stepped back, watching her eyes gloss over in murky evil.

"You think this is a bloody game, good boy? This is my life you're dabbling in," she snapped, diving out of bed and into his personal space.

Two unknown agents attempted to restrain her, only evil had consumed her. B head-butted the first agent in the temple with such volatile force, she knocked him unconscious. The second man pulled the doctor out of harm's way, only to run into B's instep as she kicked him in the face, sending him crashing into her wardrobe. Stomping toward the doctor, she watched him slip behind the door just in time.

Her hands pounded the door until her knuckles bled; the devil controlled her body now. B had no sense of clarity or pain as she belted the door.

Blood trickled from her knuckles, dripping onto the floor in decorative spots of deep red. B had become lost to the drug once more, lost enough to relish at the fallen agent's grunts into consciousness. Sneering a sinister grin toward her prey, B's heart pounded with excitement. Her Dragon-like tendencies had returned to all their glory, only amplified by ten. Taking hold of his tie, B wrapped it around his throat, choking him until he breathed his last breath. Her fire red eyes glistened like spherical sparks popping out of flames in a coal fire. She licked her lips as if spotting a tasty treat, her next target; the other agent who attacked her. Knee-dropping onto his chest, she dug her thumbs into his eyes, smashing his head off the pristine white marble floor until a sea of red satisfied her vision.

The drug made B fearless and dangerous. She was no longer bound by any moral fiber. She had one mission to kill anyone in her path to freedom.

A moment of clarity entered her mind's eye.

Keycards!

B frisked the two agents, taking their keycards before leaving wearing only striped pajamas. To her surprise, the door whooshed open, and B remembered she entered from the left, dashing down the corridor barefoot. She raced down the long corridor, rugby tackling another agent who wasn't quick enough to react to B's presence. Tackling him to the ground, B continued to the main entrance, releasing the deadbolt on the old oak door. She ran across the gravel, knowing the frozen water would kill her by shocking her to her death. She couldn't feel the stones tearing up her skin in her adrenaline rush. Her only thought was to go home. She would send her pack to rescue Erik once she reached safety. She had run about 400 meters, hurdling two fences when she felt a quickening pace behind her. Taking half a second to turn her head, B saw a safari jeep approach her. Forcing her stride, B willed herself to outrun them until another jeep circled her as if they were rounding her up. A debilitating pain seared through her thighs and her right foot failed to connect with the ground as B was lassoed, like a cowboy lassoing a bull.

B face-planted the ground in a muddy thud.

Shit!

What appeared to be fishing wire had entangled her thighs and legs. B tugged at the sharp wire with an urgency to free herself, slicing her hand.

The vehicles circled once more like vultures before halting to a stop. Four agents exited each vehicle, gathering in formation toward her.

"Stand down, Dragon. You will return with us," one agent commanded, stepping into her presence and forgetting the blade tucked into his waistband.

B reached up in one swoop, swiping the knife and jabbing it into his thigh with such force, she heard a satisfying bone crack.

The man wailed as two agents dragged him away, and the others retrieved their guns.

"You better make sure you kill me, because if I get back up, I'm ending all of you!" she screamed.

They cocked their weapons until another agent spoke up. "She's wanted alive. Mateo will kill the lot of us if she's dead upon his return tonight."

"We'll say we had no choice. That bitch just killed Keith and Kenny."

"No, we have orders!"

"To hell with that. This bitch dies now!" The agent cocked his rifle, pointing at B's head. Just as he squeezed the trigger, Erik appeared, tackling him to the ground, watching as the bullet narrowly missed B's head and embedded itself into the mud.

"Freeze Traitor!" an agent shouted as Erik kneeled in front of B, creating a line of defense.

"You take her back to her room, or you kill both of us. What would Mateo say if you freed me from my pain by ending my life sooner than he wanted?" Erik said.

B glared at him as the other agents considered his words.

"You get her back to her room. No funny business," the agent who tried to stop her from getting shot the first time around said.

"You have my word."

"Not mine, good boy. I'm getting out of here!"

Erik snapped his head to meet her pouting stare. "Not today, Dragon. You need to learn when you've lost the battle. It's the only way you'll win the war."

B snarled at him, and Erik directed his attention to the agents. "Cuffs?"

An agent tossed a pair of handcuffs at his feet, and Erik snapped them onto her wrists. "Trust me, Dragon."

Disappointment seared into every fiber of her being, weaving an intricate web of undeniable anger into the depths of her molten soul. Erik picked her up, throwing her over his shoulders before placing her into the Jeep and sitting beside her.

B remained mute for the brief journey back to the house where the smug-looking doctor waited.

"I want her restrained on my gurney. Good work Erik. Your allegiance will please Mateo when he learns about it."

B growled at him. "You were just fucking playing me?"

Erik ignored her, carrying her into the house and along the corridor to the medical room. He applied the straps securing her to the bed before releasing the wire from her thighs and removing the cuffs.

"You are a fucking traitor!" she snapped, spitting in his face.

CHAPTER FORTY-FOUR
Zanders' Return

The doors of the Uskiville bar smashed open, stunning the packed bar to silence. Everyone remained on edge in the wake of recent events. Shock filled the air as Zander entered.

"What the fuck is everyone staring at? You honestly dinnae think I'd bail out on my old lady, or my MC did you, ya bunch of wee pricks!"

The bar erupted in cheery relief, welcoming their once fallen Prez back into the fold. Hyde raced to clear a space at the top table, fetching him a cushion for his chair.

"Get to fuck with the fannying about. I'm fine, asshole," Zander snapped, sitting in the wooden bar chair with the pain rinsing his body of the little happiness he had tried to experience at returning home.

"What in God's fucking blazes are you doing out of hospital? And don't tell me they released you because I know they didn't," Jimmy demanded.

Zander shrugged, forgetting how much it hurt to move. "I'm no' sitting by while some prick is torturing my old lady. Fuck the tiny bullet hole. It doesnae matter."

"With respect, Prez, you almost met your maker. You flatlined, brother!"

"I was deed for a second. So what? Now I'm back and ready to kill!"

Frankie burst into a fit of laughter, getting up to hug Zander. "You hard fucking bastard! Glad you're alright, brother. You scared the hell out of us!"

Zander waved to the bartender to fetch him a drink. "You cannae keep a Scot like me doon. We're stubborn bastards. Now where are we on finding Welsh Cake?"

The bar went silent.

Zander took his drink from the bartender upon delivery.

"What, nobody has the balls to tell me you got nothing? Why the fuck do you think I discharged myself? Tyr informed me of the shitshow of a stunt Irish pulled. Where the fuck is he? I want words with him."

"He's up the valley. He knows he fucked up by blowing up the MC. He's reflecting," Frankie said.

Zander coughed up his whiskey, grimacing in pain and applying pressure to his wound to stop it from splitting.

"You alright man? You wanna lie down?" Jimmy asked.

Zander waved his free hand, dismissing him. "Fucking reflecting. He'll reflect on the end of my fist if anything has happened to Welsh Cake. Fucking reflecting, pfft!" He turned to the bar where Leif, Ragnar, and the other Rus Reapers were drinking. "And dinnae think I forgot about you, ya traitorous fuckers! I knew you were up to something, and let me tell you now, if that piece of shit hurts one hair on my old lady's head, I'm taking my tools to you and your club, and that includes everyone. I will wipe out your entire existence."

Leif stared at the beer-stained, slippery floor.

"Look at you, you fucking coward. You cannae even look at me."

"Celtic Warrior, I am sorry. My son—"

"Fuck your son. He's no' my concern. My concern right now is how you and your pack of savage fucking Vikings are gonnae make it up to me. I want Mateo. Your clock is fucking ticking, boys, and I dinnae care if you have to resurrect Odin himself to find him. You leave here tomorrow and meet us back in Sunnyville in two days with everything you fucking have on the guy. You fail me, it's bye-bye Reapers."

Leif stepped forward. "I know you're hurting. He took my Erik, too. The Reapers will do all they can to bring our loved one's home. We have provided Frankie with all our intel. We won't rest until we fix this."

Frankie gave Zander a nod. "They've been cooperating, Prez, and if we're going to take on Mateo, we need the numbers."

Zander raised his head, scowling with pursed lips. "Fair enough. You can breathe for now, but you're on my shit list, Viking!"

"Thank you for your grace. I'll decapitate Mateo and bring justice to our families!"

"Get in line Viking! He's mine!"

CHAPTER FORTY-FIVE
Traitors!

"Is she ready?" Mateo said from the doorway, giving nothing away regarding his brother's demise.

"Fluid and nutrient dense, vitals are stable. I'm about to administer the dose."

Confusion spiraled within him. "A little premature, isn't it, doctor? The fight isn't for two hours."

"Come, I have something to show you," the doctor said, directing Mateo's attention to the security monitors. "Dragon's condition three hours ago, 36 hours post first dose."

Mateo cast his eyes over the screen, watching B annihilate two of his best agents. He bit down on his bottom lip with an inquisitive smile.

"That was before she escaped using their keycards, raced the length of an Olympic track before plunging Gareth's own knife into his thigh, splitting his femur." He steepled his fingers. "I'm not saying the drug is solely responsible for Dragon's reactions. It appears her desire for survival is contributing."

Mateo stroked his chin. "Damn, Dragon's got game!"

"How did you subdue her?"

The doctor grinned, pleased as punch. "I sent Erik after her!"

Mateo's eyes popped like a party-popper. "And he followed orders?"

"Even took out one of your agents who wanted to kill her. Saved her life by tackling him to the ground as he fired his weapon."

"Interesting. Have him report to my office," he said, pivoting in B's direction. "You gagged her?"

"The bitch doesn't shut up, and that fucking accent grates on me! I chose a gag over a bullet," the research doctor said without glancing up from his computer monitor.

"My, my, Dragon. You are relentless if nothing else. I lack time for such childish behavior. You are here as my prisoner and personal project. There's no hope for you here other than to follow my rules to stay alive. Capiche?"

B growled like a savage beast through the rolled-up bandage wedged in her throat.

"No more games, Dragon. I'll see you at your fight. You'll appreciate your opponent, and you're welcome."

Mateo witnessed the administering of B's next dose, watching how her veins bulged from her temple, attempting to stabilize her troubled body from the trauma of the adrenaline tearing through her. Watching her eyes roll back into her head and her body convulse before stabilizing fueled him with excitement. He was ecstatic to be torturing the woman Mack loved and being progressive with his successful research. Smiling, he left the room, relishing in victory: a win for his brother, who had likely died in the explosion at his club the previous night.

Taking the elevator to his office on the first floor, Mateo waltzed over to his black leather desk chair, plonking himself down, and helping himself to a Cuban cigar. Lighting it up, he puffed away, encouraging the fiery embers to glow while blowing smoke in small circles from his twisted mouth.

That's for you, brother. Your sacrifice won't be in vain.

He basked in the glory of his successful research; Gen Force had remained in B's system in lethal quantities, and not only had B's body stabilized, but it was also believed that she tapped back into a remarkable feat of adrenaline much higher than normal values 36 hours later. These new groundbreaking results would now become a selling point to his potential buyers at her fight tonight.

He was already seeing dollar signs when Erik was escorted to his office by three agents, one of them being the agent who took a shot at B.

"Aah, Erik, I wanted to commend you on your actions today. Placing your life above my research was truly admirable."

Erik's crystal eyes glistened like the first snow drops of winter. "I didn't have a choice. Dragon dies, I die, correct?"

Mateo rose from his chair to puff smoke in Erik's face. "Yes, but you didn't disappoint did you, my Viking traitor?" He brought his free hand to Erik's face, slapping it. "Good dog! Now that I've broken you in, you could prove to be more useful in my absence here."

"Oh?"

"Yes, in fact, you'll start now. Tell me which of these three buffoons tried to kill Dragon today."

The three men quivered where they stood.

"The idiot in the middle," Erik clipped.

Mateo swaggered over to his agents, rolling his cigar between his fingers and stopping in front of the agent in question. "You threatened millions of dollars of work to stroke your ego, huh?"

"I- uh- she killed-."

"Blah, blah, blah! I don't want your excuses, agent. Now kiss my boots as punishment for your stupidity, you filthy pig."

The stunned agent froze, and Mateo grabbed his shirt, pushing him to the floor. "Do you not understand English? Kiss my boots."

The cowering agent lowered his lips to Mateo's boot and Mateo kicked him full force in the face. "Filthy, filthy traitor. Have you learned nothing from Viking here?" he pointed to Erik before swiftly turning his attention back to the crawling agent, kicking him in the ribs. "You are getting blood on my Persian rug, asshole." He glowered at the two other agents. "Imprison him next to Dragon as a warning to those who challenge me."

Mateo continued to smoke his cigar, watching the two agents drag their injured colleague from the room.

"Show no mercy to those who cross you, Viking," he said, returning to his seat. "Tell me, are the heart pills working?"

"I haven't had another heart attack, so yeah, I guess so."

"And you've finished the course of the stabilizers?"

"I have," Erik said, failing to disclose the extra tablets he was giving to B to help manage her symptoms.

Mateo smiled. "I trust you haven't informed B of your heart condition?"

Erik placed his hands on his hips. "You're asking if I've I told her she's going to die before the trial ends?"

"Correct."

"What good would that do? At present, she is fighting for her life and her freedom. If I remove her hope, she doesn't fight for anyone. She dies, then I die."

"I'm glad we understand each other."

"Tell me something, Mateo. You've had 186 unwilling participants as well as Dragon. 185 fatalities from heart failure. As the 186th, even I died twice. Has it ever occurred to you, the science is wrong, and your drug doesn't work?"

Mateo stubbed out his cigar in a nearby ashtray. "It works!"

"Until it doesn't. You've strengthened the dose for Dragon, making it more dangerous than all the others before it. She could die any day now. What happens to your precious research, then?"

Mateo pressed his palms onto his desk. "It continues and we press on with Mack."

"So, you're just going to keep going until everyone dies?"

"If that's what it takes to bottle my liquid courage, yes. Viking, Dragon's body is responding better to Gen Force than any other subject, even you on your dose. Perhaps the female body has a way of adapting." He leapt from his seat with excitement. "Think about it. A woman in childbirth endures pain at approximately 10.5 dols when her baby's head is crowning. No man has ever endured such pain. Even when shot, shock and adrenaline kick in. Dragon's figures have the potential to revolutionize global militaries."

"With you cashing in on their pain."

Mateo loosened his tie. "Dragon is here because she made the mistake of befriending Mack. Her crimes are her own, and I don't care about her pain. I care for the millions I set to make when selling her to the highest bidder. I'm showcasing her each week until someone buys her."

Erik narrowed his gaze as Mateo continued. "Mack won't see her again. Once I sell her, I'll have all the data for the global distribution of Gen Force. Dragon's benefactor will not try to replicate her because the men I deal with are more about unique trophies. She'll become a wife of a very rich middle eastern general or president if she survives. I'll sell her by week six, way before the cardiac threshold. If she dies after that, not my problem," he shrugged. "She's sold as seen."

"She'll never give up on her family. It's the MC way!"

"Oh, Viking. You've never been one to show mercy to anyone. You were happy to sell out your entire pack. Why the change in heart?"

"She's a mother. She's not a criminal like me."

"And now, she's an abomination set to make me millions, and the only one keeping you alive. Now I suggest you give her a pep talk before her first fight. The clock is ticking."

CHAPTER FORTY-SIX
B's Fight!

B was so jacked up on adrenaline, she bounced around her room like a ping-pong ball in a world championship match.

Pacing, she readied herself for her first fight. Every heightened emotion danced through her body as if to tease her about her potential demise. Only B felt invincible.

Mateo had left instructions for her to wear her 'fight outfit,' a red sports bra and tight shorts.

Who the fuck does this guy think he is? I'm not wearing that shit!

Tossing it aside, she rummaged through the closet and selected a white vest and a pair of ripped jeans. Instead of choosing the sneakers that Mateo instructed her to wear, she opted for a red pair of combat boots that someone had placed in the closet for Mack's arrival. Fortunately for B, she and Mack wore the same shoe size.

That's more like it.

B dressed and paced the room, hoping to see Erik. He spent days preparing her for her biggest fight yet, explaining the competition after peeking at the schedule. B only knew she was competing against a man named Cafu from Brazil. He was 6 foot 3 inches with a background in Capoeira.

Her nerves threatened to overwhelm her, and her patience grew thin. B just wanted it over with.

Come the fuck on. Let's go play with dancing boy, and if I survive this, that prick better have a shitload of Welsh Cakes for me. I'm having bloody withdrawals from them.

She paced again.

At least I'll break in my new boots.

The door whooshed open.

"Show time, Dragon," Mateo said upon entering. The sinister glare of disappointment flooded his face as he laid his eyes upon her. "That is not appropriate attire for tonight's event."

"Sorry Good Boy. I know sex sells, but I couldn't give a shit about what you're selling. I dance to the beat of my own drum and I'm going to be comfortable doing so."

Mateo's lips curled up on his favored right side of his face.

"You continue to test me, Dragon."

"Like you test me, asshole. Here's an idea. You get in that ring with me. The winner walks away?"

Mateo laughed, pressing his palms together. "Oh, I'm not an idiot, dear Dragon. I know I'm no match for you. I have a challenger, but it's not who you expect. There's been a last-minute change with your competitor. You will face Cafu next week, and yes Dragon, I know everything that goes on around here. The Viking isn't known for his stealth. I caught him checking the fight roster. In fact, I'm glad he did. It better prepares you. Now, Hudson will escort you to the pool. Enjoy your fight!"

B watched Mateo strut from her room.

Pool. What the fuck?

Hudson glared at her like an eagle studying his prey. "Move, bitch!" he snapped, ushering her into the corridor.

He directed B through the service entrance and across another hallway until they reached a steel door. Hudson yanked it open and pushed her inside.

Applause echoed around the cold pool room. The ancient empty pool had signs of previous trauma, combined with rust from leakage and depreciation.

B whipped her head around to see crowds of high rollers, some in military uniform, all clapping and cheering her on as the main attraction.

Jesus! It's like a twisted, bloody horror movie here.

Erik's voice called out to her from inside the pool, extending his hand to her.

"Down here, Dragon."

B gripped onto the rickety metal handrail, climbing down into the pool. The handles creaked, threatening to break as she stepped down to meet him.

"This is the ring? You're a fucking snake by the way," she snapped.

"Believe it or not, I'm on your side, and the pool has its advantages."

"Yeah, like what? Dying of septicemia from all the shit that's going to infect me here. or asbestos poisoning before this drug wipes me out?"

Erik smirked at her. "You're funny, Dragon. Keep that spirit. Ensure Mateo never strips that away from you."

B scanned the room again.

Two guarded exits. There's no way I'll be able to make a break, especially with all these brown-nosers sipping champagne and telling Mateo how he's outdone himself in his latest mad science project.

Erik placed his hands on her shoulders. "I know what you're thinking. Don't bother, for both our sakes. Mateo's clients have paid a fortune for you to entertain them. They are potential business connections from across the globe. Live to fight another day, Dragon."

B bit down onto her bottom lip until it bled. The adrenaline rushing through her system made her heart pound into her ears, triggering her. B became an unpredictable mess once more, thirsty for the blood of her enemies.

"I just want to rip his throat out, Erik. Show him the pain he's caused me."

"Channel that at your opponent tonight and you're one step closer to getting that. How are you feeling after the second dose?"

"It feels as if my head and heart are going to explode."

Erik closed his eyes. "I know the feeling well. Hang in there, Dragon. Do this and I'll have a pill ready to help with the comedown."

"What the-"

Two agents dragging their fellow agent into the pool caught B's attention. B pushed past Erik. "That's the dickhead who tried to shoot me earlier."

Erik whispered into her ear. "Nobody fucks with Mateo, B. He's showing his power here, to you and to him. The agent wronged him, and he's setting an example to those thinking of crossing him."

B stood ready for war, observing the agent's contempt for the situation as he unshackled himself.

"Good luck, Dragon," Erik said, leaving the pool.

Mateo stepped to the edge of the pool.

"Competitors. You want to leave this pool? Kill your opponent."

B cracked her neck with an increasing desire to attack the man who had shot at her. "Are you ready to dance with the Dragon, asshole? Not so big without your rifle and savage brothers, are you?"

"Ooh, ladies and gentlemen, don't you just love the sass? But can the mighty Dragon back it up? Fight!" Mateo bellowed.

The eager agent ran at B, attempting to rugby tackle her, only to collide with her knee. B gripped his short black hair as if she wanted to rip it out, tossing him over.

The agent quickly rolled to his feet, wiping his bloody nose on the back of his hand. "You're gonna die, bitch. You killed my friends."

B shrugged, her temper boiling. "Maybe their mother should have told them not to pick on women."

The agent ran at her again, bundling her into the wall. His firm grasp around her neck threatened her oxygen supply. "You think you're a tough bitch? I'm going to snap that pretty little neck of yours."

B pulled him closer, gripping his ears, and distracting him enough to knee him between the

legs. Her long legs and bony knees were her defense, creating enough distance for her to recover her breath.

Beetroot red and crying out, the agent dropped to his knees as B caught her breath. Gasping for air, she smashed his head against the pool with a loud crack. Unsatisfied with the unsettling crack and the rumble of gasps from the crowd above, she grabbed the barely conscious agent by his black T-shirt and raised her fist to strike him again. Aware he had no fight left to muster, she punched him again, feeling his cheek bone cave with the crushing blow of her fist.

Her temper boiled, knowing what had to be done.

If I want to stay alive, he needs to die.

The agent choked on his gnarly breath, suffering like a wounded animal, and B was there to put him out of his misery. Kneeling before him, B threaded her arm around his convulsing throat, dragging him into her, and took hold of her own bicep. She wrapped her other hand around the back of his head, crushing his fragile windpipe until he breathed no more. Once convinced her fight was over, B pushed the flopping man aside as if he was trash and stood glaring at Mateo.

After a split second of unease on Mateo's face, he broke into a cheer. "This is Dragon everybody. I promised you a mere taste of her strength. Look at her," he said, pointing at her. "She didn't even break a sweat. Imagine what she'll bring to the table next week."

B snapped! "How about you, Mateo? I keep asking you to face me, but you won't accept. How are all these people meant to trust in what you're selling if you won't test it yourself?"

A nervous glint crossed his face. "Oh, she's a character, this one. Everyone, if you'd like to make your way to the grand hall, we'll continue to celebrate there."

Erik jumped down into the pool, knocking her out of her evil trance, shoving her into the wall. "Are you plain stupid, calling him out like that?"

"He was sending me a message, so I sent one back, telling him he's a weak prick. I wanted to show his precious business connections how gutless he is."

"You think he gives a shit about that? He'll just increase your dose and turn you into a fucking monster until your head explodes."

"And corrupt his precious research? He won't waiver on whatever his target is. I'm priceless to him, and I'll do whatever the fuck I want if it helps me get out of here."

Erik shook his head. "How can I convince you, behaving like that will lead to a quicker death." He wrapped an arm around her, guiding her to the pool steps. "Let's clean you up and get some food."

CHAPTER FORTY-SEVEN
His Mother's Eyes

Zander woke from a nightmare in the small hours dripping with sweat. He had relived his shooting, waking in terror after remembering the fear in B's eyes while being ripped from their wedding day.

Reaching for his orange pill bottle, he discovered his arm had gone numb. He often complained to B how uncomfortable her couch was to sleep on; Zander couldn't face their bedroom without her. It would destroy him. His broken body trembled, struggling to cope with basic demands as Zander sat himself up. Unscrewing the cap then tapping the bottle, he caught two painkillers in his hand.

I wish the pain would get to fuck. I cannae function like this.

He tossed the pills down the back of his throat, swallowing them dry, and glanced around the room. A chuckle escaped him, casting his gaze to Tyr lying sleeping on the opposing couch with Valkyrie sprawled across his chest with his legs in the air.

Aww, Welsh Cake would fucking melt if she saw them now.

He picked up his phone from the table and snapped a picture.

Something to show her when she gets home.

The pain in his heart overwhelmed him; not the physical pain, the pain of missing his love. The anxiety swept through him like a tornado, destroying everything in his path, making it hard to breathe.

Five things, Zander, five things. Keep your shit together, she needs you!

He relayed the mantras that B had taught him on the first night they'd slept together, over, and over until he calmed. Thinking of her brought both joy and sadness, and Zander knew this feeling would consume him if he allowed it.

He dragged himself to his feet, once again clutching his chest to support his wounds. Walking the short distance to Madoc and Rhys's bedrooms, he cracked their opposing doors to check on them. Rhys stirred at the light shining into his room before Zander closed it, leaving an inch to make him feel better. He wanted to hear if they woke up in distress, determined to be a rock like B was for him. Madoc snored as loud as a freight train; his covers strewn over the floor showing he'd been restless in his sleep. Zander cautiously bent down enough to hook them with his fingers, picking them up to drape them over Madoc and tuck him in just like B would have. As Zander made his way out of the bedroom, Madoc called him.

"Zander?"

Zander closed his eyes, dreading the words about to exit Madoc's mouth before turning.

"Yeah pal."

"She's coming home, you know. It may take some time with you having to heal and all, but I know you'll bring her home. You must believe that, too."

Zander nodded into a choke. Clearing his throat, he approached Madoc, lowering himself onto the edge of the bed.

"Thank you, son. I needed to hear that. You know, I'll never give up on finding her. I dinnae care what it takes."

Madoc sat up to converse with him. "My mother is the strongest person I know. She'll hold her own until you find her. I heard Uncle Frankie whispering earlier, and I know about the human testing but you gotta believe me when I say my mother is strong enough to endure anything thrown at her. She has a strength like no other."

Zander smirked into a nod. "Oh, aye. She could kick my ass for sure."

"Yeah, while eating a Welsh Cake!"

Zander gave him a loving nudge. "Easy. I thought you were giving me a pep talk."

"I am, Prez. All I'm saying is, Mum wouldn't want you to go after her all broken like you are. She would say, 'You're not going anywhere in that state, Boyoh. You're as useless as a chocolate fireguard. Now get your shit in one sock before trying to fight battles you know nothing about, she would."

Zander's vocal cords erupted in laughter. "God, you even sound like her."

"I am her son, good boy," he teased.

Zander stared at him in awe, placing a hand on his shoulder. "You have your mother's strength, Madoc. I'm so proud of the way you're handling this shitstorm, laddie, and I know your mother would be, too."

"What doesn't kill you makes you stronger, and don't worry about Rhys. I got him like I got you!"

Zander's bottom lip trembled. "Come here," he said, gripping Madoc. "I love you and your brother so much. Thank you for bringing me a healthy dose of your mother. You dinnae realize how much I needed it." He kissed his head before pulling away, wiping the tear from his left eye. "Try to sleep," he said, tousling his hair.

"Good night, Zander."

Zander stood, calming himself while leaving the room. He clasped onto the door handle ready to pull it close to closure, taking one last look into the boy who had his mother's eyes.

Hang on in their darling, I'm coming to find you.

As dawn broke, Zander directed the wolves, as if preparing them for a fierce war. He instructed the Sunnyville chapter to pack up; they were heading home to Sunnyville, where Zander could heal and think.

Leif and the Reapers were heading home, too, arranging to meet in Sunnyville in two days with additional intel on Mateo. Frankie and

Marshall conversed with Gnarler, unearthing any evidence they could muster from the dark web, and Mack was still nowhere to be seen.

Unable to ride back to Sunnyville, Zander was checking his bike was secure on the trailer attached to B's truck. Bamfa had agreed to drive it to Sunnyville knowing how much it meant to B. He would spend some time in Sunnyville assisting Frankie, using their former military skills and making up to Zander for building the bomb that destroyed the club's only connection to B.

"I am sorry, Prez. I wasn't thinking," Bamfa said to a fatigued Zander.

"You were following your Prez. It's fucking done now. Just use your contacts to find me information on Mateo, and Bamfa, I appreciate you driving B's truck back to Uskiville."

"It's the least I can do," he said, taking Frankie's lead, who'd approached and gave him the nod to take a hike.

"Where is he?" Zander asked.

"Up the cabin. He's not talking to anyone."

"Not even you?"

Frankie shook his head. "I lost my shit with him. He'll sulk for a day or so and turn up thirsty for vengeance."

Zander leaned against the trailer. "We all want vengeance, Frankie, but Welsh Cake's safety comes before all of that."

"I know. He'll have a clear head when we next see him."

"Good. I've no' got time for his shit. The laddies ready?"

"Yeah, their dad is throwing a wobbly, though."

"Tough shit. They're coming home. They should return to school for a sense of normalcy. That's what Welsh Cake would do."

"Maybe so, but B isn't here, and this situation is far from normal."

Zander raised his head to the sky. "Please Frankie. Just help me out with this. I'm barely holding on here, pal. I just want them close and under my protection. We'll stay at the club to ensure their safety. The club stays on lockdown until further notice."

"That'll be hard with a business to run, Prez."

"We'll make it work; we have to. Any update with the Feds?"

"The agents on the case are bread crumbing me. Giving me shit little nuggets of information. They're investigating us more than B's abduction. They'll believe it's retaliation."

"Well, it is."

"I know. It just makes them less cooperative with us. I'm gonna reach out to some old contacts when I arrive back in Sunnyville, and Dad has someone looking into Mateo as we speak."

"Awesome. Church at 4pm. See you then."

CHAPTER FORTY-EIGHT
The Apple Doesn't Fall Far from the Tree

The Rus Reapers left at dawn, eager to get home to their families and away from Zander and his wolves.

Zander readied his pack to leave; he couldn't wait to get back to Sunnyville. Almost every time he visited Uskiville, someone became a victim of the cascade of lies. Blaze had captured him before, but this time, he almost died, and Mateo abducted his fiancée.

Tapping his fingers on B's Humvee hood, patience wasn't a quality in his alpha armory.

Come the fuck on, laddies. You're worse than your mother for making me wait!

He glanced around the retreat filled with desolate faces, understanding more than anyone about the pain they felt. Disappointment etched across their weary faces, unlike when they arrived brimming with excitement for the upcoming nuptials.

B's radiance in her wedding dress crept into his cerebral cortex; her beauty as she walked down the aisle with a glowing smile masked his torment until Madoc and Rhys's bickering distracted him from his thoughts, crippling him with reality.

"Pipe down Rhys. We're going home and that's it!" Madoc snapped.

"But mum wouldn't want us to leave Uncle Mack alone. He's upset, just like us!"

"Yeah, well, if Uncle Mack wants to sulk in the cabin, that's his choice. Mum would tell him to man up!"

Madoc slammed his luggage down in the back of the Humvee, snatching Rhys's case and throwing it next to his.

"Hey, what's going on?" Zander asked.

Madoc's vexation colored his voice. "Rhys doesn't want to leave Uncle Mack alone. Nobody has seen him. He's been hiding at the cabin since Ari took off to Portland with everyone. She left him, and Rhys thinks he's blaming himself for what happened to mum."

Zander dragged in a steady breath. The pain still cutting him like a knife every time his chest expanded. He placed his hands on Rhys's shoulders. "You want to visit the cabin, laddie?"

Rhys stared up at him with his beautiful saucer eyes. "I just want to check on him. Make sure he's alright. Everything that's happening should make us all closer, not leave people behind. My mum wouldn't want that."

"Rhys, he chose to go to the cabin. Nobody forced him!" Madoc hissed.

Zander placed a hand on Madoc's cheek. "How about we chill a sec? We can sort this." He turned his attention back to Rhys. "Let's visit before we go home. We'll make sure he's alright. After that, we head home and get some kind of normality back into our lives until I bring your mother home. Deal?"

Madoc nodded and turned to climb into the truck while Rhys beamed with a smile that warmed Zander's heart.

"Thank you, Zander."

Zander tousled his hair. "Don't mention it, kiddo. Now get yasel' in the truck. I'll brief the wolves."

He watched Rhys climb into the truck as if he was his man cub before turning his attention to his pack.

"Listen up!" he growled.

The pack sat in silence with firm grips on their motorcycle handlebars, giving Zander all the attention he demanded.

"Change of plan. We're making a slight detour before heading home."

Puzzled expressions stared back at him.

"We're heading up to B's log cabin to check on Irish. Rhys is worried about Mack, and right now, anything that distracts him from Welsh Cake is welcome. It's fine if some of you need to leave now." He snapped his head at Eddie. "Eddie, I need you to head down and check on the prospects. The relief staff for the bar and bistro finish up at six today, so we need to ensure we have cover. Ensure the staff rosters are complete for the next week, too please, pal."

"No problem, Prez," Eddie said, adjusting his brain bucket.

Zander continued. "Jimmy, you might as well head home, too, brother. Stock take, remember?"

"Oh, I can handle that," Clarabelle interrupted. "I need to be back home for Jenson, anyway."

Jimmy dismounted his bike, giving Clarabelle a wink as he did so. Stepping an inch away from Zander's grizzly bear face, he glared at him. "If you think I'm leaving here without you in the state you're fucking in, you have another thing coming, ya big bastard!"

Zander closed his eyes, shaking his head in amusement. "Of course. I forgot I cannae go anywhere without my babysitter."

"No. You fucking can't. You don't go anywhere without the entire pack. Sunnyville is cool, man. Everything is ticking over nicely. Eddie can escort Belle, and she can handle the stock take until I arrive. Eddie and the prospects can manage things while we're away. Got it?"

"It sounds like I dinnae have a choice."

"That's because you fucking don't," Jimmy teased.

Zander raised his hand in defeat. "Fine. Stay safe, Eddie. Any trouble, you call. Got it?"

"Sure, Prez," Eddie said before grinning at Jimmy. "And don't worry, Jimmy, I'll take care of your girl until you get back."

Jimmy walked the short distance to Clarabelle, gripping her by the back of the neck and taking her by surprise. Zander and the pack didn't know where to look as Jimmy dragged her into his embrace, forcing his tongue down her throat as if to stake his claim on her.

Zander's envious eyes studied the pair. He felt delighted for Jimmy, but their embrace served as a reminder of what he was missing with B.

"Alright pal, quit fucking eating her, and give the lassie a breath."

Jimmy pulled away, giving Clarabelle a wink. "I won't be long, babe. Don't take any crap from that pecker," he said, giving Eddie the evil eye.

The pack watched Eddie and Clarabelle head off, and Jimmy escorted Zander to the truck.

"Too much?" Jimmy asked him.

"Huh?"

"The kiss?"

Zander shrugged. "Jimmy, I couldn't give a flying fuck how you kiss your woman. She seemed to like it though, pal."

"So, you're just a grumpy bastard because you're hurting and missing your old lady?"

Zander glared at him.

"You're allowed to feel, man. Don't go keeping that shit locked up again. We're better than that now."

"Aye, it's just tough. I dinnae know how to support the laddies. They're brilliant, but I know they're hurting, and Madoc is too God damn strong, like his mother."

"You're not wrong. He was even giving Tyr a peptalk this morning. The apple doesn't fall far from the tree there."

They stopped in front of the passenger side door, watching Tyr in the back seat with Madoc and Rhys. They were fussing over Valkyrie, who provided them with comfort.

Jimmy placed a hand on his shoulder as Bamfa started the engine. "Time to be the father you've always wanted to be. I'm with you, brother."

Zander dragged his hands down his face. "What if I fuck up?"

"You won't! I've seen you with them. You're everything they need, man."

Zander smiled. "We're getting good at this talking shit!"

Jimmy stepped away, blowing a kiss to the sky. "Yeah, and Noah would be proud. Come on. We got this!"

"Aye."

Jimmy turned on his heels. "See you up there."

Zander opened the passenger side door, heaving his body into his seat, slamming the door behind him. "Move out!"

CHAPTER FORTY-NINE
Mack's Guilt

Mack cast another line into the murky creek. He hadn't gotten one bite from fishing this morning. The first light had woken him from another nightmare. His anxiety of old had returned with an onslaught of night terrors, waking him hour after hour after his mind tricked him into watching B die at the hands of Mateo. Each nightmare spun a web of cruelty, showing reruns of B being beaten and brutally murdered as payback for Anton's death.

The cold sweat soaked his skin, and copious amounts of whiskey seemed to fuel the fire, coercing his body into an adrenaline filled state of consciousness.

Sitting on the edge of his bed, trembling, he knew he had to snap out of it, and fishing on the creek helped him center himself. Tranquility aided his recovery, providing calm and clarity to the direst situations and Mack had hit rock bottom. Any clarity he could draw today would be a blessing.

I'm not helpful to Dragon in this state. This time I must help myself!

Mack had become too familiar with B solving his problems, only now, B was his problem. Her life was in danger again.

My cascade of lies is going to kill her if I don't fix this. Why was I so stupid? Well, there is no point crying over spilt milk. Sort your fecking life out, Mackie!

He was about to bring his beer can to his lips until he changed his mind, pouring it into the creek and crushing the can instead. Tossing it on the grass behind him, he waded through the thigh-deep water and headed back toward the cabin to relieve himself of his waders. After packing his fishing gear away, he made for the kitchen to make a coffee to contemplate his next move.

His shaky hands struggled to scoop the coffee with anxiety and alcohol, twisting up his system. Startled by the roar of motorcycle engines, he snatched his rifle from beside the front door and rushed outside locked, loaded and ready for anything.

The Sunnyville chapter took up half the cabins grounds with their entourage of bikes and trucks. Everyone waited for Zander to appear from B's truck with an uneasiness blowing through like a gusty wind. After all, Mack was responsible for the mess they were in.

Mack placed the safety on his gun before lowering it and propping it up against the side of the cabin. His heart skipped a beat as Zander exited the vehicle. Rhys and Madoc hopped out too, only Madoc stood from afar as his younger brother ran to embrace him.

"Uncle Mack, are you okay?" Rhys asked, holding him tight.

Mack gripped Rhys hard, kissing the top of his head.

"Oh, I needed that matey."

Rhys peeked up at him. "Why did you leave without telling us? We were worried about you."

Guilt rinsed his body of any remaining adrenaline. "I'm sorry, my boy. I had to clear my head. Come here," he said, ushering him to sit on the porch steps. "Look, everything that's happened to your mum, it's my fault. I made several poor decisions a few years back. Now they are coming back to bite me in the bum."

Rhys narrowed his eyes at him. "The cascade of lies?"

"You know about that?"

"Not really. It's all people are saying."

"And what are they saying?"

"I heard some of the newer members say you cursed our family?"

Mack shook his head. "And what do you think?"

Rhys bit his nails, spitting the broken nail across the grass. "I think you're my family, and sometimes family makes mistakes. I know you didn't mean to hurt anyone, Uncle Mack. You just go crazy sometimes."

Mack put his arm around him, catching Zander and Madoc's glare in the distance. "Your brother pissed at me?"

"Nah, he just thinks you're being a pussy for sulking."

Mack roared with laughter. "Fair comment. He's too much like your mother."

"Exactly, so you better move your butt and help Zander find her, otherwise we'll have two fiery dragons to deal with. My mum is enough dragon for all of us."

"So, what you're saying is, don't unleash Madoc's wrath."

"Correct. I know his name means fortunate, but you won't be if you don't find her. He's scary at the moment."

Mack tipped his chin to make Rhys look at him. "And what about you? How are you holding up?"

Rhys's bottom lip wobbled, breaking Mack's heart. "I just want her back, Uncle Mack. I want the bad stuff to go away. Please save her," he cried.

Mack brought him into his embrace, listening to his sobs as his own tears fled down his face.

"I got you, son. Let it out."

Mack knew Rhys kept everything bottled up. He only ever opened up to B or Mack. He wasn't like Madoc, he was a worrier, and young minded for a teenager. Inside, he was a terrified little boy who just wanted his mother home safe.

Mack watched Zander, Frankie, and Madoc approach after they heard his gut-wrenching cries.

"You're no' upsetting my laddie, Irish?" Zander asked as Frankie sat on the other side of Rhys.

Mack shook his head. "No, brother. Rhys just needed to vent," he said, stroking his head.

Rhys buried his face in Mack's chest, as he always did, to hide his embarrassment when he was upset.

Zander kneeled in front of him. "Dinnae be embarrassed about crying Rhysey Boy. There's no shame in it. I've cried a million times."

Rhys peeled his distraught face from Mack's chest. "Really?"

"Yeah. I miss your mother so bad; it's hurting here." He pointed to his chest.

"I thought you were just in pain from being shot."

Zander narrowed his gaze with a teasing smile. He shook his head slow, "No laddie, there's no pain bigger than a broken heart, and mine will stay broken until I bring your mother home."

"All of ours will," Mack added.

Frankie gripped Rhys's knee. "You're not alone Rhys. We've all cried tears for your mother but understand this. You have the best pack in the world searching for her. My dad is tailing Mateo as we speak."

Rhys sat up, wiping his tears with his hoodie. "Really?"

Frankie nodded. "He left at dawn, and he'll find something. All we need is one tiny breadcrumb."

"And let's no' forget, Mateo is dealing with the scariest, most clever dragon I know. Your mother will do everything she can to escape," Zander said, nudging his chin with his fist. "Now, how about we see if Irish will allow us to camp for the night? We'll fetch some tents, get a fire going, and have a bit of a laugh. That way, you can make sure your Uncle Mackie stays out of trouble?"

Rhys gave him half a smile. "I'd like that."

"Good lad. You and your brother go grab what you need from the truck, while I talk to these fellas."

Madoc wrapped a loving arm around Rhys, escorting him to the truck as Mack directed his attention to Zander.

"I appreciate what you're doing for the boys, Prez. Rhys is such a sensitive soul. He needs this."

Zander sat on the bottom porch step, resting his head against the handrail. "Then why the fuck would you abandon him? Welsh Cake told me how close you both were, yet you leave him when he needs you most."

Mack pinched the bridge of his nose between his thumb and forefinger. "I was spiraling. My mental health is taking a pounding. I needed to ground myself. I'm no use to anyone broken."

"We're all fucking broken, pal. You think I've been able to breathe since shit went down? I was supposed to marry the woman of my dreams, but you tried to steal her before the wedding, I got shot, and someone seeking revenge for something you did took my old lady. No pal, you dinnae get a fucking timeout right now. You need to fess up to yasel'. Suck up your mistakes and make this right by helping bring her home!"

Mack pressed his hands into his knees; he knew Zander was right, and he hated himself for his past indiscretions. "You're right, brother. I went on a rage fueled quest and ruined our only lead. I want to make that right. No more going off half-cocked. You'll have clinical Mackie from here on out."

"Glad to fucking hear it. Now get me a fucking drink. I'm melting here."

Tiny appeared a short while later with a truck full of tents and Rhys's telescope; as ordered by Frankie, figuring he could stargaze with the boys at nightfall. There was a slight increase in morale as the masses of wolves pitched up along the water's edge while Mack collected firewood with Frankie. They were gathering fallen branches so Frankie could tackle them with his chainsaw when Mack stopped to stare at the ground, crumpling his lips.

Frankie eyed him with curious intent. "What's on your mind Mackie Boy?"

"Our last trip here," he began. "Dragon looked at me like she saw me for the first time. Like fecking saw into my soul. It was the day I realized she loved me deep down."

Frankie dropped the enormous log from his boulder-like shoulders, wiping his hands on his wife-beater shirt before clasping a firm grip onto the back of Mack's neck. "She's alive Mackie. We both know B would never die on us."

"What if she had no choice? What if whatever shit they're testing her with kills her? What if I never see her again? Wha—"

"That's a whole load of 'what if's', brother? Stop it! B is alive! She's been prepared for this. That shit with Jericho. She's ready, brother, and the first chance she gets, she'll murder Mateo and call us."

"Maybe."

Frankie slapped him across the head, making Mack's temper boil. He raised his fist before stopping himself.

"Haha! Mackie Boy. That temper of yours has landed you in so much trouble. How about you change the narrative and switch on? You're better than this. B needs us all to be better. The FBI isn't doing shit. They don't believe Mateo is involved. They suspect we're hiding a gang conflict. We're alone in this."

"Oh, it's a war alright. I'm going to rain hellfire on all Mateos businesses. Flush the fecker out!"

"No! You're not, Mackie! You just told Prez you're going to be level-headed, and so help me God, if I have to beat you black and blue until you do so, I'll fucking do it!"

"ALRIGHT! Calm down!"

Frankie growled. "Don't test me Mackie. I haven't slept or got laid in days. I've got a team running surveillance. We don't need any more drama. When my dad checks in later, we'll have a better idea of what we're dealing with. I'll create a plan from there. We can't expect Prez to run point the state he's in, so I need you with me. Got it?"

"Funny. I thought I was next in command?" Mack said, picking up a stone and lobbing it into the creek.

Frankie retrieved the log he had placed down moments before, tossing it back over his shoulder. "Then start bloody acting like it, good boy. And while you're at it, grab that other log and bring it back to camp."

Mack's laugh echoed across the creek until he saw the log Frankie was referring to.

"You cheeky prick!" he teased, staring at the tiny log.

"If it's too heavy for you, there's a twig here," Frankie bellowed from a distance.

Mack picked up the log, along with multiple others, and headed back to camp. He imagined B appearing from nowhere to tease him or help with the fire until reality hit him like a sledgehammer. B was still missing, and he had to find her.

CHAPTER FIFTY
Clarabelle

It was close to midnight when Belle finished the Bistro's stock take and decided to stock up the Shake Shack with her latest protein bars and cookies before heading home for the night.

Eddie had just placed his local hook-up into a taxi and called out to her in the parking lot. "Are you still here, beaut? It's way past your bedtime."

"Oh, I'm almost done. I'll stock the Shake Shack and head off. See you in the morning for your black coffee and double egg and bacon sandwich."

"You're too good to me!" he teased.

"You know it. Night Eddie, and thanks for your help today. I may even make you some snickerdoodles tomorrow."

"You carry on like that and I'm gonna have to steal you away from Jimmy," Eddie shouted over his shoulder before heading back into the club.

Belle laughed, shaking her head. Despite dragging her bone-tired body across the parking lot toward the gym with a box of goods, she still beamed with pride after selling out all her recent additions that week. She wanted to make B proud by doing her bit and keeping the Bistro in top shape while Jimmy and the rest of the club focused their attention on finding her, and after ten minutes of restocking, she turned out the lights, ready to head home.

Upon leaving the shack, she heard a gunshot. Shaking, she peeked through the door to see a suited man shooting a prospect in the head. Terror froze Belle as panic swept through her. She had no choice but to watch another two prospects being assassinated on the cold and murky evening. She covered her mouth, stifling her sobs as they too received close-range shots to the head. Nausea hit her shaking body like a freight train as a familiar-looking man ordered other agents to search the grounds and watched them spread themselves across the perimeter.

He was one of the intruders at the wedding.

The Shake Shack was in the farthest corner of the compound, and Belle hoped they hadn't seen the light on as they entered the parking lot.

Oh, sweet potato pie, what am I going to do?

She eased the door closed, locking it from the inside. Panic swept through her as she carefully removed the delivery boxes from under the serving counter. Clarabelle stacked large boxes to create the impression of an empty interior and a dumped delivery at the doorway. She then clambered underneath the counter, wedging herself against the wall, placing protein packets and empty boxes in front of her. Retrieving her cell phone from her purse, she dialed Jimmy's number as she lay on the cold hardwood floor.

Come on Jimmy, please?

CHAPTER FIFTY-ONE
Bad Omen!

The senior wolves sat around the campfire drinking bottled beer except for Frankie, who was star gazing further along the creek with Madoc and Rhys as promised. The evening appeared like a prisoner of war camp, so Tiny fetched his guitar, hoping Zander would help lighten the mood with a song or two.

"This place is a bad fucking omen. Nasty shit happens every time we're here," Zander snapped, tossing his beer bottle into a pile of scattered rubbish and taking the classic guitar from Tiny's hand.

"Not every time. Dragon told me my son was alive here!" Mack said.

"Yeah, and look where that's got her?"

Mack cowered with guilt until Zander checked himself. "Sorry pal. I'm just fucking knackered and fed up. We need to work together and we cannae do that if I'm ramming shit down your throat every two seconds."

"Nah, it's fair. I keep making the same fecking mistakes. I regret not heeding Dragon's advice to keep a platonic relationship with Ari and me. If I had listened, we wouldn't be here now."

Zander sighed. "Hindsight is a wonderful thing. Besides, you cannae say that. Baby Alex came from you two getting it on."

"Yeah, she's the only decent thing."

Zander strummed the guitar, trying to fine tune it. "Sorry about her doing the dirty on you, brother. That shit must suck."

"She's a fucking whore! He's better off without her." Tiny, chipped in.

"Oof! Dinnae hold back, Tiny. Say it like it is pal!"

"He's right! She opened her legs the first chance she got, and after all I did for her. I can't talk, mind; I kissed your old lady on your wedding day. Feck, I was the last person she kissed before Mateo snatched her away."

Tiny gulped at the sight of the raging inferno dancing across Zander's face.

"You fucking want me to beat you to death with this guitar, you prick? I was trying to be nice, you dirty mother fucker!"

Mack raised his hands. "Sorry, I didn't mean it like that. It just dawned on me, that's all."

"What. That you were trying to dip your wick where you shouldn't. No wonder Ari cheated on you, ya prick!"

"She can go do whatever the feck she wants now. I'm done with her."

Zander growled, his eyes fixating on the guitar. "Fucking asshole. If you weren't Welsh Cake's best friend, I'd drown you in the creek."

"You love me really, Prez."

"I fucking dinnae."

"Will you two quit bitching so Prez can play us a tune? It's like a fucking morgue here. Come on Prez, give us one of those Flower of Scotland tunes," Tiny asked.

"Aye, alright, calm your gran," Zander said before strumming away, ignoring the pain in his chest. "Right, come on, you miserable fuckers. I've taught you this a million times," he said, bellowing the lyrics to his home nation's anthem.

The pack joined in as they had a thousand times previously; their misery uplifted as the notes echoed in the open air. Zander caught the attention of Madoc and Rhys, who had stopped stargazing to join in, receiving a grinning salute from Frankie. It was the first time Zander had seen them smile and laugh since before the wedding and once the song ended, he called out to them.

"Hey laddies, come here a sec!"

Madoc and Rhys raced over to him.

"It's only fair that we sing the Welsh National anthem too. You're half and half after all. Fancy teaching us?"

Madoc and Rhys doubled over in hysterics.

"What?"

Madoc took the guitar with all the confidence of a Las Vegas showman. "You know how long it took us to learn Welsh? All our lives and we're still not fluent. We'll sing it with Mackie and Frankie, but you have to help us with the chorus. That bit's easy."

"Alright then boys, let's show them how it's done?" Mack said.

"I dinnae know what you're on about. You're Irish!" Zander teased.

"Dragon made us honorary Welshman after she didn't believe Frankie and I could learn it. We spent an entire week learning it in my cabin to surprise her for her birthday. It was the only time I ever saw her close to tears."

"Great fucking days!" Frankie added.

Madoc started playing the tune before the four of them sang their hearts out with Frankie, teaching the puzzled pack the chorus. Laughs rippled around the campfire, even Madoc and Rhys laughed their heads off at the wolves' attempt to sing in Welsh.

"Jeez! A dragon on your flag and a bellowing roar of anthem that would frighten off anyone. Your little country has a lot of heart, boys!" Jimmy said, raising his glass to them.

"We have passion in our hearts and fire in our veins, Uncle Jimmy, but Rhys and I are special because we are ScWelsh!"

Confused faces darted back at them; even Zander cocked a brow in curiousness.

"What the fuck is a ScWelsh?" Jimmy asked.

"Half Scot, half Welsh. We're blessed enough to have two Celtic blood bonds running through us. That makes us proud to be ScWelsh!"

"Haha! I love it!" Zander said. "What's your superpower? I'm fucking ScWelsh!"

Cheers ripped through the pack of wolves, cheering on the boys for their unwavering passion. Tiny took the guitar this time, hammering the strings with his favorite heavy metal song, bringing the pack to their feet. The atmosphere became electric as everyone partied the night away.

Jimmy and Zander were just relaxing into the evening after Jimmy convinced Zander a joint would help calm his frantic mind when his phone rang.

"Oh, there she is. Look. My beautiful busty woman," Jimmy said, answering his phone.

CHAPTER FIFTY-TWO
They're coming!

"Belle?" Jimmy answered as the noise from the camp rattled in her ear. "It's late doll face. What's up?"

Relief choked her up as she turned her call volume down. "Jimmy, the club, it's under attack."

"Belle, I'm struggling to hear you. Speak up."

Two agents conversed near the shack before shots were fired, making her jump in fear and causing her tears to run like a river.

"Take him out!" one man shouted before he spoke to his fallen comrade. "Fisher, no! Don't die on me, man!"

"Was that a gunshot?" Jimmy asked, with concern in his tone.

Belle panicked. "Jimmy, they've shot the prospects and now they're after Eddie. I'm hiding in the Shake Shack. Please come," she cried.

"Lock the door and hide. Don't move or make a sound. We're on our way."

Belle laid as still as she could, clenching her eyes shut and praying to God to spare her life. She knew only Eddie remained in the club, tasked with watch duty with the prospects while until Prez and his pack returned the next morning.

Jimmy will come. I just know it!

She listened like her life depended on it for clues to whether the intruders had left, hearing only faint chitter chatter in the distance, until she heard shots again and Eddie's traumatic cry. The shots grew closer. Eddie's sputtering sound echoed through her, and what sounded like him being dragged away from the gym became louder, until she heard a thud against the Shake Shack.

"Where's the rest of your club?" An agent bellowed.

"Fuck you!" Eddie coughed.

Belle covered her mouth with her sweater, stuffing what she could between her teeth and biting down to ensure she remained silent.

"Dragon is dead. Now we want the rest of you. Where's your Prez?"

Eddie wheezed, struggling for breath.

The sounds of the dying wolf haunted Belle's innocent ears until she heard an ear-piercing gunshot, followed by a thud, just a few feet away from her. Her ears rang from the sound almost deafening her.

"Did you check there?" a muffled voice said.

Belle closed her eyes and prayed for salvation as intruders rattled the door.

CHAPTER FIFTY-THREE

B tossed and turned, shouting in her sleep and reliving Zander's shooting. She had lost her battle with the conscious world shortly after consuming her evening meal and the pill from Erik. The magic little white pill proved a godsend to her rattling body. B was aware of the strain being placed upon her; she could feel the vise-like pressure threatening her like a ticking time bomb. It was as if her body was ready to give out and Erik's pill provided her with the relief her body needed to bide her some time to escape.

B despised who she would become under the influence of the unpredictable pill but sought comfort that Erik was still fighting fit despite enduring a similar drug for twelve weeks. She also knew it provided her with the killer instinct needed for her survival and questioned whether she would have been so immoral with her opponent if she wasn't under the influence.

The war in B's head raged on with diabolical repetition, compelling her to endure Zander's demise until she woke herself with a violent shriek.

Chest panting and dripping in sweat, B found herself clutching Zander's identification band to her chest. She was unaware that she was crying until her tears fell onto her wrists, soaking them.

Kissing the identity band, she placed it back under her pillow and willed her tired body to her feet. Everything ached, as if her body could not decipher what torture it was undergoing. A hot flush swept through her like matches lighting gasoline, making her race to the bathroom. Her head pounded and chest heaved as she once again emptied the contents of her stomach into the toilet basin.

Fuck. This is gnarly. My body can't handle this.

Convinced she had nothing left to offer the toilet, B stripped naked and turned the shower cold. Cold showers had always helped her with her anxiety attacks. Research and tried and tested methods showed that cold showers iced her vagus nerve, causing a shift in her parasympathetic nervous system and calming her adrenaline-fueled body. B's former traumas aided her in fighting her invisible attacker; the drug forced through her veins by her family's tormentor.

B allowed the icy water to numb the base of her skull, dampening her intrusive thoughts and quieting her mind. She sat under the shower in meditation, concentrating on nothing but the water and her breathing. B had relied on mindfulness as her own army. Now she needed it more than ever. Resting her head against the cold tiles also helped relax her, and for a moment B found calm in her chaos and drifted off to sleep again.

CHAPTER FIFTY-FOUR
Jimmy

Clarabelle woke on the cold floor, thankful for her life. She checked the time on her cell phone.

03:17, Have they gone?

Muffled voices drew near, forcing her to hunker down.

They'll find me now for sure.

The door rattled, terrifying her as she covered her ears to drown out the noise coming from outside until the door opened. Multiple biker boots stepped inside, tossing the boxes she had placed at the doorway to conceal herself. Fear ripped through her fragile vessel until she heard a familiar voice.

"Belle?" Jimmy called.

Hysterical relief flooded through her system.

"J-Jimmy?"

Jimmy peered down, throwing boxes at Tyr to cast aside until his tear-stained face was staring into her opal, brown eyes.

"Belle. Oh, come here, babe. You're safe now," he said, dragging her out from under the counter.

Clarabelle collapsed into his arms, sobbing long, heartfelt sobs. "Oh, Jimmy, they killed them, didn't they? The prospects, and Eddie… I heard him. He was right outside. He fought so hard, and he didn't tell them anything."

"I know, baby. They'll pay, don't you worry. Wait!!! You heard them?" he said, pushing her away from his embrace to converse.

She nodded. "They inquired about your location. He didn't tell them, so they shot him. Eddie was a hero," she cried; her tears ran like a river as she stuttered through her words. "H-He killed a guy called Fisher, and the agent who took B, the tall, creepy one, he was here. He told Eddie that…"

She rocked. "H-he told Eddie."

"What Belle? Come on babe, tell me."

"D-Dragon is d-dead," she howled.

Jimmy stared at Tyr as he rushed out of the shack.

"Prez!" he roared in his gruff, Viking tone.

Belle returned her gaze to a numb-looking Jimmy. "Jimmy, I—"

Jimmy buried his head in his hands and cried.

"Oh, Jimmy," she said, hugging him tight.

CHAPTER FIFTY-FIVE
Dragon Skull

Zander stood over Eddie's body with Mack and Tiny, wiping away their tears while waiting for Frankie to get off the phone to his former superior. He had convinced Zander to allow the FBI to aid in their search for B.

Leif, Ragnar, and the Vikings arrived alongside the wolves. They secured the MC with Bamfa and Sandy, ensuring their safety from potential explosives and other threats. Marshall and Gnarler guarded the prospects and checked the perimeter. It appeared the agents came to assassinate the Sunnyville Chapter after Uskiville had locked down.

Fortunately, Uskiville was impenetrable when locked down, making Sunnyville the obvious target. Uskiville's heavy gates and electric fencing around the outer perimeter along with Frankie's high-tech security system would notify the club of a breach instantaneously. An army of one hundred men couldn't penetrate it. B had insisted on securing her family's safety upon hiring Frankie, and Frankie had to impress her with his first employment task if he wanted to stay in Uskiville.

"What's taking so long? Doesn't he have some fecking ex-cop privileges? Their bodies are decomposing before our fecking eyes," an impatient Mack snapped.

"Calm head, Irish. They'll sort it. It's no' like our brothers are gonna be the only victims of a shooting tonight. Look at where we live, for fuck's sake!"

"I'm just done with burying our family!"

"Well, this shit is retaliation, brother. It's what happens when you blow up a brother and a business in one day."

Mack rose to his feet, standing a whisker away from Zander. "You back to blaming me for this?"

Zander stepped up on him. "Well, I dinnae fucking bring death to my door. I'm no' that fucking stupid!"

Mack growled as if he was spitting feathers, forcing Tiny to step in between them. "Hold on to your fucking balls. Our club cannot afford our two Prez's fighting each other. Enough wolves' blood has been spilled."

"Maybe no'. My old lady is God knows where, getting treated like God knows what because of that wee prick. You always seem to come away clean, Irish, when your shit stinks worse than the rest of ours."

"Prez!!" Tyr bawled, coming out of the shack. "The agent who took B told Eddie she was dead!"

Zander and Mack stared at one another as a devastated Tyr stared back at them.

"Prezzz!" Sandy screeched from the MC, making all the men run towards the club.

Puffing and panting, they stopped short of Sandy, who was throwing up next to a picnic bench.

"What is it?" Zander managed.

Sandy was too busy relieving himself of the contents of his stomach to answer.

Zander rushed into the club for Leif to stand in his way. "You do not want to see this, Celtic Warrior."

"See fucking what?"

Bamfa stepped up, "Prez, maybe let Frankie handle this?"

Zander pushed them out of the way; his eyes darting straight to B's blood-soaked wedding dress dangling from a cardboard box. Fear erupted within him like an Icelandic volcano, his insides burned as if his body had created its own molten lava. Trembling, he stepped forward with Mack and peered into the box.

Zander jumped back with fear. "No! Fucking no!" he snapped, hunching over, struggling to breathe.

Mack reached into the box, his trembling hands retrieving a blood-soaked skull.

Zander spat through his agonizing screams as if his heart were being torn from his body until he channeled his anger. "You. You killed her!" he roared to Mack, who continued to stare at the skull. "You son of a bitch!" he spat, rugby tackling him to the ground, sending the skull flying.

Zander didn't give Mack a chance to gather himself. Instead, he rained blow after blow down on Mack. The anger within had transpired into hatred for his brother, who had started the cascade of lies.

"Brother!" Mack tried as both wolves and Vikings witnessed Zander's mighty wrath.

He gripped Mack by the head, smashing it off the floor. Just as he was about to strike again, Frankie forcefully thrusted the skull towards his face.

"It's not her Prez!"

Zander stopped, shuddering into a stunned eyebrow raise.

"B had a fractured skull as a child. She has a big fucking dent in her head, this skull is pristine. It's not fucking her. Now stop beating on her best friend, because when B gets back, she'll fucking torture you for hurting her Mackie."

Zander's vacant eyes and fragile mind couldn't comprehend Frankie's words.

Frankie turned the skull on his bloodied fingers. "She has a chunk out of her skull and plates after falling off her skateboard on a half-pipe. She has plates in her head. Nothing on this skull shows that."

Hyde approached and inspected the skull.

"He's right Prez. No signs of trauma, not even an old fracture."

Frankie gave him a reassuring smile. "He needs her Zander. Whatever she is doing, she's doing enough to stay alive. We'll get her back."

Zander stared at a bloodied Mack, releasing him, and sliding onto his backside. He winced from the tug on his still healing wounds. "Promise me, it's no' her."

Frankie gripped his cut. "I know B better than you all realize. I'm surprised you've not noticed the big slope on the back of her head. It's not her! He wants you to think it is. Ray is on his way. Now, I know you hate the guy, but he will ensure that forensics will inspect every shred of evidence. Hopefully, they'll find something if you lot haven't corrupted the scene." He turned to address the club. "Who else has touched this box?"

Leif raised his hand. "Only myself."

"Right. Everyone gathers at the bistro. The club is an active crime scene, and we need all the help we can muster. Hyde, clean Mackie up, Gnarler, grab a case of beer and a few bottles of whiskey. We have fallen brothers to mourn and we're doing it properly," Frankie said, taking charge while Zander composed himself.

The bikers left in haste, leaving Hyde cleaning up Mack and Frankie, pouring Zander a drink.

"You need to stop." Frankie said to Zander, pouring him a double.

"Stop what?" Blaming yourself for B's abduction. "This isn't on you. Hell, this isn't even on Mackie, really."

Zander grimaced at Mack, who remained silent through his medical treatment.

"This is on B, Prez, and if she was here, she'd agree."

"Fuck off, Frankie! That prick started a war with God knows how many one-percenter MCs and we've been getting fucked ever since. This is on Irish! How the fuck can you blame your own sister for this?"

Frankie sipped his whiskey from behind the bar, leaning against the fridge. "Because she can't help but fight people's battles for them. Boy wonder over there was like a damsel in distress about to be dragged away by the enemy and B had to fucking lose her shit with her, 'not on my watch, I'll kill everyone who touches golden boy,' attitude. If she'd let Mackie handle his own shit, he'd be there now, not her!"

Zander drank straight from the bottle. "Aye, but she never should've been in this position." He pointed at Mack. "That wee prick placed the woman we all love in danger for revenge. He wanted to be the hero for a piece of ass, but where is she now? Fucking a counselor. You picked a winner there, Irish!"

Mack batted Hyde away, stepping up to the bar and reaching for a whiskey glass.

Zander grimaced, pouring him a drink.

Mack took a sip. "You're right! I was angry and consumed with guilt. God, I believed Ari's injuries were on me and felt I had to rectify that. I see now, I was on a lusty ride fueled by vengeance, and had I known what it would do to my family," he shook his head. "Brother, I would never have gone down that road."

"A bit fucking late for that now, pal!" Zander snapped.

"I'm not giving up on her, Zander. I'll die if I have to. We're bringing her home."

"We all will, Mackie," Frankie said, placing a hand on his shoulder.

"Well, I'm no' fucking apologizing to you. That beat down was well overdue and you, God damn, know it."

"Agreed!" Mack said, approaching the bloodied box.

"Dinnae go messing with it now. Frankie has just told us to leave it!"

"I'm not. Jeez. Was there a note?"

"I dinnae think so. I think the statement was enough!"

"What's our next play?"

Frankie came out from around the bar. "We see what evidence the bureau finds and hope for a lead. I have Marshall monitoring whiskey and Welsh Cake shipments. If B's smart and remembers anything I taught her, she'll request them." He turned to Zander. "There's something else."

Zander scowled. "Yes!"

"A year after I met B, we agreed upon actions to take, should anything happen to her. Until Mackie and I entered her life, she had nobody."

Confusion scrambled across Zander's face.

"B instructed me to return the boys to the UK in such instances. She also recently appointed me as power of attorney in her absence or demise." He chuckled. "She figured dipshit there would blow all her money and her children would starve."

"Feck you! She chose you for your business expertise, that's it."

"I dinnae understand. Why are we talking like she's dead?"

"We're not giving up on her, Prez. I just think, now's the time to ensure Madoc and Rhys's safety. I'm arranging with her fuckwit ex to take them across the pond until we sort things."

"No! They're staying with me."

"And how can we guarantee their safety when we're hunting for B? We don't know who he's coming for next. For all we know, they could have discovered something in B's DNA. What happens if they need a male marker in B's lineage to make something work, or God forbid, B doesn't make it, but they need her DNA to continue? These are things we need to consider."

"He's right, Zand. I don't want this either, but it's for the best. You gotta let them go."

Zander pursed his lips and shook his head. "I cannae," he whispered. "They're all I have left from her. She'll want me to keep them safe."

"They will be, Prez. Come on. We need to do this."

Zander pinched the bridge of his nose between his thumb and forefinger and Mack gripped his head. "I know you're hurting, brother, and I know what she means to you because I love her just as much as you do. Let the boys go and we'll paint the town red with Mateos' blood. Come on. Allow the scary, psychopathic, dragon lover out of the cage this time and we'll finish this together."

Zander gripped him into a bear hug. "I'm gonnae kill everyone, and when we get her back, I'm gonnae kill everyone on Ari's list to make sure she's no' in danger ever again."

CHAPTER FIFTY-SIX

Ray arrived at the MC with a team of agents, setting them to work and making a B-Line for Frankie.

"I warned you, son, and you just wouldn't listen. Is this the life you truly imagined?"

"Oh, can it, Ray! I didn't call you for a hassle. I called you to do your job. Now, why don't you follow me and do it?"

Frankie led Ray to the club, stopping short of the entrance. "Oh, and a word to the wise. Prez is in terrible shape. He's survived a bullet to the chest, coming back from the dead to find B, so he won't think twice about putting you in the ground if you make any cocky remarks about B, and neither will I."

Frankie swung the heavy door open.

"Spoken like a true biker bad boy."

"Yeah, and don't fucking forget it," Frankie hissed.

Frankie guided Ray to the box and shared the backstory of the events prior to the shooting. They inspected the box together; Ray donned his sterile gloves and took a pen from his top pocket.

"Three people touched the skull before I arrived," Frankie said.

"Fucking great!"

Using his pen, he moved the dress until he discovered a note attached to the side of the box.

THE RED WEDDING

I'm coming for you, Mackie.
You took my brother, so I took the love of your life.
When she falls, I'm collecting my debts!

"That's enough to bring the bastard in for questioning at least," Ray said, bagging the blood-stained note. "We'll confer with Uskiville PD and the agents handling the case up north and wait for forensics to come back on the blood, skull, and whatever else they find. Do you have footage from the shooting?"

"Yeah, and a witness,"

Ray's eyes danced; his interest piqued.

"She hid in the Shake Shack. Jimmy is with her now."

"Right, I need to talk to her."

CHAPTER FIFTY-SEVEN
Belle and Jimmy

Jimmy escorted Clarabelle to his apartment, wrapping his arms around her as she cried the whole way. Removing his key card from his pocket, he swiped them in and entered, leading her to his couch.

"Here, sit. I'll fetch you a drink."

Clarabelle shook tears from her face as Jimmy brought her a large glass of white wine. Clasping the glass with both quivering hands, she barely stopped it from spilling as she brought it to her lips.

Jimmy sat next to her as she downed the glass in one.

"More please?" she requested in a voice-shaken tone.

Jimmy hesitated with a flash of concern before acknowledging her. "You got it," he said, getting up to fetch the bottle.

Clarabelle watched him pour her another glass and emptied it into her open gullet. "Jimmy," she said with worry in her tone. "Do you think it's true? Is B, you know?" her voice wobbled into tones of fear. "Is she dead?"

Jimmy wiped the tears from her face. "I hope not, Belle. If I know B, she'll be creating chaos right now. The woman is a warrior. I can't... I won't believe she's dead unless I see it with my own eyes."

Clarabelle nodded into her chest. "Jimmy, it was horrible. The sound of Eddie and the gun shot won't leave my mind, and I can't help but feel sorry for those prospects. Chuck was only nineteen. That's not much older than my son," she sobbed.

Jimmy slinked up next to her, stroking her head as she rested it on his shoulder. "They didn't deserve to die like that. You didn't deserve to witness that. I'm sorry Belle,"

Clarabelle sat up, studying him for a second. "Belle?"

"Yeah," he shrugged. I'm trying it out. "You're my Bell-e Boo," he smiled.

Clarabelle managed to smile. "I'm yours?"

Jimmy ran a hand through his hair, tousling it to one side. "I'd like you to be. I know the timing isn't great. After everything, I'm afraid to admit that I have feelings for you."

"More afraid than everything that's happened?" she grinned, unable to hide her bashful amusement.

Jimmy leaned into her. "Yeah, babe. I've had a lifetime of fucking up and being burnt. I don't want to fuck up with you. You're gorgeous!"

Clarabelle's heartbeat deafened her with its loud thuds as if it was trying to fracture her sternum, and in a moment of instinctual passion, she grabbed Jimmy's face, smothering him with her plump lips. Jimmy reciprocated after the initial shock, caressing her body as she delved into his mouth. Clarabelle began tugging at his shirt, desperate for him. Unsure whether her desire for him stemmed from nature, shock, or five years of a single life, all Clarabelle knew was she wanted him.

She reached for his belt, alarming him with her man-eating demeanor, stopping when he clasped his hands over hers. Her face flushed with embarrassment. "You don't want me?"

Jimmy smiled at her. "Of course I do. It's just..." he glided a palm through her thick black hair.

"Is this what you want, or am I merely a relief fuck? My heart can't take another pummeling, Belle. I have to be sure you're real."

Clarabelle took a breath, digesting the gravity of Jimmy's words. She never imagined an MC Vice President to be so in touch with his feelings. She expected the arrogance of a womanizer. Yet Jimmy sat genuinely scared of being hurt again.

"I'll never hurt you, Jimmy. I know how that feels. Unrequited love, never feeling good enough, well that's the story of my whole darn life." She smiled. "I like you, Jimmy. When I was in that shack, the door was going" She paused, wiping a tear. "All I could think about was you. I knew you'd rescue me, Jimmy, and you did. It's been a while since I felt like this. When I confessed my feelings in the past, I was ridiculed and laughed at. This time, I sense a mutual affection between us."

Jimmy stared into her eyes as if he had become lost in them.

"Say something," she whispered. "Tell me I'm wrong and I'll leave."

Jimmy traced his thumb across her bottom lip. "I don't want you to leave, Belle-e. I'd like to take you to bed and show you what you mean to me. If you'll have me?" he asked, standing to take her hand.

Clarabelle bit down onto her bottom lip with an innocent smile. Taking his hand, butterflies flapped in her stomach as he led her to his room.

"Sorry," he said, swiping clothes from the bed. "I wasn't expecting company. I was too busy packing for the wedding to clean up after myself,"

Clarabelle smiled, feeling the heat flush her cheeks, and Jimmy leaned in to kiss her. The soft bristles of his mustache and beard tickled her lips with delicate strokes. His nervous hands reached for her dress, lifting it over her head before he stilled to admire her.

"Wow!"

She giggled like a bashful teenager, helping him out of his cut. Jimmy pulled his shirt over his head, revealing small tufts of chest hair traveling down to his potbelly.

Nerves wreaked havoc between them as Jimmy fumbled with her bra strap and she fumbled with his jean zipper.

Relief washed through her, knowing he was as nervous as her. She imagined him being overconfident with all the bunnies he had slept with.

After relieving themselves of their clothes, Jimmy guided her down onto the bed, laying trails of soft, tickling kisses over her body before guiding her legs apart and settling between them. She peered down at him in excitement; his eyes glowed back at her as he kissed her clitoris.

Her throat quivered, releasing low moans.

Jimmy didn't break his gaze, as if he was studying her reaction for reassurance. Increasing his momentum, his long tongue stroked her entire entrance with slow intent; his own moans vibrating through her.

"Jimmy," she cried, opening her legs further to encourage him to explore.

He continued with his bold strokes, creating heat between her legs.

"Enjoy it, babe. I want to please you before I make love to you."

"Gosh, it's so good," she said, trembling.

Jimmy inserted two fingers, sucking down hard, making Clarabelle drive her hips into his face. A wave of satisfaction surged through her, compelling her to assert her dominance.

Jimmy reciprocated, feasting upon her while stretching her with his chubby fingers until she cried out. Shuddering into her orgasm, she released her grip, allowing him to remove his fingers and taste her. His bold strokes returned in frantic fashion, as if he was devouring her.

Clarabelle was panting into a state of recovery when Jimmy traveled along her torso, meeting her breasts with a feastful eye. "Oh, Belle," he moaned, sucking hard on her right breast then swirling his tongue around her hard nipple.

"Jimmy," she panted.

"I want to make you feel special, Belle. Let me please you."

Clarabelle smiled into his mesmerizing stare, enjoying every moment. Her body flushed with arousal as he gorged on her huge breasts, making satisfying grunts.

"Oh, babe. I want you now," he moaned, adjusting himself to enter her, slipping his long cock inside of her. "Jeez, you feel amazing."

What he lacked in girth, he made up for in length and energetic thrusts. Starting slowly and allowing her to feel every inch, Jimmy mesmerized her with his long thrust, taking his time to cause friction to her swollen nub.

Clarabelle cried out with delicate mews at each thrust.

"Jimmy, I can't take anymore. I'm going to..."

Jimmy grinned. "Gonna what babe? Don't be shy. You're beautiful when you come."

"Jimmy, harder, please? Faster? I can't..."

Jimmy thrusted a little harder, teasing her. "Like this, babe?"

"Yes!" she cried, unable to cope with the tension building inside her. "More, please?"

Jimmy drove into her, gliding his hips across hers with desperate, gravelly moans.

"Yes," she screamed, forcing fast and rhythmic driving movements from him as his eyes filled with emotion.

"Oh, babe!" Jimmy cried, losing control, and thrusting like a frantic lunatic. His higher-pitched moans sending shivers down her spine.

"Don't stop, Jimmy."

"Babe, babe, yes!" he bellowed, driving into her with the full length of his shaft as Clarabelle raised her hips welcoming him.

Overcome with her orgasm, Clarabelle's body twitched in satisfaction; her piercing shrills of excitement and explosive release acting like a trigger for Jimmy's climax. As he jerked hard and fast into her, Clarabelle couldn't contain the satisfied dance transcending through her body. Moan after moan, she couldn't contain her glee, crying out long after Jimmy had stilled, collapsing onto her breasts.

"You alright?" he asked, nuzzling into her breast like they were pillows.

"Yeah," she managed, staring, starry-eyed, at the ceiling.

Jimmy tilted his head in her direction. "Thank you! That was incredible."

Clarabelle giggled. "Uh, shouldn't I be thanking you? I mean, twice?" she gushed.

Jimmy slid off her, propping himself up onto his elbow, ogling her like a love-struck teenager. "I aim to please, and trust, two is just a starter."

Fear dashed across her face, making Jimmy belly laugh. "Babys steps, babe. I'll build you until you're demanding everything from me," he teased, giving her a wink.

She stroked his face. "Thank you for taking care of me tonight, Jimmy."

He cocked his head to kiss her hand. "Always."

She studied him as he appeared to lose himself in a daze. "Penny for your thoughts?"

"Sorry Doll face. You okay?"

"Yeah, you?"

Jimmy sat up, swinging his legs over the side of the bed, resting his head in his hands. "I'm worried that all this could finish us. If Dragon doesn't return..." He clawed at his face. "She's the glue here, Belle-e. The families here have just gotten themselves straight, and Zand won't recover if anything happens to her."

Clarabelle edged toward the end of the bed, covering her modesty with Jimmy's bedding. "Jimmy, what you don't see is you're the glue around here."

Jimmy removed his claw-like hand from his face. "I don't fucking think so."

She took his hand in hers. "Jimmy, I've seen you in action. You pick everyone up when they're down, even B. She mentioned your sacrifices for the club, stepping down as Prez. She told me you keep the place running like a well-oiled machine. She called you the sensible head of the business and running the club wouldn't be possible without you driving it to success."

"Was she pissed when she told you that?" Jimmy said, smiling down at her.

"No!" she grinned, taking a swipe at his knee. "B said you're a rock to everyone, and she thought I could make you happy."

Jimmy's puzzled expression made her nervous. "Jimmy, B nagged me for months and months to go on a double date with you, her, and Zander." She chuckled to herself. "She told me you needed an honest woman, and she was sick of seeing you with bunnies." Her voice crept into a whisper. "Jimmy, she'd never admit this, but it broke her heart seeing what that horrible woman did to you."

"She told you about that?"

"Only that, in her words, 'some stinking bitch, hurt my brother Jimmy to get to me.' She said how she wanted to gouge her eyes out," Clarabelle teased. "But let's not dwell on the gory details," she said, dismissing the thought.

"Yeah, T broke me alright." He pulled her up to kiss her cheek. "Dragon really wanted us to be together?"

"She did. The bistro job was her way to make me agree to meet you."

"I never pegged Dragon for a match maker,"

"I think she's a darn good one, and I kinda wish I'd listened to her earlier after what just happened. You think you could take me through it one more time?"

Jimmy's eyes lit up the room. "Yes Mam."

Tickling her, he climbed back into bed, nibbling at her neckline until a bang on the door disturbed him.

"Two seconds. Let me get rid of them."

Racing to open the door with his erection clear as day, he called out. "Tell Prez I need an hour!"

"No can do, Jimmy. Open the door. The FBI needs to talk to Clarabelle," Frankie barked.

Jimmy opened the door stark naked.

"Jesus, man, put your cock away. There's shit going down here. Get dressed and get your ass to the bistro. Shit's going sideways here, and all you care about is getting your dick wet."

Jimmy tied his hair into a top knot. "What's happened now?"

Frankie stood out, glaring over the balcony. "Put some clothes on and we'll fill you in downstairs."

CHAPTER FIFTY-EIGHT
Question Time

"Agent, how many other people have these criminals upset? There's no evidence linking me to this crime," Mateo said from the cold interrogation room.

"Your brother is dead. You believe Mackyntre Kelly is responsible, so you show up at his retreat and take the woman he loves. I have witnesses who can place you in Uskiville who say you shot Zander McGovan and Tyr Erling before abducting Blethen Jones."

"This is absurd!" Mateo's attorney slammed. "My client has an alibi during that time. He has already told you he was attending a charity event where over one hundred guests can vouch for his attendance."

"Then how do you explain? Two of your security team, showing up in Sunnyville and executing three MC members. We have security footage and an eyewitness placing your men there."

"Not mine, Agent. I'm an upstanding citizen."

Ray's patience vanished. Slamming down two mugshots he roared at Mateo. "Andy Hudson, and Carter Stanton. Two of your employees murdered these men in cold blood on your orders! And your third henchman, Fisher Donaldson, well let's just say, enough blood was found at the scene to know he's probably dead. I figure he was caught in the crossfire at the scene."

"Incorrect Agent. I relieved them of their duties after someone stole my pharmaceuticals. I suspected they were responsible for the theft and were in cahoots with my brother. My guess, they had a dispute with my brother and somehow the club blew up," he smirked. "Of course, you'll have to investigate that. You are the FBI, after all!"

Ray placed his hands on his hips, smiling at the audacity of Mateo. He turned, staring him down. "We know you've taken her, asshole. We found your note. An eye for an eye. I'm guessing he killed your brother after you took Blethen Jones. She was due to testify in a high-profile case, dirtbag. Now she's missing before we've had the opportunity to debrief her. Do you really want this kind of heat? Not good for business after all that's happened. Stocks must be taking a hit."

"My business is now highly profitable and, as I mentioned, I have no clue what you're referring to." He straightened his tie. "If my brother had beef with the MC, this is the first I'm hearing about it, and it's highly likely the men I relieved are attempting to frame me."

"And what about Erik Erling?"

Mateo tilted his head, curling his lips into the corner of his mouth. "Never heard of him?"

"Oh really? Because I have surveillance footage of you meeting him right before your cargo got seized six months ago."

"You must be mistaken, Agent."

"No, son. Erik was an FBI informant. He disappeared after NARCO seized your cargo at the last dock raid."

"Oh, the Viking. I remember. He approached me one day, asking if I was interested in undertaking illegal distribution of fentanyl. I declined his offer. Like I said, I'm no criminal."

"And what about your research refusal? If I'm not mistaken, they denied you ethical clearance for human trials in your research. It's funny how people keep disappearing around you."

"Is there a question in that statement, Agent?"

Ray stomped around the table and whispered into his ear, "You think I was born yesterday, dirtbag? I know you abducted both Erik and Blethen, and I'll reign fire on your ass if you don't talk."

"Are you charging me? I'll remind you I have an alibi for the date in question, and I've cooperated. Now my patience is wearing thin with your slanderous remarks."

"I can hold you up to seventy-two hours,"

"But you won't, because you know my attorney here does his job well and won't hesitate to complain of my hostile treatment today. Perhaps the media should hear how police brutality against an upstanding citizen while his brother's murderer is still at large, is very much alive?"

Ray knew he had nothing concrete tying Mateo to the murders or B's case.

"You're free to go. I should warn you, we will find your employees, and when we do, I'll make them talk. There's no such thing as a free lunch, Mr. Torres, and the DA will happily cut a deal to catch a big fish."

Mateo stood to leave. "Oh, I wouldn't count on finding them, Agent. I'm sure they would have disappeared already."

CHAPTER FIFTY-NINE
Naked

B woke once again wearing fresh pajamas. Confusion troubled her as she ran her hand through her damp hair.

Did I dream I showered?

Propping herself up onto her elbows, her eyes met with Erik's.

"You put me to bed?"

"I couldn't exactly leave you to drown in the shower."

B's inquisitive eyes glistened on him. "And how did you know I was in the shower, my lovely?"

Erik fidgeted where he sat. "Uh, Mateo instructed me to keep a watchful eye on you. If you die, I die, remember?"

"And you're so dedicated to your work you watched me shower, you dirty perv?"

"No, I'm just worried about you."

"I believe you, Sunshine, thousands wouldn't," she smiled, gesturing to her glass of water sitting on the nearby cabinet.

Erik reached for the glass, handing it to her with a twinkle in his eye. "I'd be lying if I said I didn't find you attractive. You are Viking-like with your blonde hair, blue eyes, and battle scars."

"Down boy. You couldn't handle me. Besides, I'm spoken for." She peered down at her engagement ring. "I was," she whispered.

"Dragon, I'm sorry. I didn't-"

B snapped into Dragon mode. "Nothing to be sorry about, good boy. I appreciate you rescuing me from the shower, even if you only did it to grab my ass."

Erik laughed. "Your ass is beautiful, but that wouldn't be where my attention would strike,"

B choked on her water. "Consider taking a cold shower or returning to your room to release some tension. Jeez, you've been here too long."

Erik slapped his thigh. "Yes, I should leave. You sure you're alright?"

B handed him her water with a smile. "I've been imprisoned, drugged, and had to fight for my life. Moreover, my only friend here is a pervert. So, I'm great, thanks Boyoh."

Erik stood providing his most seductive smile; his icy blue eyes and prominent jaw line highlighting his handsome demeanor.

"Stop looking at me like a prize pig at the fair," she teased. "Listen, good boy, that come-to-bed debonair, 'fuck me' smile may make women drop their knickers back home, but one, you're too slender for me. I like a man who can pick me up and drill me against the wall."

Erik blushed all shades of red.

"Also, two, you resemble Tyr, and he's like a son to me."

"So, you're saying I have a chance then?" he teased.

B tossed a pillow at him. "Find us our escape route, you bloody weirdo."

Erik's smile split across his face, tossing the pillow back to her. "I'll fetch some breakfast." He swaggered to the door, glancing over his shoulder with a cheeky smile. "And Dragon, fall asleep naked in the shower as much as you like. I enjoy rescuing you."

"Piss off! Pervert!" she faked a laugh, watching him leave, and trying to hide the pain searing through her heart. She missed Zander and her family, and she was willing to fight to get back to them.

CHAPTER SIXTY
Heart to Heart

Zander had just informed Madoc and Rhys of their flight that evening. Their disappointment shattered the remaining fragments of his heart. Madoc begged him to allow them to stay. His tears of despair still lingered in Zander's mind.

He had sent Mack, Tiny, and Bamfa to escort them home to collect their passports and everything they needed for the trip back to the United Kingdom; he couldn't go there without her. Instead, he sat in church comforted by a bottle of good stuff.

A chap at the door woke him from his thoughts.

"Yeah?"

Leif popped his head around the door.

"I thought I warned you to give me a wide fucking birth Viking and just know, if my women dinnae return whole, you'll go home to yours in pieces."

Leif stepped inside, closing the door behind him, infuriating Zander.

"You dinnae fucking take a telling, do ya, Viking!"

"I say my words and I leave Celtic Warrior, not before. You want to hit me?" he shrugged. "So be it. I will not fight back. Our enemy, our mission, is bigger than us."

Zander gestured to Jimmy's seat at the table.

"Thank you." Leif sat, tilting his head toward the whiskey.

"You don't want much, do you? You want a fucking cigar to go with it?"

"Yes, please?"

"Tough fucking shit! I don't have any. Now what the fuck do you want?"

Leif placed a plastic file on the table, sliding it toward Zander. "This is all we have on Mateo. It's not much. I have worked with him since he started out. His focus was primarily on making money with his brother, Anton. Anton was an old friend. He didn't approve of his brother's research and warned me months before Erik's disappearance to cut ties with Mateo."

Zander opened the file to find a copious amount of paperwork from the port regarding shipments, drug extractions and details on their business together. It also had a series of surveillance photographs, including one of Mateo getting into his helicopter.

"Why didn't you listen to Anton?"

"I couldn't afford it! Without the drug money, my family would starve. My business does not profit enough to feed an MC, and Erik convinced me not to."

Zander sipped his whiskey. "I bet he's regretting his life choices now,"

"Celtic. He was working on a plan to get us free, but I didn't know he had turned informant until Mateo's shipment was seized and we were arrested."

"Shit!"

Leif's face sank into his whiskey glass until it was empty. "That's good whiskey."

"Aye, you want more. Keep talking."

Leif continued. "Erik saved the club, but it came at a price. He knew Mateo was becoming less interested in making money from dealing drugs, Anton himself became worried. His obsession turned to his research and club members from the Rus Reapers and Greyhound MC were disappearing. Rumors washed upon our shores about Mateo taking prisoners to test on them. Other MC clubs informed us of their missing family members, all men, and anyone who asked questions disappeared too."

Zander narrowed his gaze, picking up the photograph of Mateo climbing into his helicopter. "And you think he was taking them to conduct his tests: make them lab rats??"

Leif shrugged. "Nobody misses one-percenters. Erik wanted to do something about it. Only Mateo snaked his way out of it like he always does. Anton tried to warn us, but he was too late. That's when he came for Erik, just like he did at your wedding."

"And why should I trust a word that comes out of your mouth? You set us up. I suspected you had ulterior motives, but I never imagined it would be this."

Leif sighed. "I am so sorry. I never expected him to take your woman. He wanted Mack, and after meeting him, I will admit, I was happy to exchange him for my son. I thought he would take him and release Erik. He gave me his word."

"His word. He's no' playing by biker code, pal. Mateo was never giving him back. He's probably dead."

"No. I asked for proof of life. My son was alive the night before the wedding. He looked changed somehow. Lost lots of his, uh," he gestured to his size, "muscle, but he was alive."

Zander's eyes bulged. "You think he survived the testing?"

"It's the only reason Mateo would allow him to breathe. He likes to make an example of those who cross him, instilling fear, preventing an uprising."

Zander pointed to a photograph of Mateo's helicopter. "And where does he go in this?"

Leif turned his palms up. "We do not have those answers. Erik has not been seen since."

Zander poured him another drink and dialed Frankie's number on his cell phone. "Church meeting now. Gather everyone." He placed the phone on the table and scratched his chin. It was their first genuine lead.

Leif placed a hand on his. "Celtic. I understand how you are feeling. I have had almost four agonizing months of not knowing if my son was alive. If your woman is strong like you say, she may survive this, but we must find her soon. Allow me to help, right my wrongs, please Celtic Warrior. I want to help."

Zander studied him for a second. The sincerity in his eyes showed the guilt he experienced. "No more trickery." Leif's honest words revealed his truth, he was hurting just like Zander.

"Alright Viking, you have one chance. You fuck up, you die. You upset Tyr, you—"

"Die. Understood," he said, standing to leave.

"Viking?"

"Yes?"

"Thank you. There's some mead on its way over from my house. I brewed it myself. It may not be what you're used to, but it needs to be drunk."

"I appreciate your hospitality. Please let me know how I can assist you further."

"Grab your dirtbag son. You've earned your place at church. If we're gonnae work together, there cannae be any secrets between us."

CHAPTER SIXTY-ONE
B's Survival

Unable to stomach her evening meal, B tried to sleep. The headaches and nausea were troubling her. She knew she needed an actual doctor. Her body hadn't acclimatized to the drug, making her anxious.

The door whooshed open, and Mateo entered, escorted by Hudson, and another agent, B, learned was Carter. He stood in front of her, looking pleased as punch. "I've wiped out your club," he said as a matter of fact.

B's temper flared as Mateo instructed Carter to throw a bloodied Gray Wolves cut in her face.

B snatched it from the air, studying it, and upon closer inspection, she discovered four bullet holes.

Through and throughs. Who does it belong to?

She ran her fingers over the blood-soaked cut, staining her hands with sticky red blood. Turning her attention to the front, her eyes darted to the name stitched into it.

Eddie. No!

She squeezed the cut, tossing it onto the bed. "You killed Eddie? Why? You have me, asshole. Isn't that enough?"

"On the contrary, Dragon. I require so much more from your family, especially as your darling Mackie blew up my brother's club. He killed him, Dragon. What was I supposed to do? Let them go unpunished? I don't think so."

"So, what's the plan? Wipe us all out in revenge? What then?"

"Like I said, I have bigger plans for you, and I left Mack alive. He'll be joining the next campaign. Now, you'll play ball unless you want your children to join you and Mack, too."

B laughed a sinister laugh, jostling an unnerving grunt from Mateo.

"Something funny, Dragon?"

"You think I'm stupid, good boy? You're not the first tosser to abduct me. The moment you took me, my boys flew back to the UK, and trust me, you'll dance with the devil if you fuck with the Welsh."

"And how do you know I didn't intercept their escape?"

"Similar to most men, you take pride in showing how big your cock is. You would have slapped it in my face if you had."

"So, you think I'm bluffing about your club, too?"

"No. You killed my family, and you'll die for that soon. Now, if you want to talk business and get the best of my time here, I suggest you send your baby lapdogs away, so we can talk."

Amusement danced across his face. "Now you think I'm the stupid one, Dragon. My security stays."

"No, I know you're stupid, Boyoh. You've picked the wrong MC to fuck with. You're just so far at your own ass you can't see it."

He sat on her bed. "You want to talk Dragon, let's talk."

B sat facing him with stern eyes. "You may have killed Eddie, you prick, but the club isn't stupid enough to get wiped out by a dildo in a suit."

"Ooh Dragon, the sass."

"Shut the fuck up, good boy. I'm talking and you'll listen to my proposal."

Mateo crossed his legs, making himself comfortable on her bed. "The floor is yours."

"You want me to conform? Give your research the best possible chance with maximum effort?"

"I do."

"Then you leave my club alone. No more bloodshed. We've lost on both sides. I want weekly proof of life before each fight. Live footage. I'm sure you can tap into the security at my club with your resources." She bit her lip. "I also want some Welsh whiskey and bloody Welsh cakes. Being Welsh, I'm having withdrawals here, for fuck's sake."

Mateo pursed his lips and shifted his head. "Whiskey and Welsh cakes?"

"I fucking live off that shit. I'm fighting for my life here. Give me something to enjoy."

"Welsh cakes, you say? Never had them. Okay, I can do that. The alcohol is a hard no. There are too many variables already. Alcohol could damage my research or kill you."

"Fine!" she hissed.

"Anything else?"

"Yes. If anything happens to my club or Erik, I allow my next competitor to kill me."

Mateo scoffed. "The shots alone would force you into survival, Dragon."

"You want to test that?"

He raised an eyebrow. "You'll play ball if I agree to your terms?"

B sat cross-legged on her bed. "I'll do everything required my end. Only if you want to keep me alive, you must do something about my blood pressure. My watch shows I'm massively hypertensive. I can feel it Mateo, it's like my head and chest are fit to burst. My blood pressure has always been perfect. My body will not sustain this for much longer."

Mateo leaned forward. "I'll speak to my team."

"We have a deal?"

He extended his hand. "Nice doing business with you. I'll have your proof of life ready for your next fight. You will resume training and adhere to my program as soon as the doctor has cleared you."

"And my Welsh cakes?"

Mateo made for the exit. "Dragon, if they'll help you make me look good, you can have a truck load. I'll have my people place an order."

B watched him leave, exhaling a sigh of relief and throwing herself back onto her bed, pulling Eddie's cut to her chest.

I'm so sorry, Eddie, I'll nail the bastard, but for now I need to remember what Frankie said. I need to adapt to my surroundings and live to fight another day.

CHAPTER SIXTY-TWO
Caught Out!

A week into his surveillance, Marshall hid in his clapped-out estate car, scanning Mateos hotel for potential leads. His car was full of fast-food containers. After returning from off grid, he indulged in numerous take-outs. Slurping on his shake, he caught a glimpse of Mateo entering the building.

His blood boiled knowing what Mateo had done to Eddie and the other prospects. He had grown close to his pack quite quickly following his initiation into the club, and Eddie had always been there to offer him advice on club culture until his recent demise.

Aware that Mateo would be heading to his helicopter on the hotel's roof for his weekend trip away, Marshall knew it was critical he gathered as much intel as possible if the club were ever going to find B alive.

Donning a cap from the back seat and stepping out of his vehicle, he scrambled about the trunk retrieving a high-visibility vest, toolbox and one of his many fake identification badges from his CIA days. Slamming the trunk shut, he made his way to the hotel's service entrance, hopping up onto the delivery bay and entering through the hotel's kitchen. No one batted an eyelid at his presence wearing his convincing attire, allowing him to swipe a keycard from a passing sous chef to gain access to the elevator.

Marshall struck the button for the fifteenth floor with his slender index finger; the floor directly beneath Mateo's penthouse suite. He wasn't aware if Mateo's suite was guarded, figuring he would play the fool if apprehended by one of Mateo's agents. After exiting the elevator, he stealthily climbed the last flight of stairs to the penthouse. A single agent stood guard at Mateo's door, eagle-eying Marshall, clearing his throat on approach.

"Hey man, I hear there's an issue with a leaking bathroom faucet?" Marshall said.

"News to me," the agent grunted, staring at his identification badge.

"Well, are you gonna let me in and allow me to do my job? Otherwise, you can speak to the hotel manager. Either way, I get paid," Marshall shrugged.

"Let me check with Mr. Torres."

Marshall gestured toward the door. "Please, do. I'm a busy man, so if I'm not required here, I can make tracks."

He watched the broad-backed agent open the door, calling out to Mateo standing in the nearby open-plan kitchen, who appeared to be mulling over a document. "Mr. Torres, I have a maintenance man here. Something about a leaking faucet?"

Marshall dipped his cap, disguising himself as best he could as Mateo peered over at him. He knew he was taking a huge risk entering the lion's den, but his extensive experience in the CIA reinforced that B didn't stand a chance without him planting bugs in Mateos' home.

"Ah yes. The dripping keeps me up at night. I appreciate the prompt response. I only informed the concierge ten minutes ago."

"They like efficiency here. It keeps everything running smoothly," Marshall said, entering the suite.

"It's down the hall, third on the left," Mateo instructed.

"Thanks, I'll have this sorted for you in two ticks."

"I appreciate it."

The agent led Marshal to the bathroom, standing outside the open door as Marshall pretended to work, turning on the faucet and placing his bag on the floor. He fumbled through his tools for the tiny pieces of technology, trying to conceal his nerves.

There you are.

His hand snagged a box holding a series of small listening devices, ready to implement the next stage of his plan.

Turning off the faucet, he attempted small talk with the agent who ignored him and pretended to fiddle with the plastic piping under the sink.

Where to plant these babies?

His eyes searched the bathroom along with stolen glances into the hallway, noticing Mateos affinity for illustrative art.

Bingo!

Hastily, he opened the box and retrieved two devices. He intended to put them in the hallway and, if he could, add another device in the kitchen before leaving. Suddenly, he felt a cold, hard object against his temple.

"Drop it, wolf!" the agent growled.

Marshall dropped the devices and slowly raised his hands above his head. "Nice choice. I've had my fair share of FNX-45 Tactical weapons at my head before."

"Then you'll understand I don't mess about when it comes to my privacy," Mateo said from the hallway, accompanied by another agent. "Escort the wolf into the kitchen," he instructed, walking away with poise.

The agent retreated slowly while Marshall exited the bathroom. His eyes shifted, seeking the exit when he was struck on the left side of his jaw, propelling him into the wall.

The agents rained down blows to his head, stomach, and groin before dragging a barely conscious Marshall into the kitchen.

"I trust you didn't leave a mess?" Mateo asked the agent from the door, who proceeded to aid Marshall to his knees by dragging him up by his hair: his cap had long gone through the beating he'd undertaken.

"I'll clean it up," the other agent affirmed, reaching for the cleaning equipment under a nearby counter before retreating to the hallway.

Mateo turned his attention to Marshall. "I recognize you from the red wedding. I call it that due to the amount of bloodshed I bestowed upon your club that day. You were second pew on the left next to B's security chief, correct?"

"Fuck you!" Marshall said, spitting at his feet. His double vision and closing right-eye prevented him from a more accurate hit.

The agent holding him punched him in the face, grinning with salacious satisfaction as blood spattered from breaking his nose, spraying a decorative line across the floor.

Marshall choked down the warm blood flooding his throat. His body throbbed from head to toe in immense pain.

Mateo crouched down to meet his gaze, tugging on his tight trousers to allow his movement. "Today's your lucky day. See, I brokered a deal with Dragon. I let you all live, and she plays by my rules as my next champion. I mean, of course I could shoot you in the face and Dragon would be none the wiser, but I'll humor our agreement just now. Rest assured, she's being looked after and doing far better than you are currently."

"Where is she?" Marshall coughed, coloring the white-tiled floor in a puddle of red.

"Somewhere you'll never find her. However, if I see a wolf within a hundred yards of me or my property again, I won't hesitate in slicing her throat."

Marshall shook his head in disgust.

"There, there. You can't always be on the winning side. Your club should know that by now. How is your Prez, by the way? I heard he managed to survive. Maybe he can be my next champion after I'm done with Dragon and Mack?" he teased.

"He'll be the one slicing your throat, cheese dick!"

Mateo smiled into a nod. "Safe travels back to Sunnyville. Inform your Prez, I'll be watching, and don't let me discover you here again. I'm a patient man, but even patience has an expiration date."

Right before Marshall could respond, the agent struck him unconscious.

CHAPTER SIXTY-THREE
Goodbye Laddies

Zander stood near the check-in desk with B's ex-husband's apparent smugness emanating from every orifice.

"Say your goodbyes, boys. It's time to go."

Rhys embraced Mack and Frankie, who both echoed instructions to 'be good,' before he side-stepped Zander, hugging him tight without saying a word. He reached for his hand luggage and stepped into his father's space. The sadness in his eyes spoke a million words to Zander, who fought to keep it together.

Madoc stepped toward him after man-hugging his uncles, conveying his last plea. "Please, Zander. Let me help. I'm old enough, and I know you need me."

"Aye, you're right, pal. I need you both, but I cannae do this with you here. I'll spend my waking hours worried about you, and I must focus if I'm gonnae find your mother."

A single tear fled from Madoc's face, making him grimace.

"Hey, you get to be mad, okay? You're allowed to cry, Madoc."

"No. I'm strong like her. She wouldn't cry."

Zander pulled him into a warm embrace, placing his head on his. "Wanna know a little secret? Even your mother cries when you're no' watching."

Madoc blinked back the single tear.

Zander nodded. "She cries when you laddies make her proud, all the time, and knowing you're safe will make her happy."

"You bring her back, Zander. Promise me?"

Zander kissed his head before hugging him. "You have my word. The next time you see me; your mother will be ready to cwtch you to death."

Madoc held onto him until his dad peeled him away. "Time to go son, we'll miss our flight."

Madoc shirked away from him in disgust, grabbing his knapsack, and taking one last glance in Zander's direction.

"Promise it'll be soon?" he shouted as his father guided him to the check-in desk.

"Aye, we'll have her home in no time," Zander shouted back, watching them disappear airside.

He froze to his spot as anxiety smashed him in the chest like a sledgehammer.

"Let's go, Prez," Frankie said, patting his back.

Zander didn't respond.

Mack tried to help. "We got this, brother. Once they're safe, we can go to war."

"I made a promise. What if I cannae keep it?" Zander whispered. His breath was shallow and erratic.

Frankie gripped his cut. "What did I say about that negativity? Bring back the old psychopath, big man. We need the man who gave us nightmares after we walked into the Pitbull's club to a massacre. You single-handedly slaughtered their young'uns."

"Yeah, brother, we need you and your tools. Time to let the devil out."

"I need someone to hit me?" Zander asked.

Mack and Frankie shared glances.

"I need someone to snap me out of this funk. Come on, fucking hit me."

"We're not hitting you in an airport with armed sec-"

Crack!

Mack punched him square on the nose, riling him beyond provocation.

Zander foamed at the mouth, lunging at him with Frankie struggling to restrain him.

Mack doubled over with laughter. "That ought to wake you, you Scottish prick!"

"I'll kill you, you piece of shit!"

Mack chuckled at a seething Zander. "Not now, you won't. Security is coming our way. Now let's get the fuck out of here while we still can?"

CHAPTER SIXTY-FOUR
Make it Rain

After another dead end, Zander, Frankie and Jimmy sat outside the bistro drowning their sorrows with a keg of beer and copious shots of Welsh whiskey.

"I cannae handle this no more. The laddies were greeting on the phone to me earlier. They are fucking distraught. I'm no' sure we made the right choice sending them back to the UK."

Frankie sighed from his diaphragm. "It's what B would want. Besides, knowing they're safe brings focus here."

"Aye, suppose you're right. It's just so fucking tough. I cannae breathe without my lassie, the helplessness enrages me: knowing she's out there and I cannae reach her."

Jimmy slapped his back, sliding his hand to the back of Zander's neck. "We'll find her, brother, or we'll fucking die trying."

"Thanks pal."

"We got you, brother, and we will bring her home. Mateo will slip up. Let's be ready when he does."

The bistro doorbell rang upon opening, directing them to the rich aromas of Clarabelle's latest masterpiece as she exited the bistro.

"Chow time, boys. All that liquor won't do anything but poison your mind. Now eat, B would hang me upside down and turn me inside out if she saw you fellas getting wasted like that." She set the tray of southern-fried chicken, brisket, slaw and fries down onto the table. "You gotta keep your strengths up. Now come on, eat up. Make sure these plates are empty when I return."

Zander raised an eyebrow at Jimmy, whose quick hand grasped Clarabelle's. "Thanks doll,"

Clarabelle hunched over to kiss his lips. "I'm right inside if you need anything else."

Jimmy gave her a smiling wink. "I need plenty, but I'll wait!"

Frankie and Zander grinned at the affectionate display unfolding in their presence and Zander couldn't help but feel the pain of missing B. Jimmy's and Clarabelle's exchange posed as a brutal reminder of his missing old lady.

"Going well?" Zander quizzed, as Jimmy watched Clarabelle leave.

"Sorry... what?" Jimmy asked.

Chuckles erupted as the men tucked into their feast.

"With Clarabelle?" Frankie asked. "Prez asked if it's going well?"

"Oh, yeah. Fucking brilliant, all things considered."

"She alright after Eddie?" Zander asked, shredding chicken like a wolf feasting on its prey.

"Yeah. She has her moments, but she's good. We're consoling each other."

"I bet you are!" Frankie teased.

"You can't say shit. You can't keep your hands off Tiff," Jimmy blasted.

"You're right I can't. Those curves bring me to my knees, and when she teases me with her Spanish in the bedroom…. Jeez, have you ever heard a woman scream in another language when she comes? Fuck, that's sexy."

A wide grin spread across Zander's face, radiating his pure happiness for his brothers. Everything they were experiencing correlated with his relationship with B. He wished he could join them in their contentment rather than drown in his sea of hurt. The painful tides crushing his waking thoughts were taking a toll on him.

"Prez?" Frankie called, waking him from his daydream.

"Sorry pal."

"Nah, brother, we're sorry. Sitting here gushing about our old ladies when B's missing. Sorry man."

Zander pushed his plate aside. "Dinnae be daft. I'm happy for yous. I'll have Welsh Cake back in my arms soon." He stood, tucking his chair under the table. "I'm gonnae check the security footage again, see if we've missed anything."

"You've checked it ten times. It's a bust. There's nothing new on there, Prez."

"Aye, well, there's no harm in checking again," Zander said, walking away.

A black four by four screeched into the parking lot, curling around the bistro's entrance. Jimmy and Frankie jumped to attention, drawing their weapons as the back door flung open and a body landed at Zander's feet.

Marshall grumbled in incoherent slurs. Swelling clamped his eyes shut, and smears of dry blood coated his face and hands.

"Dad!!" Frankie bawled, rushing to his side.

"I'll fetch Hyde," Jimmy roared, racing toward the club.

Frankie and Zander glanced over Marshall's beaten body, lifting him up, rushing him inside the club.

Marshall gasped in pain.

"You need a hospital, dad. You might have a fractured skull."

"No hospitals. I'm supposed to be off grid, remember."

"Fuck that! Your health is more important. I'm taking you in."

Marshall gripped Frankie's shirt. "No fucking hospitals!"

Zander wrapped an arm around Frankie. "Hyde will patch him up. It's one hell of a beat down, but your dad can handle it, pal."

"She's alive, Prez!" Marshall muttered.

Zander's eyes whipped to the broken man lying on the surgery gurney.

"Mateo. B cut a deal with him. Our lives are spared for her own.

She's his champion now on condition we stay alive," Marshall struggled.

"Easy Marshall," Hyde said, tending to the four-inch slice on the back of his head.

Zander and Frankie shared sinister glances.

"If we go near, he'll slice her throat. We must execute this correctly."

"We aren't doing shit until you're back on your feet. Now, rest up dad, I'll be back in a sec," Frankie said, kissing his head.

Zander departed, taking Frankie with him.

"How is he?" Jimmy asked, meeting him in the bar.

"Fucked. He dinnae want the hospital, though."

"The man knows his own mind, Prez," Jimmy clipped.

"Like hell he does," Frankie said, tossing a bar stool from his path. "I'm gonna slay that Cuban cunt!"

"Get in fucking line, pal. Leif and I have first dibs after we rescue our own," Zander said.

Jimmy dished out three beers for each of them.

"No' for me, pal. I need a clear head. I cannae expect to out-think that slippery prick if I'm wasted all the time. No' after what he's just done to Marshall."

Frankie washed down his bottle in one. "Whatever works for you, Prez. Keep them coming for me, Jimmy. I'm on the fucking warpath tonight."

"Did your dad discover anything?" Jimmy asked, twisting the cap off a second bottle, handing it to him.

Frankie glared at Zander, who smashed his fists into the bar. "Why does she have to play the hero all the time?"

"Come again?" Jimmy asked.

"Fucking Welsh Cake, making a deal with the fucking bastard devil to keep us alive when she should be worrying about herself!"

"Wait. What now?" Jimmy asked. The puzzled expression on his face provoked an explanation from Frankie.

"B has made a deal with Mateo. She'll do his bidding if he leaves us alive."

Zander shook his head in disgust.

"I wouldn't expect anything less," Jimmy said.

"What?"

"Oh, come on. This is Dragon we're talking about. She witnessed Mateo's capabilities firsthand, and I feel sorry for the poor schmuck who is pitted against her."

"It's no' just that though, is it pal? If our intel is correct, Welsh Cake will be jacked up on God knows what. We dinnae know what effect that'll have on her." Zander ripped his hand through his hair, swearing at the ceiling. "Fuck! Why is it so hard for her to be the victim and allow us to rescue her?"

"Steady on, Prez. It's not like B had a choice. She's making executive decisions to keep everyone safe. It's admirable," Frankie said.

"And it's not like we have any leads. Marshall risked his life just to be told to step off. From where I'm standing, your old lady is doing right by everyone."

Zander pulled up a bar stool, slumping onto it, pinching the bridge of his nose between his thumb and forefinger. "I worry she's met her match with Mateo, and I dinnae know how we're meant to find her. She always feared the Cascade of Lies would bring about her demise, and this was another consequence of Mack's brutality. None of this has been her doing, yet she's embraced every attack as her own. We need to unearth the shit he caused. Maybe retracing his steps will provide a breadcrumb to her. At the very least, we may discover what shitstorm is heading our way next."

"So, we can be the heroes for a change?" Jimmy asked.

"I dinnae give a rat's ass about being a hero, Jimmy. I just want to bring her home. Without her, my soul is shattered."

Jimmy grabbed his head with both hands, kissing his furrowed forehead. "Don't falter now. Get ya head straight. She's coming home."

CHAPTER SIXTY-FIVE
You Own the Other Half

Mack was sitting on B's back porch in Uskiville, staring into the starry night sky and drowning his sorrows with another can of beer. He had just tossed his eighth can into the pile of empties when Junior appeared with a suitcase in tow.

"Junior?" Mack said, standing to attention.

"Dad!" Junior cried, embracing his father.

Mack checked him over. "I've missed you so much, son. How did you get here? I've tried ringing your mother to speak to you, countless times, but she won't pick up."

Junior dumped his case and sat on the outdoor couch. "She's not my mother anymore! Dad, I can't look at her for cheating on you. I had to come."

Mack pulled a chair up, sitting in front of him. "Hang on a sec, Junior. I haven't exactly been the husband of the year, either. I don't want you falling out with your mother over this."

Junior tossed himself back onto the couch, scratching his head. "It's a bit late for that, dad. Mr. Perfect has already moved into the old house. Setting up household rules like some prison. Remy, of course, thinks he's wonderful because mom is so happy with him. Parading around the house like I don't know what. Well, they can both bite me!"

Mack sat on the sofa next to him, offering him a beer.

Junior narrowed his eyes to him. "You know Aunt B would kill you if she was here right now."

"Yep. She'd slap me about the head and tell me I'm being a terrible parent and ruining your soccer career."

"True."

"So, you want a soda instead? There's some of Rhys's favorite in the fridge."

Junior waved his hand, dismissing him. "I'm good. Can we just sit for a while?"

Mack relaxed against the couch. "Whatever you want, son."

They sat without speaking for a short while until Junior broke the silence.

"Dad…"

"Yeah?"

"Have you ever told Aunt B you love her?"

Mack took another gulp of beer. "Yep."

"What did she say?"

"She turned me down flat. Aunt B was very different back then. She wasn't like she is with Uncle Zander. She feared love."

"What changed?"

I disappointed her with the Mauler incident, and Uncle Noah showed her a world I tried to shield her from. When he passed away, I feared she might shatter once more until Zander touched her heart like I never could."

"I don't understand."

Mack rotated his body to face him. "Love is complicated, son. In short, I made mistakes and drove her right into Uncle Zander's arms."

"Do you think she ever loved you?"

"She loves me, Junior. I know she does. The problem is her love for Uncle Zander, and he won't be as foolish as I was to release her. Besides…. I keep letting her down. Dragon deserves better than that."

"You gotta find her dad. She fought for you when you had no one in your corner. We've lied, deceived, and Aunt B didn't deserve any of that. Bring her home, dad please?"

"Aww. Truth is, son, I don't know where to look."

He crushed another can in his hand. "This is all my fault, son, and I can't make it right."

Junior sat up, staring him down. "Dad, you love her, right?"

Mack smiled into a definite nod. "With half of my heart, son. You own the other half."

"Then don't give up on her. She never gave up on finding me, just like she's never given up on you and all your mistakes."

"Gee, thanks!"

"Dad, she jumped to your defense against Mateo before any of the Wolves. She loves you. I see the way she looks at you. That's gotta mean something."

"You're not wrong. I just have to figure out where Mateo has taken her."

Junior stood gazing up at the ridge, casting his mind back to the night B found him after her argument with Mack. "If you were Mateo, where would you take her?"

"Um... With his links to the Greyhound Reapers, probably north. I'd go somewhere where I could execute my plan without being interrupted."

"Then that's where you look."

Mack hauled himself onto his feet, tapping his fist onto the porch pillar. "It's not as easy as that, Junior. Mateo has access to planes, helicopters, and all kinds of resources. Dragon could be anywhere."

"But, close enough for him to leave the hotel on Friday and return on Sunday for work on Monday?"

Mack gave him an inquisitive stare.

"I do my homework, dad. Rhys, Madoc, Remy, they're all doing the same. Madoc has been conducting his own investigation from Scotland, sending Uncle Zander everything he finds in the media or online. We all want her home. So, think dad. Where could he have taken her?"

Mack cocked an eyebrow. Rubbing his chin, he stepped inside B's cabin, sitting at the breakfast bar, and opening her laptop. Entering her password, he began searching for a map of America in the search engine.

"Junior followed with a curious gaze, watching him turn on the printer to print out multiple copies of the map to scribble on.

"What are you thinking, dad?"

"He gets on the chopper wearing a thick jacket. She's somewhere colder than here, for sure. He's prepared for the weather, yet we're still in T-shirts here."

"Alaska?"

"No, he doesn't seem the type to stray that far. He's closer than that, I know it! We just need to find out where."

CHAPTER SIXTY-SIX
Model Student!

Weeks went by with B, annihilating her opponents with Mateo's proof of life providing the motivation she needed.

The doctors stabilized her blood pressure except for fight nights, forcing B to persevere through the comedown with the help of Erik's pill.

By Monday mornings, she was raring to go and ready for her sparring sessions with Erik. They reminded her of her time with Mack and Frankie, only she forced herself to shut down all her emotions until proof of life on fight night. It was then she used them as fighting fuel.

The club appeared to be running smoothly, providing her hope that her family could survive without her if she fell short in her next fight. Her opponents became bigger and stronger as B lost bodyweight and muscle mass: a side effect of the drug. B's body had also undergone extensive trauma with each battle to save her own life. A fractured wrist, steroid injections, a dislocated knee, and a hairline fracture to her eye socket, not to mention the internal damage to her homeostasis. B knew her body was struggling, she'd forgotten what it felt like to feel healthy, only B felt nothing other than adrenaline and rage on fight night. Aware she was fighting for survival, B allowed her dragon tendencies to wreak havoc and destroy her enemies, allowing her to live to fight another day.

The more B fought, the more she lost herself to her inner dragon, becoming accustomed to her surroundings. Anton's methods for conditioning tore fibers of B's moral compass from her existence and, with each life she took, she lost a little more of herself. Her thoughts redirected themselves from her family and friends to focusing on the strengths and weaknesses of her next opponent. B had switched to survival mode, conforming to Mateo's regime. She was unaware she was becoming a priceless military weapon who could be sold to the highest bidder at any moment.

Mateo requested that B and Erik meet him at the medical suite, informing her he wanted to ensure her wellbeing personally after their business agreement. She hadn't seen Mateo for almost two weeks following a break in the competition because of his brother's funeral. B still, however, had to ingest her weekly dose of the drug and welcomed a week off her thuggish brawls to heal from the injuries she had sustained.

The doctor informed Mateo of B's latest test results.

"Her body won't cope with any more shots. Make the sale tonight to continue the research with the Irish man."

Mateo stroked his chin. "Pump her with anything to stabilize her. We'll give her a placebo for tonight's fight. If I know Dragon, she'll fight to the death, anyway. We get her through this fight, and I'll make the sale." He studied the test results on the ancient flickering computer monitor. "The buyer gets placebo shots: fill them with vitamins and minerals or anything to keep her alive long enough to ensure he doesn't come looking for a refund if she kicks the bucket. Ensure she has a better concoction of daily meds to stop her ticker blowing out for a few weeks. By then, we'll have put the money and resources into the Irishman, and he won't fail me."

B entered with Erik distracting their attention.

"Aah. Dragon. Right on time. Dr. Shankland will administer a drip to combat your weight loss and palpitations. Just potassium and some other vitamins. We want you at your best for this one. It'll be your biggest challenge yet."

B sat in the medical seat without challenge. "Let's get on with it, then. Erik and I need to prepare for my fight."

Mateo's amusement lit up his sadistic face. "If I didn't know better, I'd think you're enjoying your new routine, Dragon."

"Simply trying to get through the day, Sunshine. Besides, I enjoy kicking Erik's ass."

The research doctor inserted a cannula into B's forearm, without a flinch from B, who gave Erik a cheeky wink. Fixing the bag of yellow liquid above her head, he tapped away on his keyboard before muttering to her. "I'll be back when the bag is empty. You may resume your day, but without training. Save your energy for your fight. You'll get your shot before the fight, as usual."

B nodded, watching Erik track Mateo and the research doctor exiting the room.

Turning back to her, he pulled up a chair. "I'm getting closer to the office every day, Dragon. Hang in there."

B raised an eyebrow. "You're worried about me, good boy. Don't be, I'm no damsel, and I have every confidence you'll make that call."

Erik tightened his topknot, his eyes unconvinced. "I'm glad you do. I'm busting my ass to earn access to the upper levels."

B changed the subject. "Erik, do you honestly think this drug differs from what the military already possesses?"

His gaze narrowed in on hers as if he was pondering her question.

"Think about it," she said. "If you were in an active war zone, I would imagine a soldier's fight-or-flight response would have kicked in. Let's say you take an adrenaline shot after getting injured, and it makes you feel invincible where you no longer feel pain. At worst, it gives you extra time. At best, you get rescued. What makes this drug any different from what's used currently?"

Erik closed his eyes; the shame written across his face. "Nothing Dragon. It's a concentrated dose responsible for too many innocent deaths." He sighed. "You're an anomaly dragon. You shouldn't be here.

This drug has killed so many. Mateo is selling a lie and you're convincing people otherwise with your bad bitch weekly slayings."

"That's enough idle gossip Erik, let her rest," Mateo said, making his presence known from the doorway. "Come, I have work for you to do and Dragon requires plenty of rest ahead of her fight later."

Erik stood in frustration, directing his death glare at Mateo. "She's got a God damn IV hanging out of her arm with whom knows what pumping through her veins for your gratification."

Mateo curled his lips. "Your point?"

Erik's Adam's apple bobbed as he swallowed his apparent distaste. "As her coach, I am advising the fight to be postponed. She's not stable. It's too dangerous."

"Crossing the street can be dangerous. I have duly noted your advice, now please run along. Carter is waiting. There's plenty of work you could be doing. Dragon doesn't need her hand held."

Erik turned to B, pursing his lips before snapping his head back to Mateo, lunging across the room with Viking-like strength. Shoving him into the wall, he spat through gritted teeth. "You sick son of a bitch. End this now or?"

"Or what?" Mateo laughed, shrugging him off.

Erik backed down, glaring at B before storming out of the room.

"Just as I thought," Mateo sniggered before turning his attention to B.

"What the bloody hell are you not telling me, asshole? Provoking a response like that at Mr. Calm there, tells me you're hiding shit from me. Transparency, asshole, right now!"

Mateo stepped closer, tilting his head with a joker-like grin. "Now, Dragon, remember our deal. Proof of life for your cooperation. You want to keep your family breathing; you'll be ready to fight."

CHAPTER SIXTY-SEVEN
Race Against Time

Erik bypassed Carter's office, diving into the lift unnoticed, swiping Mateo's key card to the first floor.

Come on, come on, she's running out of time!

The lift chimed like an old grandfather clock upon arrival at the first floor, and Erik raced across the landing. Burying his head past a waiter, he made for Mateos' office, swiping his keycard on the old oak door frame, allowing himself to slip inside.

His heart pounded against his ribs; the heavy thuds threatening to explode his fragile heart out of his chest like a nuclear blast.

I'll happily die making this call if it means my father finds this place and wreaks havoc on that sick son of a bitch.

He raced to the old-fashioned telephone, dialing nine before punching in his home telephone number.

"Hello," his mother said, answering the phone, slowing his heart rate with her calming tone.

"Móðir?" Erik gasped. He never thought he'd hear the soft undertones in her thick accent again.

"Erik!" she gasped.

"Fetch the Prez. I have little time. I am a prisoner in a mansion near Lake Whatcom."

"Leif," she screamed. "It's Erik. Come!"

THE RED WEDDING

Keeping one eye on the office door, Erik waited for his father to take the call.

"Erik?"

"Prez, Mateo will kill me for this," he said, his voice wobbling. "Bring the wolves. Dragon won't last much longer. I need to make this right. She has kept me alive, and I will return the favor. The small wisp on the map before you reach Lake Whatcom. You'll see a red fishing boat named 'love machine.' There's a tree line guarding Mateo's private estate just after that. You enter there."

"Slow down, my son. Thank the Gods you're alive!"

"Prez, listen!! The perimeter has six men on a six-hour rotation. The next shift change is at eight p.m. Thirty guests will arrive at seven-fifteen. They'll be disarmed upon entry, no cells, no nothing."

He took a breath to steady himself.

"Leif, I d-"

"B will fight at eight-thirty pm in the basement pool. I'll be coaching her, and she won't waste any time killing her opponent. Later, she'll shower and change in her room before being presented to the buyer. You'll find her along a dark corridor in the basement and you'll need a keycard from the guard to enter her room."

"I understand."

"You need to blow this place after that. Mateo cannot survive. 185 before me died, father. Most of our tribe have succumbed to the fate of this drug. I've seen the files. Magnus, Ivar, Ulf: they did not dishonor and abandon you, father. Mateo took them, and I will not allow him to cull our bloodline. This vile creature has spilled too much of our blood, and B's body cannot handle another shot. I see her body failing and she is none the wiser."

A powerful spew of anger ripped from Leif's raspy throat. "I'll gather our forces. We will slay the man who dared come for our families."

"Mateo will sell B to the highest bidder this week, and she will be lost forever. She needs a hospital once rescued, she won't survive without one. Her heart is more fragile than she knows. Promise me, Prez, promise me you'll save her!"

"We will save you both, my son."

Panic swept through his body listening to Mateo's agents conversing outside the office door. Erik was painfully aware it would be a matter of time before Mateo returned to his office and realized he had lost his keycard.

"I love you," he said, wiping his tears on the back of his hand. "I'm sorry I failed you. You have a granddaughter. She's with her mother, my old handler. Father, please, ensure she's looked after and promise me you'll honor my wishes and rescue Dragon. I need your word, and if I don't make it, take my body home so I can go to Valhalla."

"NO! I will not concede. You will live, my boy. We're coming. Now go before you're caught! Be safe until I see you again. We are coming with an army of wolves. The Rus Reapers and Gray Wolves will make the lake bleed red with Mateo's blood."

Erik ended the call and rushed to the door. Biding his time, he waited for the circling agents to depart from the first floor.

Once they reached the elevator, Erik slipped out unseen, heading straight for the stairs. Sneaking down, he raced along the hallway toward Carter's security office. Turning down the narrow corridor, he clattered into Mateo, sending him crashing to the ground.

"You Buffoon. What are you doing?" Mateo snapped. His blotchy-red face angered in embarrassment.

"Sorry, I was looking for Carter." Erik said, lifting him up with one hand and planting him on his feet.

Mateo dusted himself off. "Idiot!" he said, taking a step to leave.

"Mateo!" Erik said, reaching for the fallen keycard lying on the floor. "You dropped this."

Mateo grimaced at him, snatching it from Erik's grasp. "Wait! There's been a change of plan. Come with me."

CHAPTER SIXTY-EIGHT
Zander

Zander's psychological state had almost dipped into disrepair since the last lead with Marshall confirmed Mateo's intentions for B, and despite altering his lifestyle choices, dropping the liquor habit, and choosing to train at B's gym twice a day, Zander's mental health declined. Weeks of anxiety attacks had taken his toll on the fiery Scotsman. The thought of B going through hell to survive, enduring brutal attacks while under the influence of an unregulated drug, brought tears to his eyes. He tried everything to stop the onset of another debilitating panic attack that saw him clinging to his sheets and gasping for breath each night. The only comfort he found was reliving the night he and B first slept together, picturing her on her knees in front of him, palming his chest. Her soft voice guiding him back into himself and calming his frantic soul. Zander held onto the image in his head so tightly, scared he'd lose her forever if he let go. He wanted to be strong for her return, fighting against every intrusive thought that reared its ugly head. He wasn't strong enough to embrace them and let them pass, choosing to use his strengths by powerlifting instead. The exercise was a temporary fix until the sun faded, darkness fell, and the Prez felt unprecedented weakness.

B's absence cut his heart out of his chest and fed it to a savage pack of wolves, unlike his trusted brothers, who picked themselves up after B's abduction and losing their brothers. They aided Zander as best they could, with Jimmy and Frankie at the forefront, ensuring Zander ate and stayed up to date with the search for the love of his life.

Friday morning was no different. Zander directed his attention to Frankie's face as he entered the gym. It bores the same bleak expression it had in the past few weeks foretelling the lack of any new lines of enquiry. Ray had been a bust from the start. The FBI faced a crossroads without evidence linking Mateo to B's abduction and with Carter and Hudson in the wind.

Frankie had already explained that even the attempt to track any potential Welsh Cake orders fell short because delivery went to subsidiary businesses that could not be traced back to Mateo.

That slick fucker is good: I'll give the bastard that!

He mopped the beads of sweat from his brow into his already drenched cream t-shirt.

How did they knock out the security cameras at Uskiville that day? Maybe the excitement made everyone complacent? Fuck! We should be returning home from our honeymoon now, and Eddie and the prospects should still be alive.

"Hey Prez, smashed another PB yet?" Frankie said with an encouraging slap to his sweaty back.

"Hit 792 for four reps this morning. My chest is still sore, and healing but I get why she's so addicted to lifting," he grumbled.

"You'll be pulling tanks soon, man."

"I'd rather be smashing heads, brother. You got anything for me today?"

Frankie swiped a paper towel from the counter, wiping the sweat-covered gym bench before sitting. "Nothing Prez. It's driving me insane. B's out there somewhere fighting for her life, expecting us to find her, and we got zip!"

Zander gripped his shoulder, squeezing it. "Dinnae beat yourself up! I know everyone is hauling ass trying to find her. We'll no' give up on her pal. I'm bringing my lassie home."

"When did you become the sensible head? The weights are doing wonders for you."

Zander cracked half a smile. "Being in here, knowing how much she loves this place. It makes me feel closer to her. Ridiculous right?"

"Nah, brother. It makes perfect sense. Do you fancy grappling instead of doing chest later? It'll do you a world of good to release your frustration, and it'll help me to be honest. I haven't brought myself to grapple since I grappled with B last."

"Aye, pal. Sounds good. I'll no' be as good as her though," he laughed. "My Welsh Cake is a beast!"

Chuckles echoed across the cold gym floor just as Tyr belted his way through the glass gym door, almost ripping it off the hinges.

Frankie jumped up next to Zander, whose attention snapped to the burly Viking.

"Tyr, what's happened?"

Tyr hunched over, catching his breath. His hard, choking breaths making his sentences incoherent.

"Leif... Lake Whatcom... hustle."

Zander locked eyes with Frankie before returning a heavy gaze to Tyr.

"What?"

Tyr stood, his vibrating chest slowing so he could communicate coherently. Tears fell from his eyes as he spoke. "Erik called my dad. We must go now. Móðir doesn't have much time."

Zander's jaw dropped. Gripping Tyr's bulging biceps, he spoke with calm intent so as not to frighten an already frantic young man.

"Easy, son. Start from the beginning. I need cold, hard facts here."

Frankie grabbed a bottle of chilled water from the fridge, handing it to Tyr as he explained the exchange between Erik and Leif.

Within minutes of Tyr's explanation, Zander had called an emergency church meeting and had every able rider mounting up for B's rescue mission. Because of his lengthy rehabilitation, Sandy would watch over the club with two remaining prospects.

Zander had just climbed onto his bike when Frankie stepped in front of him.

"Just so we're one million percent clear, you're positive you don't want me to bring Ray in on this?"

"No, I dinnae, pal. I'm gonnae end this today and bring my old lady home. I'm no' wanting red tape interfering. Mateo will no' slip away with her."

Frankie raised his palms. "War it is then?"

"You're damn right. Now let's fucking go. Irish and the Uskiville chapter are meeting us enroute to Leif."

Zander's burnout left thick tracks as he led the Wolves out of the parking lot, ripping up the highway, stopping only to refuel at the rendezvous point with Mack. Anxiety threatened Zander's physiological state, forcing him to swallow his fears, trapping them to the pit of his stomach: nothing would stop him from reaching the love of his life. His heart panged and panged like an air raid alarm with every mile passing, the desperation on his face clear of the pain engulfing his every synapse since B's disappearance.

"So, we're taking a boat?" Mack barked into his microphone, snapping Zander into the present.

"Aye! Leif has a plan. He'll explain more when we reach the diner on the outskirts of Bellingham.

"And do we trust him?"

"Tyr told me he wasn't lying, and I trust Tyr. Now move your assless chaps and open your fucking throttle. We're running out of time!"

CHAPTER SIXTY-NINE
Dragon Slaying

Mateo led Erik back to his room, gesturing to him to enter.

Erik's puzzled expression prompted a delirious smile from Mateos lips.

"Don't look so confused, Viking. I simply want a conversation. Sit. Kick back on your bed," he said overly calmly.

Erik sat with unease sweeping through his exhausted body. His heart skipping beat after beat was nothing out of the ordinary since he was still recovering from his latest heart attack. One of the many side effects of the trial.

I'll be back shortly to explain my ideas for your future progressions here. Viking, you've impressed me, and I will soon reward you.

Three hours passed with Erik racking his brains trying to figure out Mateo's motives for locking him away from B. There usual fight day included fight prep and the usual pre-fight banter before B transformed into a killing machine, slaying her prey.

What's your game here, Mateo? What are you doing with Dragon?

Staring at the ceiling trying to make sense of Mateos' actions, the door whooshed open frightening him into a bolt upright position. Planting his feet on the cold concrete floor, he glared at Mateo pacing the box-sized room as if he was trying to contain his excitement. His bright and vibrant face reinforcing that Erik's prediction of trouble was correct. Carter and Hudson appeared in the doorway along with the research doctor.

"What is this?" Erik asked.

"Exactly 10 extra pills? Did you honestly think my staff would betray me?"

"Sorry, you've lost me."

"The extra pills you received from the doctor here after you begged for more. Your tests didn't warrant extra pills, yet you were handed an additional prescription."

Erik shrugged. "I asked for them because I was still having symptoms. He gave them to me. He's your doctor."

"After you asked for a few extra?"

"He helped me out. So, what! He could have declined my request."

Mateo chuckled. "Wait you thought you made a friend here. You're more stupid than I thought."

Erik shook his head. "What are you suggesting because all I'm guilty of is asking for extra pills after you blew out my ticker."

"Ahh, only they weren't for you, were they? Your last bloods revealed they weren't in your system."

Erik's color drained from his face as Mateo sat beside him. Placing a hand on his shoulder, he winked at him. "Methods of deduction, Viking. I authorized your prescription refill, but the last pill ran out on the day the new champion arrived. Only the doctor here gave you ten more because of your claim to be suffering. Ten pills, ten weeks of you trying to build an ally if the tournament had lasted the duration. The exact number of pills to provide relief after each of Dragon's fights. I knew you'd feel guilty about your brother's ill treatment back home. Dragon helped him, so it's only right you'd want to return the favor by helping her. I do my research too Viking."

Erik bit his lip, turning to Mateo with a salacious grin. "You knew I'd help the next champion. Why not stop me or give her the drug yourself."

"RB83 isn't produced in liquid form, and I knew I couldn't trust you to crush it into her food or trust Dragon to ingest it without vomiting it up." Dragon was more than willing to try it from an MC brother. You built her trust that day you helped her." He slapped his back. "You're just as culpable for Dragon's slow demise as we are. You just thought you were helping her."

Erik's fiery demeanor lit up his soul. "You twisted bastard!"

"I like to have fun while I work. We were unsure if the drug would stabilize her. We wanted to experiment with the drug's efficacy between doses. If it didn't help, no harm done," he shrugged. "We would have collected the Irishman if Dragon had died in service. Plus, we wanted to test your loyalty to me, and you failed Viking."

"I'm loyal to my club and my family. I'll never be loyal to you, asshole! You're sick! You've murdered my family and almost two hundred innocents!"

A hysterical laugh escaped Mateo's vibrant throat. "No, I'm a genius. Thanks to my social experiment, I now know the perfect dosage to control Gen Force or shall I say the newly improved, rebranded Adreno Warfare. More lethal sounding, right?" he teased. "And now for my next trick," he said, nodding to Hudson who swiftly stepped from behind him, jabbing a needle into Erik's neck.

Betrayal shocked the unsuspecting Erik, clasping his right palm to his neck and experiencing the instantaneous effects of the familiar drug he had once been accustomed to. His pupils dilated as Carter slapped the cold, steel cuffs on his wrists.

"That's right Viking. You have one last battle. Let's see how Gen Force fairs against Adreno Warfare!" He slapped his cheek. "You do have one last fight in you champion right? Soon, you'll face Dragon in the ring. The boss level, baby!" he said jumping to his feet and shadowboxing. "Daddy wants you home and I'll take pleasure in informing him that the old lady of Zander McGowan murdered you as payback for his betrayal." He laughed. "Oh, the havoc he'll wreak on the wolves, on your own brother."

Battling the drug threading through his nervous system, Erik told himself otherwise while growling. "No! I won't do it!"

Mateo whipped his head back in a laughing frenzy. "Fight. Don't fight. Regardless, Dragon will emerge furious and prepared for slaughter. It's kill or be killed, and I win either way. Now hand over the excess pills, Dragon won't be needing them anymore."

Erik quickly grabbed the orange pill bottle from under his bed, feeling the adrenaline coursing through his veins. She was alone now, and he knew only one of them would leave the drained basement pool. The drug enthralled his system as if he was being controlled by the Gods somehow. He despised that he had missed the hit so much, succumbing to the crippling addiction of his former habit.

Mateo gripped his hair. "That's right Viking, let the red mist wreak havoc over your mind."

Erik thanked Odin for preempting a move from Mateo, praying his father would reach them on time.

Hurry Prez! We're running out of time.

CHAPTER SEVENTY
Rendezvous

Zander stepped off his bike at the dilapidated diner, removing his sunglasses to greet Leif, palming his hand with unwavering power. "Leif. Thank you for setting this up. Is everything ready for us? I want my old lady home where she belongs."

"All is ready, Celtic Warrior. We will bring them home!" Leif said, bear hugging him with gratitude.

They walked towards the diner accompanied by Mack, Ragnar, Jimmy and Frankie, and Zander wasted no time in eyeballing Mack who clipped the back of Ragnar's heel, tripping him up.

"Dinnae fuck with me today, Irish. Your antics brought us here, and I'm telling you now, if you even breathe in the wrong direction and fuck things with your childish fucking antics today, I'll fucking slaughter you."

Mack grinned, "What? It was an accident?"

"Aye, right then. Leave the laddie alone. He's paid his dues. We need everyone singing from the same hymn sheet today."

"Understood." Mack said with a glint of humor in his eyes.

Zander turned to Leif. "What did he say about Welsh Cake?"

Leif's eyes turned gray like a bleak weather forecast. "Mateo will sell her to the highest bidder after her fight tonight. I'm unsure of her condition or what she has undergone. Only Erik insists she see a doctor as soon as we rescue her. There was fear in Erik's voice: a fear I've never heard before. Only he can answer the questions surrounding her treatment."

Zander rested his foot against the creaking diner porch, leaning against it for support. "She's alive though?"

"This is true. Erik confirmed that your old lady will fight again tonight. You know as much as I do. We must leave now if we're going to save our loved ones."

"Aye, agreed. Is the boat ready?"

"I fueled and prepared three RIBs. It's the best I could do at such short notice."

"Are there regulations on RIBs in that area? I dinnae want to fall at the last hurdle, pal?"

"I have no idea. We have no other choice."

"Better than nothing, I suppose. Before we go, let's review the plan with everyone."

CHAPTER SEVENTY-ONE

B had just returned to her room after receiving her infusion of vitamins and minerals. Taking a moment to relax before the research doctor called her back for her shot, she sat on her bed with ready eyes. B was eager to meet her next opponent, even without the administering of her next dose. She had grown accustomed to the palpitations and left-sided chest pain. She had even grown used to the agitation and the throbbing headaches; B knew the drill by now. Take the shot, digest the security footage showing her family carrying on without her, and take her rage out on her next opponent. The fight was already a done deal in B's mind. Like the previous weeks, B was prepared to end her fight, knowing she would survive another week.

A wave of nostalgia washed over her. Erik had kept her mind occupied, but now he was gone. For the first time in weeks, her thoughts wandered to her old life. Slipping her hand underneath her pillow, she reached for Zander's identification band and the LVAD wires cut by Mateo's henchman to end his life. Studying them, a mixture of anger and resentment punctured her heart. Her thoughts flickered like an old camera reel showing Zander's rugged handsomeness wearing his kilt on their wedding day; how he'd undressed her with his eyes once he set his gaze upon her in her white lace wedding dress. She swiped away a stray tear, frustrated with herself for allowing herself to feel.

Erik, where are you, good boy?

Her mind wandered to Madoc and Rhys.

Where are they? Did Frankie send them back to the UK? How are they coping with my absence?

She threw her pillow across the room as her mind collated a collage of her loved ones.

Mackie, Frankie, Tyr, Jimmy. Did they even try to find me?

Her temper boiled like a pressure cooker; the flood of toxic hurt overwhelmed her limbic system, enabling her returning feelings to traumatize her. Gripping her head, she instructed her mind to stop.

Get out! Get out! I can't deal with this right now.

The door slid open with B, straightening herself up to meet Hudson's gaze. His designer suit clung to him as he marched her into the nearby research room. B stopped dead in front of the old television combined DVD player, waiting for Hudson to insert the security footage pertaining to her family's proof of life.

Hudson inserted the disk just as he had in the previous weeks. Stepping back, he allowed the footage to play.

B's vexation reached a breaking point.

"What the bloody hell is this?"

"Problem, Dragon?" Mateo asked, stepping inside the room.

"Too right, there's a problem. This is week three footage good boy. You're taking the piss thinking I'd fall for that."

Mateo grinned, pulling on his suit lapels. "You got me, Dragon. I didn't collect footage this week."

"And why the bloody hell not?"

Mateo shrugged. "This is your last fight, Dragon. I won't be needing your services after tonight. We're moving forward with Mack. Nothing personal."

B's hackles went up in a fit full of rage, lunging at him, forcing Hudson and an emerging Carter to restrain her.

"Take her for her shot before heading to the pool. It's show time."

B fought to twist her head back at him. "Where's Erik, asshole? We had a deal."

"And I honored it until it no longer served me. Relax Dragon. Erik is waiting at the pool for your arrival."

CHAPTER SEVENTY-TWO
Rescue Mission

Two rigid inflatable boats snook along Lake Whatcom, creeping to their destination less than ten miles away.

Zander turned to address the Wolves and Reapers on his team. "We're all clear on what we're doing, yes?"

Acknowledging heads nodded.

"Bamfa, you have the explosives?"

"Yeah, Prez, I'm ready to blow shit up for Dragon."

"Aye, well, make sure you're ready when I give the order. This fucker and everyone in that pretentious fucking mansion is gonnae die. We're cleaning house tonight."

He spoke into his microphone to Leif while travelling in the rib to his left. "You ready for this Viking?"

"I am ready, Celtic Warrior. Let's bring them home."

"You're going to the pool, correct?"

"Correct. When we arrive, Dragon will probably be in her room. We'll need the keycards, so it's imperative we take out the agents on guard duty. Divide and conquer my friend. You head for B's room, and I'll cover us by going to the pool. Hopefully, Erik will still be alive when we find him."

CHAPTER SEVENTY-THREE
Gen Force Versus Adreno Warfare!

The cold corridor to the pool reeked of betrayal. B feared the worst after no sign of Erik and sensing the unease in the atmosphere. Carter and Hudson remained mute tonight, a far cry from the usual abuse they hurled at her.

Each step closer to the pool room created unwavering doubt in her mind.

Something's off.

A loud, gut-wrenching crowd bellowed toward her.

What the...

B entered the pool room taking a double take as the crowd acknowledged her arrival with a mass of cheers, only it wasn't they who unnerved her.

A bare-chested, raging Erik howled louder than any wolf she had ever heard, rattling her eardrums.

Blinking, B couldn't believe her eyes. Erik's unrecognizable disposition and his venomous stare startled her to her core.

No way!

Turning to Mateo's widespread grinning face, the penny dropped for a devastated B. Her last fight would be against a drug-induced, animalistic Erik.

She climbed down into the ring, witnessing the essence of his brutality as he battered his own chest and head, psyching himself up for his fight against the mighty Dragon.

B had no words. To her it was another twisted power move from the man she despised.

The satanic look in Erik's eyes explained everything.

He's injected you, too!

Erik's eyes raged war upon her without breaking his stare, waiting for Carter to remove her cuffs.

Mateo diverted their attention with his introduction.

"Ladies and gentlemen, we have a special treat for you tonight. Witness the ultimate showdown: Dragon vs. our all-time champion, the Viking. The battle of all battles. Are you ready?"

The crowd screamed in encouragement as B tried to comprehend the reality of the situation.

"Let the mayhem begin," he bellowed. "Viking, Dragon, kill!"

Erik charged toward her with cheetah-like speed, picking her up as if she was nothing and throwing her into the wall.

Unable to collect herself after having the wind knocked out of her, B felt warm, fresh blood trickled down the back of her neck.

She attempted to compose herself. Breathe B, breathe.

Choking down her oxygen, she forced out her words as Erik returned after encouraging cheers from the crowd.

"Erik."

Erik stamped on her fractured arm, forcing her to feel a faint splinter of pain. When he tried to kick her in the stomach, B grabbed his foot, twisting it and kicking his grounded foot out from under him, provoking the crowd who welcomed the entertainment.

Erik crashed to the ground and B dived on top of him, hooking her feet under his legs. Displacing her weight across his torso, she drove her shoulder into the side of his head, applying shoulder pressure to his jaw to keep him fixed in place, just as she used to with Frankie and Mack.

"Erik, it's me, Dragon. Stop this!"

Erik foamed at the mouth, trying to wrestle her off. Only B's flare for technique ensured he wouldn't budge. Her only grace was that Erik had lost as much weight as she had on their journey with Mateo.

"Listen to me goddammit! We're on the same side. We need to work together to get home to Tyr, our families," B tried.

"Dragon," he seethed. "I'm juiced. The wolves are coming! They're on their way to take you home. You must kill me. Mateo is going to kill me anyway after this. We both can't die in vain."

B's distracted consciousness gave Erik enough room to toss her off him, clambering on top of her to choke her. The danger in his eyes informed B he was struggling to restrain himself.

"Fight back, Dragon, or I will kill you," he growled. "Please, I wish to go to Valhalla. Only you can provide me with that."

B clawed at his eye with her left hand before punching him in the ribs until he released her.

Choking on the stale pool air, she crawled to her feet while Erik came to his senses.

Infuriated by the situation, she booted Erik in the stomach.

"Get up, you piece of shit! You betrayed me! I thought we had each other's back, but you sided with him!" she shouted, pointing at a gleeful Mateo.

Erik palmed the wall, using it as a crutch to stand, laughing at her. "That's right Dragon. I'm a Viking. We look out for our own kind. I did what I did to stay alive."

B side stepped into a circling dance with him as his eyes brimmed with confidence. He made the first jab to her mouth, jolting her head back and splitting her lip open. B raged, spitting out the excess blood and wiping her mouth on the back of her hand.

Erik moved in for a second jab, forcing B to block him with her fractured arm, reminding her of the weakness. She delivered an uppercut with her good hand, connecting with the base of his chin with a clatter.

Erik stumbled backwards, shaking his senses back to him.

"You die now, Dragon," he roared, storming toward her and before he could grip her, B judo threw him onto his back.

Keeping hold of his arm, she dived into an armbar position to disarm him. Grappling with him had taught her his weaknesses. He was just like Mack to her, a bull in a China shop, allowing B to pick her critical moments of attack.

B wrenched his arm, squeezing and raising her hips until his elbow popped and wrist snapped.

"You won't be punching me now, asshole."

Erik roared in Viking pain as B released his arm, forcing him to roll away in retreat.

The crowd roared, knowing what was coming. The same signature move she did to end all her fights.

Erik bawled in pain with his back to her, as B threaded her arm around his neck. She had stepped into dragon slaying mode.

Erik tried to roll away until she clasped him into a body triangle like a vise, wrapping her stronger arm around his throat. Pulling him into her chest, B took hold of her opposite biceps to secure him into a head and arm choke, placing her held arm around the back of his neck to tighten her grip.

"Dragon," he struggled in a choking whisper.

"Good night, good boy, and thank you," B said, squeezing the life from him.

Tears rolled down her face, feeling Erik resist against her. His feet jerked and spasmed until his lifeless body stopped.

The crowd's cheers dissipated into silence, witnessing B's gentle release, and her last goodbyes to him.

Hudson entered to check his pulse and B released a banshee war cry. Refusing to allow anyone near her fallen friend, B threw herself at him in a fit of abnormal rage.

"Don't bloody touch him!" she screamed hysterically, punching him in the throat and tossing him to the ground. Hudson never saw it coming as B kicked him in the face, watching his head bounce off the side of the pool, knocking him unconscious.

The crowd gasped, throwing confused glances at a grinning Mateo, allowing the carnage to unfold. B knee-dropped onto the unconscious man's chest, releasing sickening cracks from Hudson's caving torso. B became a woman possessed, punching him in the face with repetitive blows.

Carter entered the pool to intervene, dragging her off his best friend, only there was nothing left of Hudson's face.

Carter slammed B into the side of the pool, enticing her inner dragon to pursue him with eyes raining fire upon him as her next victim.

The regrettable uncertainty in Carter's eyes staring back at her filled her with confidence as she stepped forward. "Touch him and you die."

Carter grinned with malicious intent. "Oh Dragon, I'm gonna end you like I ended your brothers."

B ran at him, tackling him like a football linebacker. The pair scrapped like two men in a bar fight, grabbing, choking, gouging, and punching at whatever they could. Carter gained the advantage, hammering his fists onto her chest with a face like a possessed gorilla.

B's body struggled and her chest tightened with every strike. She bucked and bridged up into him, jostling him onto his back. Her strength had always come from her hips. She glimpsed at the baton attached to his belt. With one hand around Carter's throat, she watched his eyes track her movements. Flipping the popper to release the military grade baton, she pressed it to his jugular, removing her grip and placing two hands onto the stick to crush his windpipe. His purple face and red eyes burst a thousand blood vessels, while his feet danced to the lack of oxygen. A mighty crunch rattled from his Adam's apple. B had killed the Sunnyville slayers without even realizing.

She stood glowering at the stunned-to-silence crowd with her crazed demeanor, frightening everyone until Mateo spoke with a nervous disposition.

"Well, what can I say, folks? Didn't she put on a show? Huh?"

Echoes of nervous laughter coupled with the odd Dragon chant reverberated back to him as he turned to B.

"Dragon, you are a force to be reckoned with."

Overcome with grief, B couldn't allow herself to gaze upon Erik: it was too painful. Her only ally's lifeless body lay just two feet away from her. Her eyes shifted to a reflective light coming from Hudson's corpse. A small hunting blade secured to a holster on his left ankle shimmered back at her. In a moment of insanity, B ripped the blade from its holster, pressing the blade to her jugular.

Gasps ricocheted off the cold blue walls as the crowd resonated with her pain.

"Now Dragon, let's not be hasty. Your victory has secured a new home in Saudi Arabia. Abbas here is your new owner. You never have to see me again."

B pressed the knife into her, puncturing the skin enough that blood trickled down her neckline. "I want your word that Erik's body goes home to Leif. He deserves to go to Valhalla. You owe him that, at least. You send him home! He's earned that."

Mateo's voice softened as he raised his hands, trying to diffuse the situation. "That was always the plan, Dragon. I promised Leif, I would return him when I'm done with him, and I will."

"I want to say goodbye. Give me that and I'll do what you please?"

"You'll be compliant?" Mateo asked.

"I will."

"Very well. Say your goodbyes, shower, change into something nice and I'll have you escorted to the grand hall. You dine with us tonight, champion."

B tossed the blade to the floor, turning to Erik. Her salty tears engulfed her battered face. The shot amplified her sorrow as her fight-or-flight response remained in full fight. Anger, guilt and hurt consumed her, making her shake.

"My prestigious guests, follow me to the grand hall," Mateo announced, assigning guards to accompany B back to her room.

B's eyes burst from their teary banks as she knelt, kissing Erik's forehead. "I've got to go, good boy. I'll be seeing you real soon, though. Sleep tight!"

Screaming in agony at the ceiling, B felt two hands on her biceps, lifting her up.

"A valiant victory, Dragon. Allow me to escort you back to your room. We'll ensure the Viking goes home," an agent said, recognizing her sorrow.

The other agent helped steady her as she climbed the pool ladder. Taking one last longing look over her shoulder at Erik, she released her last tears and headed down the corridor to her room.

"Get cleaned up, Dragon. We'll return once you're ready, to accompany you to the doctor for a check-up."

CHAPTER SEVENTY-FOUR
Strike

Zander slit the throat of the last agent guarding the perimeter, dragging his lifeless corpse behind the tree line.

"That's the last one," he said, stripping the agent of his comms and keycard. "Bamfa, Marshall, Gnarler, you're up. Everyone else, set your watches, it's go time!"

The pack of Wolves and Vikings stealthily made their way to the mansion unseen, listening to the agents on the stolen comms. They braced themselves against the side of the building. "Celtic Warrior, you go. Take your team and we will cover. We shall hit the pool and make our way to your location," Leif said, before directing his men toward the building.

Zander provided a curt nod before signaling his pack to enter the building.

The deserted basement reeked of death, provoking a wave of uneasiness amongst the pack.

"I don't like this, Prez," Frankie said.

"Aye, you and me both, brother. Keep your wits about yous."

Zander raised his fist, halting his pack. "Agent approaching. Three o'clock. We need to cross into that corridor unseen. We'll never make it if someone raises the alarm now.

"To late, he's almost upon us. I'll take him with Tyr and Sims. We'll find somewhere to store him out of sight. You, Mackie, and the others get to B," Frankie said.

The agent turned the corner, meeting a blow from Frankie's forehead, dropping him. Tyr and Sims helped drag him back down the corridor, once again swiping his comms and keycard.

"Go!" Frankie whispered, sending Zander down the adjoining corridor.

Zander's nerves threatened to overwhelm in as they reached the dark corridor to B's room. Torment coursed through his anxiety-riddled body; anticipating seeing B again after five weeks of torture took his breath away.

Please be alive, darling. I'm almost there.

His legs picked up speed, drawing him closer to her. "Silencers on," he commanded, expecting trouble. They were two-thirds down the corridor when two agents entered their line of sight, and Zander swiftly took them out. The pack began racing to their destination, with Jimmy and Tiny dragging the bodies out of sight, dumping them in a nearby empty security office.

Zander stopped dead outside B's door, catching his breath. "This is it."

CHAPTER SEVENTY-FIVE
Desolate

B stood clothed under the ice-cold water, tracking the waterfall of bloodied water to the drain. The chilly water numbed her senses enough to catch her breath and stop her thinking. It was the only time B experienced peace, feeling her skin tighten under the icy pitter-patter of the shower water. Every Friday night, she neared a meditative state, and tonight was no different until the bedroom door opened. Unnerved at muttering voices, B slid the sliding shower door open, stepping out of the shower to peak through the crack of the door.

What the fuck? Military-grade combat boots. Abbas ain't taking me nowhere!

Pouncing out of the shower room, B rugby tackled her unknown visitor onto the bed, throwing punches as she did so.

"You're not taking me anywhere, asshole!" she wailed.

Fist after fist struck her attacker in an angry frenzy.

"Dragon, Dragon. It's me? Mackie," Mack said, raising his hands in defense as the door whooshed opened again and Frankie rushed to drag her away, wrapping his arms around her.

"We're here B and we're taking you home."

B inhaled Frankie's familiar sent, as he clung onto her releasing a sigh of relief. B's feet stuck to the floor like cement as her shattered mind tried to connect with her vision. Whipping her head around the room, her eyes blinked in rapid succession at the sight of half the Sunnyville pack including Tiny. She glanced across the bed to meet Zander's gaze, wiping them in disbelief.

"Welsh Cake," Zander whispered.

"No!" B shook her head. "No, no you're dead." She bolted backwards into the shower room, slamming on the shower, and backing against the wall as the water bounced off her puzzled head.

Gripping her head and sliding down the wall, B screamed. "He's dead. This isn't real!"

She rocked back and forth in a shower puddle with the spray raining over her like a torrential downpour.

Zander handed his gun to a terrified Tyr with devastation written on his face. He walked into the walk-in shower, crippled in silence. Dropping to his knees and hovering his hand over her head, he whispered in her ears. "Welsh Cake, it's me, darling. I would never give up on you. Please dinnae tell me you gave up on me!"

CHAPTER SEVENTY-SIX
Unrecognizable

Zander reached up, turning the shower handle, shutting off the water. Casting his eyes upon the woman he loved engulfed him with pain; B was almost unrecognizable. Her curves had long gone, and her eyes and cheekbones had sucked into her skull.

"Welsh Cake, it's me darling," he whispered.

B's sobbing shattered his heart into a million pieces, making him tremble as he stroked her head with one hand and lifted her chin with another. Her blood and water-soaked clothing hung off her as her open wounds wept a lighter shade of red.

B peered up with devastated eyes. "You're not real. This is my fucked-up mind tormenting me before I die!"

Zander gave her half a smile, releasing tears of his own.

"Oh, darling, I'm real. I told yer' I dinnae work without you."

"No, no!" she cried, sucking up her sobs and wrapping her hands around her knees.

Frankie popped his head into the shower, holding up the ID tag and LVAD wires, staring at B in concern.

Zander dropped his head in despair. "He lied to you, darling," he said, removing his bullet-proof vest and handing it to Frankie before unzipping his black hoodie. Unbuttoning his shirt, he took her icy hand, placing it on his scarred chest.

THE RED WEDDING

"You feel that?" he said, gazing into her eyes. "I told you Blethen. It only beats for you. I would never leave you behind. You have always been my reason for breathing."

B ripped her hand away. "No, no. I can't take anymore." She struck the side of her temple, screaming until Tyr rushed in, pushing past his Prez, and grabbing her hands, placing them onto his face.

"Móðir, please," he cried. "It's Tyr. Let us take you home."

B studied his face for a second, taking her a moment to recognize his baby-faced dimples and eyes likened to Erik's.

"Tyr," she cried.

"Yep," he nodded, smiling down at her in relief.

"It's really you!" She gripped him hard, reality hitting her like a ton of bricks. Clambering to him, crying a song of relief as Zander sat back, hurt, and confused.

"Tyr, Erik. He's in the basement," she said.

"Leif and the Rus are looking for him."

"I'm sorry, Tyr. I had no choice. It was the only way to give him a chance to survive."

Tyr shook his head. "He's not dead?"

B shook her head. "I hope not. I tried to choke him unconscious. We must reach him before the agents. I killed two agents trying to get near him. I couldn't let them check his pulse. They would have forced me to kill him. Tyr, Mateo has plenty of agents. Please? If he's alive, he's in danger."

Frankie spoke in his comms. "Leif, what's your location?"

"Just woke my boy, Frankie. He's alive. Do you have Dragon?"

"Yeah, but we're still in her room."

"We'll get to you as soon as we can."

"Negative. Get to the rib. The clock is ticking. We'll get B out."

"Understood. Please place Dragon on the comms," Leif said.

Frankie narrowed his eyes.

"B, someone wants to talk to you," Frankie said.

B gazed up at him as Tyr and Zander stepped aside to make room.

Crouching down, he removed his earpiece, popping it into her soggy ear. "Speak into my chest," he instructed.

"Dragon," Erik called, with a groggy undertone in his raspy voice.

"Erik!" she gasped, the relief in her voice shot panic through Zander's soul.

"Thanks for not killing me."

Tears belted down her face. "I thought I had!"

"Ha! Listen, we're going to get your pills. Neither of us will survive the night without them."

"Don't. Just get out of there, please?"

"Dragon, one-hundred and eighty-five people died before us. The trial is the devil's work. I had a heart attack before your arrival. We need those pills. Now haul ass and I'll see you on the other side."

B dragged her hands down her face, batting away her tears. "Don't you dare die, Viking? I'll fucking kill you all over again if you do."

"I can't make any promises."

"Erik, wait! Thank you for making the call."

"It was the least I could do. Now go on."

Frankie removed the earpiece, placing it back into his ear. "You ready to go home B?"

B pursed her lips, still unsure of her reality.

"Come on," he said, pulling her off the wet shower floor, squeezing her tight. "I missed you, sis. I'm sorry we took so long."

B remained mute as he led her out of the shower. Her skeptical eyes tracked Zander, still unsure whether she was dreaming.

"Put these on," Tiny instructed, offering her dry clothing and boots.

"Tiny?" she whispered, as if she was remembering who he was.

"Glad you're alright, Dragon," he said, kissing her cheek and stepping aside.

The others turned around as Frankie and Mack ripped her wet clothes from her back and Zander stayed at arm's length, scared to go near her.

His eyes tracked her bare skin, breaking his heart at the sight of the healing scars covering her frail body.

"Hyde patch her up," Zander ordered. "Quick as you can."

"We got company," Jimmy said, keeping watch. "End of the corridor."

THE RED WEDDING

"Did they see you?"

"Nah."

"They're coming for me," B said, throwing a sweater over her head with Mack's help. "To escort me to the grand hall."

"Let them come," Mack said, stepping in front of B and pulling Jimmy inside. They huddled close to the bathroom while B sat on the bed, patched up and clothed.

Once again, the door whooshed open.

"Time to go, Dragon," the first agent said, removing his handcuffs from his waistband.

A fist connected to his temple, knocking him to the ground. Mack stood over him, punching him again to ensure he stayed unconscious.

"He's out Prez," Tiny said, dragging him off.

"Take his key card, just in case," Zander ordered.

"Right darling," he said, turning to her and extending his hand. "We're leaving."

Zander scanned her face, watching her inhale a deep breath. Her terrified eyes shifted from him to the bathroom before she rushed inside the walk-in shower, almost slipping as she hunted for the LVAD wires and Zander's identification band.

"I have them," he said, following her and dangling them from his hand.

She snatched them from him, clutching them to her chest like an item of precious jewelry.

His voice wobbled in desperation. "I'm right here, darling. Please?"

B's unconvinced eyes did not falter until Tyr interrupted them. "Time to go Móðir," he said. offering her a hand.

Zander's brain flitted between devastation and confusion. He had imagined their reunion to be momentous, envisioning B running to embrace him like a knight in shining armor, with tears of joy escaping their relieved eyes. He followed her every step as Tyr kept a firm grip on her hand while she clasped the items pertaining to his fake death in her other hand.

I'm right here and that sick bastard has messed up her mind so much she's struggling to believe it.

The pack hustled down the narrow corridor to bump into three unsuspecting agents. Terrified he might lose her again, Zander threw himself in front of her, holding onto her while his pack of Wolves took out the enemy.

"They know we're here Prez," Jimmy shouted, firing his weapon down the opposing corridor where six more agents stormed toward them, opening fire.

"This way," Tiny directed, forcing them to alter their escape route.

Shots ricocheted off the walls, clipping Frankie on the shoulder.

"Shit. I'm hit!" he growled, grabbing at his flesh wound.

Zander and Tyr transformed into human shields, protecting B as they made for the main entrance.

Shooting the agents in their path, they entered the lobby, just ten feet from the grand hall doors.

Zander halted them, placing his finger over his lips to silence them. "Frankie, get her to safety. You walk straight out the front door to Gnarler, Bamfa and Marshall. The rest of us will cover. I'm no' leaving until I put a bullet in Mateo."

B gripped his vest, shaking her head. "Mateo wants Mackie. He's his next target. I'm not risking losing anyone today."

Christ, even when she's traumatized, she's trying to save everyone.

"Alright darling, I hear you, but dinnae worry, we're all going home tonight." He turned to Frankie. "Get her out, now," he said, kissing her cheek. "I'll be right behind you, and we can talk about tossing that shit you're carrying around with you. It's no' mine."

B's vacant expression worried him. He had never seen her so vulnerable. Snapping himself back to the present moment, he reloaded his weapon and instructed the pack to escort B and his brothers to the front door.

Tyr had just swiped the keycard to unlock the front door when four agents appeared, opening fire.

"Go!" Zander bellowed, taking the first agent out with a headshot.

Frankie raced B outside, insisting she did not stop despite the sound of frantic gunshots from the enemy coming from inside the building.

CHAPTER SEVENTY-SEVEN

Frankie and B raced across the field to the tree line where Bamfa, Gnarler and Marshall were waiting.

"Dragon!!" Bamfa roared, opening his arms to her.

B embraced her old friend. "Hey buddy. Nice to see your face."

"Glad you're back in one piece," he said, releasing her so Gnarler could take his turn while Marshall checked Frankie's wound.

"It's just a scratch, Dad. I'll be fine. B needs to board the boat."

Marshal covered Frankie's wound with a dressing from his survival pouch, before releasing him and turning to B. "Come here, kiddo!" he said, hugging her. "You alright?"

B held him back, fighting the urge to cry in front of Bamfa. "I am now, sunshine!"

"Right, to the boat now!" Frankie said, his favorable tone suggesting he felt better with B making her way to the RIBs.

Marshall kissed her cheek, releasing her to Frankie, who threaded his good arm around her and led her through the tree line.

They stopped at the shoreline, where Frankie stepped into the shallow water. B took a step when Frankie stopped her.

"Here, I'll carry you. You were close to hyperthermia when we found you earlier."

"Fuck off!" she laughed, pushing him out of the way.

Frankie crouched and threw her over his good shoulder in a fireman's lift, grimacing and stomping through the water to the RIB.

"Frankie. Put me down! You big jerk!"

"I told you. I'm looking after my little sister." He set her down on her backside in the boat and climbed in, sitting behind her, wrapping his arm around her to kiss her cheek.

"It's so good to see you, B."

B tilted her head to his. "Thank you for not giving up on me."

"Never. Besides, Marshall found the Welsh Cake trail. Well done. Too bad it didn't lead us to you. That was a brave thing Erik did. Zander has been going out of his mind with worry. He wouldn't have lasted much longer before he lost it."

"He's really alive?"

Frankie couldn't help but chuckle as he rifled through the first aid kit. "Of course he fucking is! He's like a cat with nine lives. He died, flatlined twice. Woke up and tried to fight the doctors to leave so he could find you," he smiled. "Then they sedated him and as soon as he came around, he discharged himself. He's never stopped looking for you, B."

"I got him shot Frankie, and then I believed Mateo when he told me he killed him."

"Is that why you're clutching onto them hospital mementos?"

B drew them to her chest, squeezing them. "Yes."

"Can I see them?"

B jerked her head to meet his gaze. "No, because you'll throw them away."

"Your damn right I will! They aren't real B, Prez is!"

"I don't deserve him. My guilt gave up on any hope he was alive."

"Well, start making up for it. You owe him that, at least. When he arrives, you embrace your Prez like you fucking mean it, or did you find someone else back there?"

B moved away from him. "What? No! God, that's sick."

"Glad to fucking hear it. It's bad enough with Mackie and Prez."

"What if he doesn't love me anymore? I've changed, Frankie. Look at me. I'm a monstrous killing machine. The stuff I've done here..."

"You mean, just like he was when you met? B, you might not

remember this, but that big Scot of yours is the most dangerous man I've ever met, and he worships you. Do you think he gives a shit about what you did to stay alive, cos I sure as hell don't!"

B sighed.

"Hey!" he said, sitting back beside her and packing his wound with a dressing. "You survived. That's all that matters to me, Prez and the rest of the pack."

"Did I though?"

Frankie narrowed his gaze. "I'm not following you."

"Frankie, my body is barely functioning. Something is very wrong; I can feel it."

CHAPTER SEVENTY-EIGHT
Burn It Down

Zander and his pack took cover in the lobby's stairwell, dodging shots from the enemy who rallied in numbers in front of the locked grand hall. The agents were Mateo's only defense against the Wolves. Concerned shrieks rang out in between gunshots, no doubt the increasing fear enveloping the unarmed guests.

"They got us pinned!" Jimmy shouted.

"Keep picking the feckers off, they'll drop soon enough." Mack said, shooting an agent in the chest. "See?" he joked, placing himself in a vulnerable position to take out another.

"Always the fucking comedian. Let's no' forget why we're here Irish."

"Really? We're doing this now. Can you not wait until we're on the fecking boat already?"

Zander dragged Mack behind the staircase wall for cover, just as two agents opened fire.

"I'm just saying I'm sick of saving your ass and cleaning up your shit."

Mack reached around the wall, shooting another agent in the head.

"How many times? I meant none of this."

"Aye, I understand that, but you saw the state of Welsh Cake. That's your doing, pal. That Cascade of Lies shit... You need to come clean about all of it. I did some digging, and I know I've only skimmed the surface. When we get home, you're spilling your guts!"

"Will you two can it, for fuck's sake? We need to survive this first. Worry about your bitch fight after, will you?" Tiny spat, setting his gun to automatic. "Fuck this! They're going down!"

Tiny stepped out enough to unleash a round, assassinating three more agents before taking a gliding shot to his side.

"Shit, Tiny!" the pack chimed.

Zander and Mack pulled him down the stairs, where Sims and Hyde covered the other corridor. Hyde pounced on his injured brother, removing dressings from his kit to pack his wounds. You're alright, brother. "We'll fix you up. Just hang in there."

"Watch him!" Zander snapped. "Stupid prick! Nobody dies today!"

Racing upstairs, he replaced his magazine and unleashed another round.

"There's too many. Let's head back through the basement. We can blow this place," Tyr asked.

"No chance. That fucker dies tonight," Zander growled.

"The kid's right, Prez. We have to get Tiny out of here," Mack tried.

Zander released an unwelcome growl. He knew his pack was right. Mateo was within touching distance, yet he knew he couldn't risk any more lives.

"Alright," he huffed. "Let's-"

An explosive array of shots ripped through the agents, killing them all in one swift movement, stunning the Wolves. Leif's thudding footsteps appeared from behind the dead agents with his army of Vikings.

Zander stepped out, embracing him. "Now that's a fucking entrance. They had us pinned. Thank you, brother."

Leif's taken back expression piqued Zander's humor. Taking his hand, Leif found his words. "Always, brother. Now let us destroy this monster together."

They locked eyes until Zander noticed Leif's missing sons. "Wait. Where's Erik and Ragnar?"

"Erik insisted they go to the pharmacy. He and Dragon are in danger. Mateo has created an abomination of a drug named Adreno

Warfare. Erik must gather pills to save their lives. Without them, he fears both he and your Dragon will meet their makers."

Zander erupted in a fit of rage, storming to the grand hall.

Leif's Reapers and Zander's Wolves exchanged handshakes, showing a united front.

Leif grabbed the cuff of Zander's sleeve. "What is your plan, Celtic Warrior?"

Zander hovered outside the door, inhaling his ready breath. His face turned sour with sinful rage. "I'm gonnae slice his throat and then we burn them alive. The bomb can take out the stragglers."

He snapped the handle on the hall doors, kicking them open. Suited guests and their wives huddled together in the hall's rear, cowering in fear. Zander's gaze shifted from left to right, landing on Mateo in the center. Zander's scent reeked of revenge, sprinting full pelt into a jumping punch to Mateo's jaw, knocking him onto his back. Mateo clambered backwards, mute with fear. "Now, Zander, you're a business-man. Let's discuss this!"

"Not so fucking big without your agents, are you arse-wipe?" Zander snapped, gripping him by his lapels and head-butting him. "I'm gonnae fucking torture you like you tortured my family."

Screams of terror whistled across the room as Leif ordered everyone to surround the guests just like Mateo had at Zander and B's wedding.

Zander stood over Mateo as he tried to defend himself.

"Come here, you fucking scroat!" he bellowed, parading him in front of his guests. "This wee cunt here: your fucking entertainer is nothing but a murderer."

"Please, we have children," a terrified woman interrupted.

"Oh, you have children," Zander said, handing Mateo off to Leif, who crushed his ribs with a mighty bear hug. "Funny that? The wee prick who stole her away on our wedding day left my future wife's two laddies traumatized. You see that big bastard? Well, his son and half of his fucking family were abducted and killed for your fucking entertain-ment. While you sipped on champagne and ate fucking caviar!" He waved his arms as if he was in a theater production. "How fucking dare you! *We have children,*" he mocked, kicking Mateo in the face and reveling in the crowd's dissatisfaction.

Approaching the woman, he wiped his chin on his hand. "Tell me something, do your children know that Mummy and Daddy watch people get violated and murdered for fun? How fucking proud they must be!" He circled the hall. "From my perspective, you're all culpable and as guilty as this sick fuck. Do you even give the dead a second thought as you parade around with your champagne and designer wear?"

The profound silence empowered him. "Well, allow me to entertain you one last time. Watch one of your own meet his maker and tell me then how entertained you are." He turned away from the crowd, addressing his pack. "Teachable moment, brothers! Anyone try's playing the hero, shoot them in the fucking head."

Hysterical cries gathered in the hall, creating piercing acoustics as Zander went to work on Mateo.

"You ready to play with fire, Viking?" Zander asked Leif.

Leif grinned: He finally had something to smile about. "Make him feel and I will burn this place to ashes!"

Zander retrieved his blade from his belt, placing it between his teeth.

Mateo's hand reached to grab it, promoting a smile from Zander's lips and provoking a jab to the face.

"My research will live on. Others will continue my work."

"Not anymore," he said, ripping off his shirt. "Tyr, Jimmy, come hold this fucker while I go to work. He's wriggling like a wee fanny."

Jimmy and Tyr forced Mateo to his knees, facing his guests. They stretched his arms out to the side, pulling him with brute force.

Zander flicked his blade between his fingers, catching it in his hand and dragging the blade diagonally down Mateo's chest.

Mateo cried out in a soul piercing yelp.

"Auch, I'm just getting started," Zander teased, dragging the blade across the opposing side of his chest to create an x. "No' funny, is it? Being tortured while everyone witnesses your pain."

Sweat poured from Mateo's face. His body jerked against the strain of being stretched by Jimmy and Tyr as blood dripped down his chest.

Zander gave Leif the nod, who instructed his men to douse the hall in petrol, soaking the thick, velvet curtains and wooden bookshelves.

In the room, desperate shrieks echoed as guests looked to flee, yet Reapers blocked the door, keeping everyone captive, and gunning down those who didn't conform.

"You threatened my world, now I'm gonnae burn yours. No one will remember your name, asshole. You'll be nothing but a scorch stain by the time I'm finished. But first, you'll suffer, and when you're lying in a pool of your own blood, watching your world burn, remember who's responsible. Fuck with a wolf, and you get ripped apart. Fuck with a Viking, you get burnt. Time to meet your maker, Mateo."

Horror diced across his face. It was clear Mateo never suspected his demise.

Zander dug his blade beneath his collarbone. "First you'll bleed into your chest, then you'll drown in your own blood, all while you watch your sadistic fucking empire burn." Mateo released a guttural cry, as Zander circled him before pushing the blade into his back, cracking his spine.

Tyr turned away, unable to witness the sadistic revenge bestowed upon the man who had imprisoned and tortured his family.

Zander continued, relishing Mateo's downfall, whispering in his ear. "How does it feel to be helpless, asshole? Payback is fucking beautiful." He shouted to Leif, "Play with fire, brother. Play with fire!"

Leif and his men lit the curtains and books, setting them ablaze and watching the flames spread like it was a living being.

Panic erupted as the Wolves and Reapers rushed towards the door, leaving only Zander, Jimmy, and Tyr behind. The Reapers continued to open fire on the guests, trying to flee while men cradled their wives.

Zander stood towering over an almost lifeless Mateo, careful not to slip on the pool of blood forming beneath him. "Time to die, ya wee prick. This is for Welsh Cake," he said, plunging his knife into his chest.

Mateo exhaled his final breath.

"Let's move!" Zander said, as Tyr and Jimmy dropped Mateo's

corpse. Ushering them to the exit, Zander covered his mouth from the billowing smoke and ducked falling debris.

They raced to the exit, closing the grand doors.

"You're killing them all?" Tyr asked.

"They sat by watching Welsh Cake and Erik get drugged and beaten. They dinnae deserve to live pal, and I'm no' leaving survivors who can testify against us. Now run!"

CHAPTER SEVENTY-NINE
Pharmacy

Erik and Ragnar made their way to the laboratory where he and B had undergone their mistreatment. Erik's mind raced, the adrenaline from his last injection of the savage drug wreaked havoc on his metabolic systems. The synchronizing thuds deriving from his head and heart hurried him along the narrow corridor once more, using the fear of another potential heart attack as survival fuel.

"Here," he said, dragging his brother from the corridor toward the laboratory door to hide from a circling agent.

"Wait until I tell you to go. We enter, get the drugs, and leave. You hear me? No kamikaze shit!"

Ragnar chuckled. "I'm glad you're still the same autocratic VP asshole and this place hasn't changed you."

Erik placed an ear to the door, listening to the muffled voices inside. "This place has almost killed me a thousand times, brother. Don't underestimate the lurking evil. You'll lose your life if you try your showboating here."

"What's the matter, brother? Upset little bro had to come save your ass?"

Erik glared at him. "Just keep your fucking head down. We raid the drugs cabinet and leave via the way we entered. That corridor over there houses the security for the entire building."

Ragnar checked his watch, grinning at his brother's dead-pan expression. "Hurry, big brother. This place goes boom in about eleven minutes."

Erik removed the key card hanging out of Ragnar's top pocket. Swiping the door open with one clear whoosh.

The research doctor stared at him in horror.

"Surprised to see me alive, doctor?" Erik sneered, picking up an unnamed bottle of chemicals from the counter with his uninjured arm.

The research doctors' eyes tracked his movements "Vi-"

Erik smashed the bottle across the side of his head, knocking him unconscious with blood dripping from his wound.

"Yesss!" Ragnar cheered. "Big brother's back!"

Erik raked through jars of medication on the shelf to his left, tossing the unwanted containers onto the floor until he came across the large container marked ADRENO WARFARE RECOMP. "Got it! Let's go!" he said, placing the orange container down his sleeve.

"What about him?" Ragnar asked.

"Give me your gun."

Ragnar raised an eyebrow. "Waste of bullets. The place is gonna blow."

Erik reached for Ragnars holster, removing his side arm, pulling on the trigger. He released five rounds into the research director's head and chest. "I refuse to leave that to chance. We must ensure this killing ends today. He mercilessly murdered our kin, devoid of guilt." He kicked the dead man's bloodied head, trembling with a body full of combustible anger. The torture he and so many others had experienced at the peril of Mateo forced images of his dead enemies in the blood-spattered pool. Enemies he had never chosen as his own; victims that Mateo had hand-picked for him to murder to survive. He clenched his fist before side-swiping it across the counter, clearing it of the chemicals situated there. He tore the old computer monitor from the desk, smashing it on the floor in a rage of hyperventilation.

Ragnar placed an endearing arm around Erik's shoulder. "They will not hurt you anymore, brother. It's over! We must leave!"

Erik reached into the filing cabinet to retrieve his and B's files, stuffing them into the back of his pants. "Now we can leave!"

Billows of smoke engulfed the long, dark corridor, obscuring their vision. Coughing and spluttering, they palmed the walls, feeling their way to the end of the corridor.

"The stairs!" Erik shouted, pushing his brother ahead.

Ragnar raced up the stairs with Erik on his heels until a large wooden beam fell from the fiery ceiling, blocking his path.

"ERIKK!"

"I'm alive, brother," Erik coughed. "Go! I'll find another way!"

"I'm not leaving you!"

"Ragnar, please. I promise I will find you. Now go!"

"We meet at the tree line," Ragnar shouted from a distance.

Erik glanced at where the ceiling once stood. The burning rage of angry flames hovered above, dropping debris as if hell itself had risen. Covering his mouth with the top of his shirt, he stumbled back down the stairs and crawled along the smoke-filled corridor with his broken arm dragging along the floor. His eyes stung from the thick smoke and his breath became jagged.

He remembered the large wooden fire door to the rear of the basement in a mess office where the agents congregated. Reaching the end of the corridor, he clambered to his feet, dragging his oxygen-deprived body into the office. The room appeared empty with the light from the open emergency exit, providing him with anticipating hope. His movements transpired into a scurry; Erik could almost smell the fresh air as he dragged himself to the building's exit. He had just reached the open door when the ground shook beneath him and a deafening blast ripped through his ear drums.

CHAPTER EIGHTY
Mourning the Dead

The Wolves and Reapers ran from the burning building, leaving screams of peril behind them.

Approaching the muster point, they reconnected with Bamfa, Gnarler and Marshall who had planted the explosives. "You got two minutes. Get to the boats!"

"Where are my brothers?" Tyr asked.

"No sign yet," Marshall replied.

"I'll wait here for them. I'm sure they are right behind us."

"I hope so. We've rigged the timer. We can't stop the blast," Marshall explained.

Zander, Leif, and the others raced through the tree line to the boats, climbing aboard where B had just finished applying another dressing to Frankie's injured arm.

B's gaunt expression made Zander sick to his stomach. She could not make eye contact with him, choosing to rest her head on Frankie's chest. Frankie provided Zander with his best sympathetic glance, no doubt feeling remorseful that he was consoling B when Zander should have been doing so.

Zander sat beside her, frightened to touch her, and forcing a flinch from her bone-tired body. "We're just waiting on Leif's laddies to appear, darling, then we'll get you home."

B gave a slight nod to her head as he watched her tighten her grip on the LVAD wires she refused to leave behind.

Shaking his head, he relieved himself of an exasperated sigh. "Please talk to me, Welsh—"

His conversation ended abruptly at the sound of a bomb blast.

B scrambled to her feet, almost knocking him into the water, seeing her head snap to the other RIB before directing her attention to the tree line. "Where's Tyr and his brothers? Marshall, Bamfa? Gnarler was up there too. Where are they?" she cried.

Zander rose to place an arm around her, shouting to Mack in the next RIB. "You see anything?"

"Negative. Just billowing dust. You want me to go look?"

"No. Give it a minute."

Ghostly silence loomed, with all eyes fixated on the tree line. Zander's heart smashed into his sternum. They were nowhere to be seen.

Thick smoke wafted toward them from the blast and B's already trembling body shook. "Are they—"

The sound of snapping branches and a series of coughing rants approached them, and everyone ripped their weapons from their sides in one skittish movement.

Emerging from the tree line first were Bamfa, Gnarler and Marshall, who, despite being coated in a thick ashy residue, appeared unhurt.

"You good?"

"Still breathing," Marshall joked.

"Where's Tyr and the others?"

"No clue. Tyr set off looking for them prior to the explosion. The place is decimated. We can't see shit. Thought it best we meet here!"

B dived out of the RIB, wading through the water toward the shore.

"Welsh Cake!" Zander shouted in a gasping shriek before heading in after her.

"Welsh Cake!" he tried again, listening to the panic in her exasperating breaths.

B dragged herself from the water, enabling Zander to appreciate how weak she was. The sight of her so drastically changed from the fiery-eyed, curvy Firestarter unsettled him. B was typically strong and stealthy, contrasting with the frail woman standing on the shore with desperate eyes.

"Tyr, Erik!" she screamed, her voice weak and strained.

He grabbed her waist. "Hey, they'll be—"

"Get off me!" she snapped, trying to push him away.

In a moment of madness, he snapped, snatching the LVAD wires and identification bracelet from her hands and tossing them in the water.

"No!" she cried, trying to escape his firm grasp.

"Hey! Hey!" he shouted, grabbing her jaw to ensure she met his gaze. "I am right fucking here, darling. That shit you're clinging onto, that's Mateo's lies."

"No, no! I need them," she cried, stretching her hand out as if to reach for them.

Zander placed his head to her temple, closing his eyes. "You dinnae, darling. Please, I'm right fucking here. Please?"

Tears trickled down his face, soaking her cheek. His heavy body pressing into hers, holding on for dear life. "Please, Blethen. Come back to me. I've missed you so fucking much!"

The softness of her skin glided across his stubble-ridden cheek, waking him from his torment.

Her tear-filled eyes stared back at him, full of hurt and trauma.

Their gazes met, transpiring into a strong-hold stare of uncertainty, as if B were remembering who he was. Her hands grasped the back of his head, pulling him in to taste him with her delicate tongue. Moaning in combustible relief, Zander devoured her mouth with every flurrying memory of their historical relationship flooding through his hippocampus. They didn't exchange any words, just indulged in a long embrace.

A voice of anguish broke them free of one another.

"Tyr?" B called, releasing herself from Zander's embrace.

"Oh, God!" the voice cried.

B and Zander ran toward the voice with Leif and half of the pack on their tales. The unsettled, thick smoke hampered their view as they coughed their way toward the painful cries.

"Someone's on the ground," Zander said, "Get behind me."

THE RED WEDDING

He retrieved his side arm from its holster, hoping it hadn't gotten too wet from wading through the water after B. Thud, after thud rattled in his ears; the anticipation threatening him with a cardiac arrest.

Holding her hand with one of his and pointing his gun at the other, he turned past a great oak tree, almost stumbling over Tyr.

B gasped in horror.

"Shit!" Zander said, ripping off his vest to relieve himself of his hooded sweatshirt.

B dropped to her knees, wrapping her arm around Tyr.

"The windows blew out just as I reached him," Tyr said in boyish sobs. "Ragnar took the brunt of it," he cried over Ragnar's corpse.

B pulled him into her chest, holding him like a mother to her son as Zander placed his sweatshirt over Ragnar's body.

Leif and Mack were the first to arrive, panting at a stop. Leif's eyes darted between Tyr and the body.

"Who?" he stumbled. "Who's under that hoodie?" he panicked.

Zander palmed his chest. "Ragnar. Leif, I'm sorry."

"No. He went with Erik. Where is Erik?" Leif tried in confusion.

"No sign of Erik yet but trust me pal. You dinnae want to see it. How Tyr carried him this far in one piece, I'll never know. He's gone!"

Leif barged past, using his Viking strength, buckling to his knees in front of Ragnar's dead body.

Trembling, he pulled back the sweater to understand for himself. "No! My son!"

Tyr, still inconsolable, reared his head away from B's chest. "I'm sorry. I tried to save him."

Leif reached over, gripping him by the back of his neck, sending both B's and Zander's hackles up.

"This is not your fault, boy! You understand me!" Leif roared before breaking down into a sob, clutching Tyr over his dead son.

Zander dragged B from the ground, embracing her. "Give them a minute, darling, yeah?"

B stumbled away. "Erik didn't make it, did he?" she whispered.

Zander kissed her head. "I'm sorry, darling. I dinnae think anyone is left alive back there."

B nodded into soft tears, shaking her head.

Zander rubbed her back with Mack approaching from her left side, cuddling her. "I'm so sorry, Dragon."

In a moment of frustration, B pushed him, slapping him across the face.

A stunned Mack glowered at her.

"How dare you apologize? Fuck my life, Mackie! Do you even understand what you're apologizing for?"

"Dragon!"

B picked up a nearby rock and threw it at him, striking his chest as he failed to bat it away.

"You're a fucking arsehole! How many times have I almost died because of you? Hell, I still don't know if Erik's gone, and I have no pills to fucking keep my heart pumping in my bloody chest!"

Zander raised an eyebrow at Mack, stepping toward her.

Your funeral pal!

B threw another rock at him, striking him in the knee.

"Ah, feck, Dragon. Cut it out. I'm sorry for all of it, alright?"

B punched her hands in the air. "Well, that's okay then! As long as Mackie says the magic bloody words, everything is just fucking peachy." She glared at him. "You're a fucking prick. How many more lives will your Cascade of Lies take?" she laughed. "Jeez, Mackie. Blaze, Jericho, Mateo…. Just how many maniacs did you cross? Because I'm so fucking over this shit!"

"Dragon..."

B stormed into his personal space. "You're supposed to be my best friend, Mackie. It was us against the world and you destroyed it all. I'm glad I left Uskiville because it means I never have to look at you again!"

"You don't mean that. You're pissed! We'll talk when you calm."

A gasp rippled through the air from the gathering Wolves and the Reapers mourned their fallen brother.

"Not this time, Boyoh. We're done. If I survive this, you're out of my life for good!"

"What do you mean, if you survive?" Erik shouted from behind her.

B's body swiveled in shock, casting her eyes upon a soot-covered

Erik. She ran to him without hesitation, diving into his embrace, leaving a jaw dropping Zander behind her.

"You're alive!" she cried.

Reaching into his pant pocket, he retrieved an orange pill bottle. "Take your medicine, Dragon." He smiled at her, twisting off the cap and handed her a single pill from the pot and popped one himself. "I think we're even now. You saved my life, I saved yours?"

B took the pill dry. "Erik," she said, taking his hand. "Ragnar... he didn't make it."

Erik's eyes bulged from his head.

"I'm sorry, my lovely. I'll take you to him," she said, taking his hand and leading him to his family.

CHAPTER EIGHTY-ONE
Embrace and Sorrow

B led Erik to his grieving family, with Zander walking behind them and keeping a watchful eye. B stopped short of the grieving Vikings, her sympathetic smile proving enough to make a tear-filled Erik crack a smile from his mourning expression. An awkward silence loomed as Erik turned to meet her gaze. "I have much to explain, Dragon. For now, we rest and grieve with our family," Erik said, rubbing her shoulder with his good hand and forcing a smile from his mourning expression.

B smiled, nodding subtly, allowing Tyr to rush into his brother's arms. Witnessing their embrace brought a tear to her eyes. She had never believed she and Erik would see their family again and as Tyr's face unfolded and shattered in his big brothers' arms, relief washed over her like a warm embrace, knowing she was out of harm's way.

The crisp sound of a snapping branch from over her shoulder startled her.

"Sorry, darling," Zander said, extending his hand to her. "How about we leave them and get you back on that boat? I cannae rest until your home safe."

B stared at his hand, contemplating his words.

"Please, darling?" he pressed.

B pursed her lips, pushing his hand away, wrapping her hands around his boulder-like frame.

Zander released an earth-shattering sigh, holding her tight. "Oh darling, I missed you!" he said moaning into her ear and kissing the side of her head before leading her back to the boat.

"Wolves, move out! Allow Leif and his family some time."

Tyr stood to attention, ready to follow.

"No' you pal. Stay with your Viking kin."

Tyr nodded, turning back to his Viking family.

"And Tyr?" Zander called.

"Yeah?"

"Dinnae take this the wrong way pal, this place is gonnae be crawling with blue blood any minute. We cannae be near when the cops arrive, and you need to bring your brother home."

"I understand. We're right behind you, Prez."

The Wolves waited in the RIBs for Leif, Tyr, and the Rus Reapers to return with Ragnar's body. Zander could feel B's pulse rattle in her chest in vibrating waves of restlessness. Peering down B appeared to be resting only her body told him otherwise; it worried him.

What have they done to you?

He kissed her head, making her stir.

"Sorry darling, I dinnae mean to wake you, get some sleep."

Zander watched her sit up and lock eyes with Erik.

"Hey, you okay?" she said to him.

Erik glanced at the other RIB carrying the Reapers, including Leif and Ragnar's corpse, before smiling at her. "I'm okay, Dragon. Thank you. We have much to talk about."

B slipped from Zander's embrace to sit next to Erik, causing anxiety to breed contempt within his troubled soul. He listened to their conversation where Erik divulged everything about their time in capture and held her hand.

Wait, have they been... Are they?

A million questions entered Zander's mind, fearing B had been unfaithful. His heart hurt: he had spent every waking moment pining for her and now it appeared her love lay elsewhere.

CHAPTER EIGHTY-TWO
Catching Her Breath

B had fallen asleep in the RIB, resting her weary head on Erik's shoulder. Erik spent most of the trip persuading B to go straight to the hospital. Zander also tried to encourage her to do the same despite B's lack of acknowledgement that he was present. It angered Zander that B refused point blank to see a doctor even after Erik had stressed her about the danger she was in. Zander believed it was B's oppositional defiance prohibiting her from obtaining the medical help she needed. He did not believe for one second that fear was the root cause of her unwillingness to seek medical help. B explained that she no longer trusted doctors, and all she wanted to do was go home to her boys. Fear and nausea whistled through Zander's regulatory processes like a dreary melancholy whisper; the woman he loved rested her head on the shoulder of another man with her precarious mental state prohibiting her from seeing the reality of her life-threatening predicament.

Zander shifted his eyes from her as Erik caught his gaze.

"She's been through a lot," he said.

"Aye, haven't we all?" Zander said, stroking his chin.

"You're what kept her alive?"

Zander grimaced, expecting the worst. "Looking at her now, I'm guessing it was you, pal."

Erik chuckled. "My relationship with Dragon isn't what you think. She shut that shit down before the words ever left my lips."

Zander smirked, throwing a passing glance at Frankie.

"It's true Prez. I asked her outright. B wouldn't lie to me," Frankie said.

Erik continued. "Dragon believed you were dead. She clutched those hospital items as if she was drawing strength from them; drawing strength from you."

"It's true Prez. She blames herself for you getting shot. Imagine what weeks of guilt have done to her," Frankie said, shaking his head at his sleeping sister.

"Dragon never let go of those items. Every time I entered her room; she would clutch them. She would place them under her pillow once I entered, refusing to show her weakness. That hard-faced, resting bitch face would decorate her pretty face and it was game on."

"Sounds about right!" Zander scoffed.

"Dragon made a deal with Mateo to keep the rest of the club safe and to add fuel to her fire on fight nights. Without a doubt, she knew her sons were safe. However, she needed to see that the MC could continue without her. I've seen no one so fearless. The things I saw Dragon do to survive might well haunt me forever." He closed his eyes to pause. "That drug.... what Dragon has coursing through her veins is an abomination and it's going to kill her if she doesn't get medical help."

Zander stared longingly at her. "I dinnae fight this hard to lose her when I've just got her back."

"Then get her to the emergency room. God knows how either of us has survived."

The RIBs found dry land a farther ten miles downriver where Erik jostled B awake.

"Come now, Dragon, we're half-way home."

B tried to stand only her knees buckled; the effects of the pill Erik had given her had taken over.

"Come here darling," Zander said, scooping her wafer-thin body into his chest and carrying her to the truck.

"Everyone meets back at the club for a debrief. Erik, can you link up with Hyde, our resident doctor? Fill him in on everything you know about the trial. He'll be better equipped to help you both."

"Of course,"

"Wait! Celtic Warrior," Leif interjected. "My wife needs to see her son. We need to bury Ragnar. Please? Can this wait until after we've grieved?"

Erik placed a hand on his father's shoulder. "B and I may not have time to waste. I must do what I can. We have a short supply of the combative drug and both B and I are fragile. Take Ragnar home Faðir. Tell Móðir I will return. Please?"

Leif gripped his son's head. "I am proud of you, my son. Come back to us soon."

Zander directed Erik to the front passenger seat next to Hyde after ensuring Hyde traveled with him and B in case B needed medical treatment.

Cradling B in his arms, he once again felt her erratic heartbeat rage at war against his chest. She clung to him tight in a state of unconsciousness, and he held her close, relieved to have her back in his arms.

Oh darling, I've missed you. Dinnae leave me now!

Jimmy pulled up outside a phone booth at a nearby gas station, distracting his attention from his sleeping old lady. "It's time Prez."

Zander allowed a deep sigh to rip from his lungs. "Welsh Cake," he said, waking her.

B's eyes sprang open, ready to attack. "Hey, hey, you're alright. It's imperative you make a call to the club."

B stared at him, confused by his request.

Zander could not help but smile. Stroking her cheek, he whispered to help her calm. "I need you to ring the club, darling. Tell the prospect you've escaped from Mateo's mansion, and you need picked up, okay?"

"Why?"

"The police will have questions regarding your escape, darling, especially with about forty dead people in the rubble. We'll work on your story later, but we need to create a timeline and alibi for us wolves."

B took a moment to digest Zander's words before nodding. He watched her drag her hands down her face to wake herself.

"We'll fix this, darling, I promise," he said, planting a soft kiss on her neck. "We're right here. As far as anyone is concerned, you escaped and hitched a ride here, okay?"

B pursed her lips and nodded before using the last of her strength to eject herself from the truck. Zander handed her some change and remained out of sight in the unmarked truck, fearing being seen on any potential security footage.

It felt like an eternity to Zander, watching B not twenty feet away. The distance almost overwhelmed him, given their recent reunion.

"You alright, man?" Jimmy asked.

Zander covered his mouth with his hand. "Look at the state of her, Jimmy. It's breaking my heart. I dinnae think she even remembers who she is?" His voice wobbled with upset.

"She knows, brother. She's just catching her breath. Give her a second to adjust and I guarantee the fiery Dragon will appear."

He watched her hover towards the truck.

"I'm scared, pal. What if we're too late?"

Jimmy reached around his seat to grip Zander's shoulder. "Don't you dare give up on her now? We've all fought to the death to bring her home. You straighten the hell up and be her pillar of strength. If she wobbles, make her stable. If she cries, cry with her, but show her how strong you are. Show her that nothing comes between your love for her. You guys are endgame, remember?"

Zander bit down onto his lip, sucking back his tears in time for B's return. "Come here, darling," he said, pulling her into the truck.

"I spoke to a new lad who pretended to call out to you. Apparently, you're on route to come and rescue me,"

Zander lifted her onto his lap, inhaling her hair. "Always, darling. I'm sorry I took so long."

B nuzzled into his neck once more. "Take me home Scottie, I'm so tired."

CHAPTER EIGHTY-THREE
Home

An exhausted pack of Gray Wolves arrived at the MC a little after 3 a.m.

Zander's unsuccessful attempt to take B to a hospital led him to return her to the club, where Hyde could monitor her until morning. Hyde provided Erik with a room at the club for the night after checking him over, before heading to his onsite office to make a call to his former colleagues for guidance on both Erik's and B's current condition. B needed to see a specialist doctor, and Zander knew the police would arrive as soon as they got wind of B's return, but in the present moment everyone required rest. Any evidence linking the Wolves to Mateo needed to be destroyed by Mack, who provided B and Zander with some much-needed alone time to figure out their next move.

Zander carried B into his room at the club, sitting her down on the bed to remove her clothes.

"Shower," she mumbled.

"Dinnae worry aboot showering, darling. You've spent half the night soaking wet."

"Please, I need a shower. I want that place removed from my skin," she said more coherently, waking herself.

Zander slipped her hoodie over her head. "Whatever you want. I'm just happy you're home."

B helped him strip her naked and Zander removed the now dirty dressing from her elbow, tossing everything in a trash bag along with his clothes and boots, leaving the trash bag outside his room for Jimmy to take to Mack for incineration.

After stripping himself naked, and picking up her wafer-thin body once more, his heart sank studying her protruding ribs. B's curvaceous figure had diminished, and bruises, healing wounds, and scars covered her body.

"Scottie, I'm a mess. I expect nothing from you, especially after I almost got you killed."

Zander set her down in the bathroom to turn on the shower. Taking her hands and bringing them to his lips, while meeting her gaze, he whispered to her. "You are still as beautiful as the day we met. And you dinnae get me shot darling, that's on the asshole who took you away from me on our wedding day."

B stared at the tiled floor, struggling to compose herself, and Zander released a hand, sliding the palm of his hand around the back of her neck to clasp her hair, bringing her close.

"Blethen Aryanwen Jones, I have never stopped loving you. I've missed you so much!"

B's bottom lip trembled. "How can you still love me when I gave up on us? Watching Mateo shoot you like a dog... I thought you were dead, and I broke. Scottie, I am broken, and I'm not sure if anyone can fix me this time!"

Tears trickled down Zander's face. "Oh, darling. I've fought every single day to get you back. I dinnae care what we've been through or how broken either of us are, as long as we're together. We'll fix this. I promise!"

B's shaking body matched the tempo of her gushing tears. "I'm so sorry, Scottie."

Zander scooped her into his embrace. "Dinnae ever apologize. You've nothing to be sorry for. I love you so much darling, let me help you. Trust me to fix this?"

B hugged him tight as Zander held her and kissed her neck. "Let's get you cleaned up and into bed."

Zander led her into the steamy shower, positioning her so the shower water rained down onto her head and back. He reached for her shampoo, squeezing out a healthy blob into the palm of his hands before gliding it through her hair and massaging her scalp. He couldn't help releasing a moaning gasp as his hands slipped through her soapy hair.

B opened his eyes to meet his glistening gaze as if she was seeing him for the first time.

He smiled with a warm heart. "There she is. I missed you Welsh Cake."

"Kiss me?" she whispered.

Zander ran his hand through her hair once more, rinsing off the excess shampoo. "You never need to ask, darling," he said before covering her lips with his.

B whimpered into his mouth, delicately entangling her tongue with his, with one hand cradling her head, while the other guided her closer to him.

"Let me make you feel better, darling," he said, reaching for her body wash. His eyes remained locked on hers as he traveled his hands all over her broken body, careful not to get soap in her wounds.

Rinsing her, she still seemed perfect to him despite her appearance. "Dinnae be nervous, darling. I got you!" he reassured her, after seeing the fear creep back into her eyes.

She ran her hand through his hair as he dropped to his knees, kissing every inch of her body. His lips and tongue glided off her soaking skin as he caressed every inch of her, from bottom to top until he met her gaze again.

"Feel better, darling?"

"Almost," she smiled.

Zander cocked an eyebrow, providing a humorous smile. "Almost?"

He studied her as she adjusted her stance to lean against the cold shower wall, pulling him close.

"Make love to me, Scottie. I need to feel you inside me."

Zander stood, pressing his palms against the wall above her head, taking a moment to compose himself. The blood rushed to his lower extremities, forcing his erection to press against her.

"Your no' well. I'm scared I might hurt you."

B caressed his cheek. "Nothing can hurt me anymore, good boy. Make me whole again, please?"

Zander stared into her longing eyes. "Safe word, darling. I need to know if you remember it. I dinnae want to lose you again."

He kissed tears from her eyes. "Tell me you remember it."

"Black," she whispered.

"Oh, darling," he moaned through trailing kisses to her collarbone. "You scream black if things get too much, okay?"

"Yes!" she whispered, gasping as he picked her up, pinning her against the wall. His mouth devoured hers with a soft swirl of his tongue as he wrapped her legs around him.

Lowering her down on to him, he placed his tip inside her, waiting for her response, feeling her body twitch with excitement as he hovered there. "Oh Blethen, I've missed you."

B gripped his back with all the strength she could muster, "Scottie, I..."

"Want more? I know."

Inserting himself halfway inside her, he watched her pant before devouring her mouth again.

"More, Blethen?"

"Yes!" she cried.

Zander's hard cock throbbed as she tightened around him. "You ready for all of me?"

"Yes, please!"

"Anything for you, Welsh Cake," he said, filling her with his long shaft.

B whimpered, forcing matching sharp gasps from the depths of Zander's soul. Pressing himself against her, he kept his thrusts steady and even, careful not to hurt her.

Her heavy breaths and high-pitched cries rang in his ears, beckoning him to drive into her with firmer thrusts until she quickened.

"Oh, darling, I feel how ready you are. Release for me. I got you."

"Scottie," she cried over and over as his stern thrusts stole her orgasm.

His body weakened in healthy pleasure as her vice like clamp ripped his climax from his relieved body. Releasing the pressure of the past five weeks into her fragile body was like a home coming to him. All the feelings he had bottled up for weeks had culminated within and he was giving into them, pouring himself into her. His climax was like no other; tantric-like and Zander laid everything bare, giving himself to her while staring into her eyes.

B's eyes fixated on him. Trying to recover, her body fluttered as the remnants of her orgasm raced through her like an electric shock.

"Feel better now?" he smiled, catching his breath.

"Almost?" she teased again.

"How can I change that?"

"Make me yours again."

Zander kissed her lips. "You'll always be mine, Blethen, but if you want me to do that for you, I will happily oblige."

"I do. I need it, Scottie. Make me scream Prez again. I need you to want me to do that."

Zander smiled into a relinquishing sigh. "You sure you're up to it?"

"Yes, make me your old lady again, please?"

Zander set her down to wash her body once more before grabbing a towel from the towel rack. Wrapping the soft cotton towel around her, he began drying her as she wrestled with his lips.

"Oh, fuck. Dragon wants to play tonight?"

"Yes, take me. Tame my inner Dragon, Scottie. Take me like you mean it!"

"Oh, Christ. Promise me I'll no' hurt you."

B took his hand and kneeled before him, just inside the bedroom. "That's exactly what I need. Pleasure and pain." Peering down at her with lustful eyes, he caught his breath as she took him into her mouth, sucking on it as if she was trying her best to please him, while one hand massaged the length of his shaft.

Zander gasped. "Fuck, Dragon, I'm almost ready to go again."

B feasted on his enlarging cock, bringing it to the back of her throat, indulging in every inch until he was erect. Removing him from her seductive mouth, she licked her lips before dragging her tongue down the length of his shaft.

"Oh..."

"Ready for me, big guy?" she said, wearing her devious Dragon smile.

Zander dragged her to her feet. "Tell me what you need, Dragon."

"Take me until I can't take anymore."

Zander's jaw dropped.

"Take me like you planned to on our wedding night. I want to feel and remember everything tonight."

"Oh, darling. Maybe we should rest. I won't relax until you've seen a specialist."

B sighed. "Please make me yours, Prez. Just one night without a doctor. They're all I've seen for weeks, and I don't want to miss a beat anymore."

Zander gripped her head, sucking on her mouth before travelling to her breasts. "Oh, Dragon, I'm gonnae give you what I think you can handle, darling, but dinnae worry, I'll make you scream the club down."

He guided her to the bed, setting her down to lick her twitching nub. "Oh, so ready for me, sweetness. Let me feel you." He inserted two fingers inside her. "Perfect. Fucking perfect."

"Yes, Prez. I need everything. Bring out the toys if you like?"

Zander gently flipped her over, bringing her to her knees. "Oh, Dragon. I think I've died and gone to heaven." He reached into the top bedside drawer, removing her vibrator. "Only one tonight. We'll play with the rest once I know you're alright."

Switching it on low, he teased her entrance. "You like that, darling?"

B's body convulsed with soft moans. "Prez!"

"Dinnae worry, by the time I enter you; you'll be screaming for more."

B backed her ass into him.

"So eager. I love it! You want this, Dragon?" he said, placing himself at her entrance, teasing her.

"Yes Prez, make me yours!"

The excitement overwhelmed him as the pre-cum dripped from his swollen cock, showing his eagerness. Zander tugged hard, encouraging his erection, and pressing further. "Are you ready for your Prez, Dragon?"

"Yes," she cried, struggling as the vibrator tantalized her nub.

"Prepare to bite down, Dragon. I'm giving you the ride of your life," he said, penetrating her with his throbbing cock, thrusting with intention and provoking a hard gasp from both parties. Increasing the tempo on the vibrator, Zander pressed it hard against her nub, forcing a shriek of pleasure from her delicate vocal cords.

"You like that, Dragon?"

"Yes, Prez,"

He thrusted again. "Oh, fuck, Dragon. This is amazing!"

"More!"

"I got more, darling," he said, thrusting hard while teasing her with the vibrator, circling it over her precious mound.

B screamed, gripping down onto her silk sheets.

"I'm gonna come."

Zander switched off the vibrator, tossing it to the side to grip her hips, penetrating her. He felt how weak she was, unnerving him into a slow stride.

"Harder, Prez. Make me yours," she pleaded again in desperation.

"You're already mine," he gasped. "Now breathe, Dragon. I can feel your rampant heart through my thrusts."

Fear forced him to slow to a stop. Removing himself, he kissed the length of her back before turning her over to meet his gaze.

B's disappointment confronted him. "You don't want to make me yours again?"

"I dinnae need to. You've always been mine. Now let's slow things down, so I can make love to my wife."

"I'm not your wife, Scottie. We didn't exchange vows."

"Fuck the vows. You're mine! Always have been, always will be. We're way past fucking you through your pain. I'll make love to you until you're ready to talk, but no more pushing shit aside. We're better than that now."

B welled up.

"Hey, hey. You're alright, darling. I'll no' let you out of my sight ever again."

B's sniffles turned into sobs as Zander dragged her into his embrace. She clung to his chest like a frightened child, releasing her anguish in relief.

Images of remember-when's and first encounters flooded his memory bank, reminding him of their connection and all he had missed. "Oh, darling," he cried, allowing his own tears to soak her wet hair. "What has that bastard done to you?"

B shook her head, muffling her cries in his chest hair, forcing Zander to tighten his grip around her.

"I'm so sorry, Welsh Cake. You dinnae deserve any of this. We'll fix everything, okay?" Bringing his hands to caress her cheeks, he pressed his forehead to hers to kiss her lips. "I thought I lost you. I promise to protect you forever. Please believe me. I love you so much."

B howled into his chest, releasing the last of her pent-up adrenaline before settling into south whimpers. It hurt Zander to see her suffering, swallowing back his tears, the lump in his throat threatened to choke him as he held her, crying themselves to sleep after the exhausting day caught up with them.

CHAPTER EIGHTY-FOUR
Nightmare

B had only been asleep an hour when a brutal nightmare took hold of her subconscious and B found herself back in Mateos' drained pool, facing all of those she killed. Amongst the dead, both Zander and Erik faced off with her, blaming her for their deaths. Her mind painted a tormented image of Zander cursing her as he bled out from his gunshot wound, challenging her decision to stand up for Mack.

B tried to talk to him as the other victims approached to beat down on her, suffocating her with body blows.

Where's your precious Mackie now? An evil voice spoke.

B fought for her life, convinced she was back under Mateos control as the dead tore pieces of her flesh in a revenge attack.

Wrestling in her sleep until she bolted upright, B woke with a shrieking scream so piercing it woke the rest of the wolves. She turned to face a frightened Zander, trying to console her, making her dive off the bed and back into the room's corner. She slid down onto the floor, holding her head in a fit of fear and anguish.

"Welsh Cake, it's okay, darling. It was a nightmare," Zander said, sitting back on his heels and stroking her head to comfort her.

B sobbed into her knees in a repetitive song. "I'm sorry! I'm sorry! Scottie, I never meant to hurt anyone."

"Hey, hey. What did I say? This isn't your fault."

"It is my fault. I tried to protect Mackie and got everyone killed. Eddie, the prospects, my competitors. They're all dead because of me."

The wolves barreled into the bedroom, capturing Zander's distraught face and B's broken body.

"What's happened?" Jimmy asked.

Zander sighed into a headshake, barely composing himself. "Nightmare. I dinnae know how to help her. It's destroying me."

Mack barged past his fellow wolves to stand in front of B. "Let me talk to her. I know her better than anyone."

In the blink of an eye, B had risen to her feet to lunge at him. "This is on you, Mackie!" she screamed, swinging punches into his defensive hands.

"Dragon, what the fuck?"

B grabbed his throat, digging her broken nails into his skin. "You keep putting everyone at risk. People have died because of your fucking lies. I don't even know what's real anymore."

Zander reached around her waist, dragging her away as Jimmy removed her hand from his throat.

"Calm the fuck down, Dragon." Zander barked, pinning her against the wall.

B snapped out of her trance, surprised at his demeanor to see Zander's face soften.

"Breathe. Just fucking breathe, please?"

B steadied her breath without breaking eye contact.

"You want him to leave? Consider him gone," Zander said.

"Hang the feck on a minute..." Mack snapped, rubbing his clawed neck. "Don't put fecking words into her mouth. I know she's mad but we're family. Allow Dragon to decide what she wants."

B whipped her head in Mack's direction. "You've destroyed everything I ever was. My confidence, my sense of self, my fucking strength, Mackie, and for what? To get into the knickers of a cheating slag!"

Zander released her from his grasp; the hurt in her tone provided enough evidence to suggest she was in pain and less inclined to attack.

Mack remained quiet.

"Look at the state of me, Mackie. You can see my bloody bones!"

More Wolves bustled into the bedroom after hearing the commotion, trying to avert their eyes, choosing to look everywhere other than at a naked B. Zander reached around the bathroom door, unhooking his bathrobe to cover B's modesty as she continued to berate Mack. "I'm not safe when you're around. What do you want from me, Mackie, because I have nothing left to give?"

Mack took a step forward. "Dragon, please? I never meant..."

B palmed the air, stopping him in his tracks. "To hurt me? Yeah, I get it. Just like you intended no harm from Blaze, Jericho, or the saga that threatens me daily. Mackie, I can't do this anymore. I can't have you in my life putting me and my loved ones in danger."

Mack cleared his throat, struggling to speak as his tone wore thin. "Dragon. What are you saying?"

B wiped her tears on the sleeve of Zander's robe. "I'm saying I don't want you in my life anymore. I'm saying..." She stopped, composing herself with a large exhalation. "Mackie, I don't feel safe with you and the Cascade of Lies wreaking havoc on every waking moment of my life. Tell me, who am I facing off with next? Who comes next to harm the ones you love?"

Mack shook his head. "Dragon, I won't let any harm come to you. Listen, I hold my hands up. I made a massive mistake with Ari and the Cascade of Lies thing. All I'm asking is for a chance to make amends. I've provided Jimmy with everything I can remember regarding Ari's list. We're gonna create a plan, sort this whole mess out."

B shook her head, reaching for Zander's hand, who took it in solidarity and spoke to Mack. "At what cost Irish? We've been through hell and we're so lucky that Welsh Cake survived this. Mateo abducted her on our wedding day, for fuck's sake, after you pulled a stunt to take her from me. Now, if my old lady wants you to leave, that's her decision to make."

"Nah, you're wrong Prez. We made a pact. Best friends don't quit. Isn't that right, Dragon?"

B stared into his eyes. "Maybe, tonight they do!"

Mack blew air out of his cheeks to the gasping sounds of his brothers. B always kept Mack close, even when he angered her. Only things were vastly different tonight.

He stepped into her personal space, kissing her cheek. "It's okay, Dragon. I understand. Just know, I never meant to hurt you. I would die for you! Consider me gone until you need me again."

B watched Mack walk toward the door where Frankie propped himself up against the jamb, staring at her with sympathy. He turned to follow Mack, and B broke down as soon as they left.

Zander ushered her to the bed, holding her. "I got you, sweetheart. I get how difficult that must have been for you."

"Scottie, I can't do this anymore. I close my eyes and I'm right back there."

Tears rolled down Zander's cheeks, holding her. "I got you, darling, and I promise I'm never letting go, ever again."

"We all got you, Móðir," Tyr said, dragging a load of pillows and blankets into the room and tossing them at his brothers.

Zander and B stared dumbfounded, watching the Wolves hunker down around the bed with pillows and blankets.

"Cut you and we all bleed, Dragon," Jimmy said, squeezing her hand. "You may be a Dragon but you're also a wolf and part of our pack!"

Tiny rested his head against the wooden bed post, clasping his injured side. "You're our favorite pain in the ass, Dragon, and we love you for it. We're here for however long it takes to get you back to the sassy bitch you are."

B choked into laughter. "Thank you."

Zander leaned back against the headboard, clamping her to her chest. "Rest darling, we're all here to protect you."

"I don't want to close my eyes. I'm scared I'll lose myself again if I do."

Frankie reappeared in the doorway with his hands on his hips. "And you think your pack of wolves will let that happen?"

B pursed her lips as he entered, sitting next to her on the bed and putting his feet up to relax.

"We gotta get that head of yours screwed back on right, so you're ready to ring your boys in the morning,"

B nodded. "I thought you left with Mackie."

Frankie's eyes remained fixed on the television that Tiny had switched on. "No. I sent him back to Uskiville. I've warned him of the repercussions of his actions time and time again, and I'll tell you what I told him the night Junior went missing... my loyalties lie with you." He turned to face her. "You're my sister B. I've missed the hell out of you and right now, my primary concern is getting you well again."

"How are my boys?" she whispered.

"They have your blood running through their veins; they're holding up. I'll ring them in the morning after you've seen Hyde's doctor friend. B, I'm not giving them any news until I know you're okay. It's unfair to tell them you're okay and something happens to you. It'll destroy them all over again."

Zander squeezed her tight. "She'll be alright, Frankie. Let Welsh Cake rest tonight."

"Oh, I'm not trying to rile her. I'm telling her she's seeing that specialist tomorrow, even if I have to drag her scrawny ass there. Her boys need their mother back. Playing this bullshit roulette game won't wash with me."

"I've had my fill of psychopath doctors."

"Tough shit! Now, apparently, you may need a doctor to save your life. B your chest is rising and falling quicker than a hooker's panties. That shit needs fixing, and I don't care how scared you are. You're doing this for your boys."

B went quiet, prompting a room full of stares from the surrounding pack.

"And you'll all be there to keep me safe?" she asked.

"Front and fucking center, Dragon," Tiny said. "Now shut the fuck up and get some sleep!"

B smiled. "I love you too, you big prick."

The room erupted into roaring laughter as Tiny grabbed her foot. "There she is!"

B sat up straight. "Thank you, all of you. I never believed I'd make it back, and I thought I'd lost..." she stopped to gaze at Zander. "Anyway, I'm so grateful to you all. Genuine, like."

Jimmy spoke from Zander's favorite chair as he sipped his whiskey. "Dragon, you picked this club up after Noah died, when only Zand believed in you. Now we're returning the favor. So, rest. You've got a busy day tomorrow."

The room hushed into a calming silence, allowing B to rest, comforted by a protective wolf pack.

CHAPTER EIGHTY-FIVE
Mack's Guilt

Bamfa and Gnarler accompanied Mack on the trip back to Uskiville while Tiny stayed in Sunnyville, after showing concern for B for the first time.

Frustration rippled through Mack's body as he tore up the highway, drifting into every bend in the road like his life depended on it.

She's just upset. She'll come around. Best friends don't quit!

The tender loving words he and B always spoke, conveying their need for one another, repeated in his head the entire ride home like a record stuck on repeat.

He pulled up to the deserted retreat, remembering past times when he and B were uninterrupted and happy.

I wish we could turn back time.

"You alright, Prez?" Bamfa asked, pulling up next to him.

"Good, brother, nothing a night's sleep couldn't sort."

"Today was a lot. You sure you don't want to hit the bar?"

Mack climbed off his bike, clasping Bamfa's back. "I'm grand. I promise. Dragon will come around. I'll give her a few days to calm herself. I'm off to bed. Catch you in a few, brother."

Mack dragged himself up the porch steps, retrieving his keys from his pocket and unlocking the door to his empty house. Junior had gone to visit Adam and Joe, and Ari had left no trace of herself or their other children after fleeing back to Portland with her counselor boyfriend. Mack's gaze swept the cabin, evoking a sense of loneliness. He had come full circle, back to a life of solitude and it scared him.

CHAPTER EIGHTY-SIX
Heart Failure

Zander woke up to an empty bed in a familiar panic. The sound of wolves snoring disoriented him as he headed into the bathroom to look for B and found himself sick to his stomach when he discovered she was gone.

He threw on his clothes and boots, climbed over the sleeping wolves, and left the room. He was halfway down the hallway when he saw Jimmy heading towards the stairs leading to the roof with two hot beverages.

The confusion on his face made his brother smile. "She's on the roof. I came to make us a drink?"

"And you left her up there alone. For Christ's sake Jimmy. She's fragile," Zander snapped, trying to rush ahead.

"She's fine, asshole. Dragon hasn't seen the sun in five weeks, and she's worried about seeing the doc later. Don't go freaking her out. I clocked her leaving the bedroom this morning and followed her. We had a good chat and let me tell you, your old lady is more compos mentis than you realize."

Zander stopped short of the roof door. "She is?"

Jimmy laughed. "She's overcome with fear and guilt and angry as shit at Mack. She never expected to see you or anyone else, but now she fears the doctor will take it all away. I think she knows something's wrong with her."

Zander narrowed his gaze. "Of course there's something wrong, pal. She's a bag of fucking bones and cannae keep her eyes closed longer than five minutes without being traumatized by whatever the fuck happened to her up there."

Jimmy shook his head. "There's more to it than that. Dragon has endured multiple challenges. This is different. She senses something is wrong." He handed Zander two mugs of tea. "Go talk to her. Find out what's scaring her because it ain't no guilt or demons."

Zander took the mugs, leaving Jimmy at the door. He wandered over to B, who sat wrapped in a blanket, watching the sunrise.

"Morning darling. Tea?" he said, handing her a mug.

"Morning. Sorry I skipped out. I figured you needed your sleep after putting up with me last night."

Zander sat beside her, wrapping his arm around her shoulder. "I comforted my wife, something I never expected to do again. I'm no' putting up with you. It's always a pleasure, never a chore, Welsh Cake."

"Sleep bloody evaded me, and all I could think of was seeing the sun rise one last time."

Zander studied her calm face, staring out into the distance as if she had accepted her fate. He placed his mug away from him, taking hers, too. "What do you mean, one last time?"

She shrugged. "I've been pumped with drugs that have eaten away the muscle in my body. My heart is a muscle, Scottie, and I've felt myself slip further away these last few weeks. Nobody knows what was in those drugs, yet I feel what they're doing to me."

"We dinnae know anything, darling. Hyde has been up all night on video call with his friends from Fresno Heart and Surgical Hospital. They're working on a plan as we speak."

B took his hand. "Scottie, I'm hanging on by a thread. I'm just grateful I got to see you again. To see the sun again. Now, I only desire to see my sons. That's why I'm hesitant about going to the hospital. I don't want to miss my chance of seeing them again when I have so much to say."

Zander's voice weakened with a shuddering pang to his healing chest. "Now, listen here, Welsh Cake. If you think I came back from the dead to save you, and have you given up on life, you have another thing coming."

"Scottie," she whispered.

He lifted her onto his lap. "No! You dinnae get to give up now. We have a whole life to live. Our story dinnae end here. We get married properly this time, have lots of Celt babies and grow old together. You hear me! Dinnae dare fucking give up on me Blethen because I will never give up on you!"

Tears fled down her face. "I'm scared Scottie."

He pinched her chin between his thumb and forefinger. "I know, and that's okay. Perhaps it's time to let Dragon die, so Blethen can live a healthy life. Death and rebirth are what's needed here, darling. Release the fears you've bottled up for years. Give them to me. My shoulders are broad enough to carry all our worries."

B placed her forehead to his. "I'd like that. I love you, Scottie!"

"Oh, darling. Allow this death and rebirth to happen. Let me take your hand, unscramble your brain, and lead you into a better future. This time we're both coming back swinging and we're no' gonnae miss. My darling, you are the missing piece to my life puzzle, and I never want to lose you again."

B held onto him with all her strength, kissing and caressing his face.

He delved into her mouth, proving his love for her with passionate kisses. "Let's watch the sun come up together and get you fixed. We need to make up for lost time."

B readied herself for a trip to the hospital with Erik. Her favorite jeans hung off her hips and her white vest hung from her bony frame. She did her best to make herself presentable, covering her dark circles with concealer and applying mascara to make herself feel more human. The minor changes she made to her appearance, along with a healthy squirt of her favorite perfume, lifted her mood despite Hyde's insistence on placing her fractured wrist in a sling, just as he did with Erik.

The thought of seeing another doctor paralyzed her; her feet remained fixed in place at the foot of the bed.

Get a grip, good girl. Fix yourself up for the boys.

Zander entered with a belt in hand. "Thought you might need something to keep your jeans up," he smiled. "I mean, I prefer them around your ankles..."

B cracked a smile, allowing him to thread the belt through her jeans, buckling it at the front.

"Tight enough?" he asked.

"Yeah, thanks. Who does it belong to?"

"Hyde. He's the only one with a woman's figure around here."

B giggled, making Zander smile as he caressed her cheek.

He kissed her forehead. "I'm so grateful for getting to see you smile again. These last five weeks have been soul destroying."

"You can say that again. I've just arrived back and now I have to leave again."

Zander ran his fingers through her hair. "Hey, we're heading to the hospital to get you fixed up and we're all right there with you. I'm no' letting you out of my sight."

"What if something occurs before I reunite with the boys? Scottie, I just want to go home and wait for them."

Zander held her, rubbing her back. "Listen. This friend of Hyde reckons he can stabilize you. He'll fix you right up and then we'll head home, ready for their return. No more drama."

"And you'll stay with me no matter what?"

"I'll stick to you like glue, darling. Last little hurdle now and we're home to fatten you up."

B nestled her head into his chest. "You don't like the skin and bone?"

"Darling, I love you no matter what, but I want you to be healthy and I miss your bum," he teased.

"Ha! I miss my bum. I miss squats, my abs and feeling strong. Honestly, if it weren't for Erik, I'd be dead already. I owe him my life."

Zander led her to the bed, sitting down and pulling her onto his lap.

"About that. Erik became the hero I've always desired to be for you, darling."

B straddled him, staring curiously.

"I dinnae blame you if yous had a relationship with him. I mean, with all you went through."

B slapped him across the face and stepped off him in a whirlwind of unrepentant anger. "Urgh, for fuck's sake, Scottie. I thought I'd lost you. I have been literally fighting for my life while mourning the love of my life. The thought of riding a Viking never bloody entered my mind. Jeez!"

Zander rubbed his face. "Point taken, darling. Fucking hell. You've no' lost that much strength. You almost took my fucking head off my shoulders!"

B's dragon-eyed pout diminished into a fit of laughter, encouraging a roaring chuckle from Zander.

"Fucking knob!" B cackled.

Zander stood, placing his hands around her skinny waist, embracing her wafer-thin frame. "Sorry."

"Scottie, the malnourished look doesn't float my boat, sunshine. I mean, we're both wasting away. Not to mention, he'd never be able to match your bedroom skills. Nobody could pin me against the wall and make me scream like you do."

Zander blushed, biting his bottom lip, melting B's heart. She wrapped her arms around his neck, reassuring him of her love for him. "I thought I'd lost you and it killed me. I never want to feel like that again. You will always be the one for me, Zander McGovan.

"That's all I needed to hear. Now shift your ass so the doc can fix you. Hyde's getting grouchy on account of being up all night."

B conversed with Zander, Hyde, Erik, and Jimmy on the drive to the local hospital where Hydes former colleagues agreed to meet B and Erik, fearing another 219-mile trip might take its toll on their already compromised health.

Escorted by the entire pack of wolves, led by Frankie in Zander's absence, they traveled a short distance down the highway and into the hospital parking lot. Stepping down from the vehicle, B squeezed Zander's hand.

He whispered in her ear as they walked into the reception area. "I got you. We'll soon be walking out this door. Once the doc fixes you up, we'll call the laddies and get them on the next flight."

The pack waited in the parking lot except for Zander, Hyde, Tyr, and Jimmy, who escorted B and Erik into the building.

B tracked Hyde's movements as Doctor Cassimino and Doctor Harper greeted him like a long-lost friend. Hyde made small talk, handing over the files Erik had retrieved from Mateo's laboratory to him. They laughed and joked before Hyde escorted them both to meet B and Erik.

"B, this is Doctor Luis Cassimino and Doctor Daniel Harper. They're old friends of mine. We served together before returning to Civvy Street. Luis here is a cardiothoracic surgeon, and Daniel is an endocrinologist consultant. They both want to help understand what's going on with Erik and yourself."

B extended her hand. "Thank you for making the trip. I appreciate it."

"Not at all. We owe Hyde our life, repaying a favor will make him shut the hell up for five minutes and stop him reminding us of how he dragged us to safety after an IED almost killed us," Daniel said.

"You think you can help us?" Erik asked.

"We have some theories. Your situation is unique. Even yours differs from B's. We need to conduct some tests, but we'll do our best."

"Your best?" Erik joked. "We require more than just theories and your best efforts. I've already had one heart attack, and my parents have already lost one son this week."

"Erik," Tyr cussed.

"No, baby brother. Dragon and I have been through hell. I need to be certain we're in capable hands."

B turned to him. "Hey, Viking, you're scared. I get it. I'm scared too, but I trust Hyde with my life. If he thinks these guys can help. I'm all in." She pushed off Zander using him as a pillar of strength to stand. "Lead the way. I'm over this already."

After blood and urine tests, CT scans, magnetic imaging, ECG's, X-rays and an array of other tests, the doctors sat in a nearby conference room with Hyde and the local consultants to discuss B and Erik's treatment plan before reconvening with B, Erik, and Zander in their private room.

"We have your test results. Both of you are presenting with adrenal disorder symptoms with similar test results. Whether these self-regulate following discontinuing the trial drug is unknown at present," Doctor Cassimino said.

B and Erik stared at the doctors, listening attentively as if they were scared to miss a beat.

Doctor Harper stepped forward. "The issue we're having is the unknown variables within the medication. The files don't explain or note the ingredients in the dose you were given. Now we've sent the combative drug off to the lab to provide us with more information as there as so many anomalies within your results. B, you have a hair-line fracture to your wrist and have lost almost fourteen kilograms of weight, and your dramatic muscle loss is cause for concern. Individuals with adrenal disorders generally experience severe fatigue, bone and muscle weakness, tremors, and blood pressure issues, which we can treat. However, we don't know the production process of the medication injected into both of you. I've also contacted the relevant authorities, who may investigate Mateo, and maybe they'll find other records of the trial."

"Not possible, I'm afraid. Everything else was destroyed in a fire," Erik said without emotion.

"Well, in that case, we have to treat you both as we find you. It's the best we can do. As for the good news, no tumors, or abnormalities detected in either of you. Your scans are clear and apart from some deficiencies and blood pressure issues, there are no other signs of anything sinister going on for you B. We'll aim to keep you here for a few days and treat your symptoms as your body withdraws from the drug."

"I have to stay here?"

"It's the safest option Dragon," Hyde said, leaning closer to provide comfort. "Besides, the docs want to start you on medication to stabilize you and aid in your weight gain. Your organs are still healthy but you're struggling."

Zander held her tight. "We got this, darling. I'll ring the laddies and have them brought here, and I'll no' leave your side."

Relief washed over her. "I'll be alright?"

"We think so. Let's just see how the next few days go," Doctor Cassimino said.

"And Erik?" she asked.

The doctors shared uncertain glances.

"What?" Erik asked.

Doctor Cassimino approached him. "That heart attack you had. It was because of a slight tear in your aortic valve. The breathlessness you're having is a symptom of your heart struggling. We need to operate today to fix that. Our concern is your body's ability to cope with surgery after everything it's been through. We fear waiting could be fatal."

B gasped. "But you can fix him, right?"

"We can do our best. There's risk with any surgery, but this is your best option."

Erik smiled in disbelief. "So, I survive hell and I'm still dicing with death?"

Tyr's pale countenance met his brother's gaze. "Erik, you are stronger than this. Get the surgery and you'll be back to your best. You are a Rus!"

"What are my chances of survival?"

"The general survival rate is around 94%. Only your body has undergone unknown trauma. As a betting man, I'd say you have a 52% chance of survival, but that's a guess," the doctor confirmed.

"And if I refuse the surgery, I'm a dead man walking? Not to mention the finite detail of no medical insurance."

Doctor Cassimino sighed. "It's anyone's guess how long you would last."

B slapped his thigh, snapping him out of his pity party. "Listen good boy. I'll cover the costs. Your story doesn't end here. You have a child to father. Now get the God damn surgery before I do it myself. And none of us want that."

Eric shook his head. "I don't know, Dragon; I've seen your handy work. I reckon you could pull it off."

"With my tremors, no chance, my lovely. Get fixed up and maybe I'll consider supporting Daddy Leif's business."

Zander grabbed her elbow, directing her attention to him. "Whoa, hang on a minute, before you disappeared you wanted nothing to do with them and now you wanna help because you've bonded with boy wonder here?"

"We all suffered losses because of Mateo. Now, we must rebuild. Scottie, this is the least I can do, given that Erik kept me alive. Without his pills, I would have died in the first week."

"I'm sure he's a real boy scout, darling. Glad to hear you found your hero," Zander said, walking out.

"Scottie...." B called out, watching the man she loved exit the room.

Frankie entered, wearing a bemused expression. "Sorry for the intrusion. B, Ray, my former supervisor, has arrived to take a statement. He went by the club before calling me here. He wants everyone's statements while they're fresh."

Doctor Cassimino interrupted once more. "Well, B can go to the side room but don't take too long. We're keen to start her on an IV to help her body cope a little better." He turned to Erik. "As for yourself, I'm booking an O.R, so you need to hang tight, and we'll be back."

"I'm not leaving him," B said to Frankie. "Ray needs to gather our statements here."

Erik nudged B's chin. "Go, I'll be alright. Tyr's here and you should patch things up with your Prez."

"No chance, my lovely. I'm staying right here until you're out of surgery and in recovery. We started this together, and we'll finish it together. Prez has waited weeks to see me. If he wants to sulk about me standing by my friend, he can bash on." She turned to Tyr. "Maybe now is a good idea to ring your dad. If my son was having open heart surgery, I'd want to me there, especially after the loss you've all suffered, and I'm guessing you mother wants to see her son before his surgery."

Tyr glanced at Erik, asking for his approval.

"Dragon's right, Tyr. Go, we'll be here when you come back."

Tyr left the office with Frankie and while B and Erik waited for his return after fetching Ray, B made use of the quiet they had.

"So, serious question. How are you holding up?"

Erik shrugged. "To be honest, I'm still surprised we made it out alive. It's not quite sunk in yet."

"Probably because you've not returned home yet. Last night almost broke me, Erik, and it wasn't until I had a bedroom full of supportive bikers that I realized I was home and safe."

Erik raised an eyebrow: his salacious, grinning demeanor forced a giggle from B.

"Not like that, knob head. They came in after my night terror to comfort me. I'd forgotten what that felt like. I'd forgotten what it was like to be held by a loved one. It's funny," she said, standing to pace the room as she pondered her existence. "Ordinary interactions, the comfort of normalcy, made me realize the preciousness of life. I won't waste another minute."

"What are you trying to say, Dragon?"

Placing her hand on his shoulder, she stared into his clear blue eyes. "I'm saying we've had so much taken away from us and it's a miracle we survived, but we did."

"Uh, huh," he said, humoring her.

"Piss off," she teased. "All I'm saying is, we survived for a reason. It's why I know you have nothing to worry about with open heart surgery, and when you're done and you've seen your child and you realize that too, I'm hoping we can be friends and maybe do business together. We didn't build the bond we have to be in each other's lives for a season, and I didn't meet Tyr for no reason either. The universe has brought our families together and I want to explore what it is we're meant to achieve in this lifetime."

Erik took her hand in his. "Dragon, your mind fascinates me. I just hope you're correct. It's a lot of money to waste on a surgery for a dead man walking."

"I'm not wasting money, good boy. I'm investing. We should always value human life over money, and I value our friendship. We're survivors and you're going to promise me you won't die on me. Valhalla doesn't get to steal you for a while yet, Boyoh!"

CHAPTER EIGHTY-SEVEN
My Time Has Come

Mack allowed himself a moment to immerse himself in his surroundings, taking one last look at the place he called home before placing a manilla envelope addressed to Junior on the dining room table.

Zipping up his cut, he sighed and left to find Bamfa on his porch.

"Morning Prez, how you doing? You spoke to Dragon yet?"

Mack's stomach churned at the mention of her name. Mack strongly believed that B's safety could only be ensured by his absence from her life.

"No. Here," he said, handing him an envelope addressed to B. "I'm gonna visit Alexandra. Can you take a trip back to Sunnyville and hand this to Dragon, please, brother? Nobody else. You hand it directly to Dragon. You understand me?"

Uncertainty flashed across Bamfas disheveled face, wearing the same exhausted appearance as every MC member wore following their war with Mateo. "Does it have to be today? I'm shattered. I was hoping to spend the day with my girls."

Mack sucked in his bottom lip, unable to make eye contact with his brother. "Yeah, it does. In fact, do it now, so I know she's received it."

"What's this about Prez? We're worried about you. You and B, you're written in the stars. We all know it here in Uskiville. Why don't we hit the road together? I'll talk to her."

Mack suppressed the lump in his throat, giving his brother's arm a gentle squeeze. "Nah, leave her be. She needs her rest. You know I like a flare for the dramatics. Truth be told, it's just a love letter. I'm going to spend a few days with Alexandra, and I hope Dragon will come around after reading my letter."

Bamfa's face remained unconvinced by Mack's words, angering Mack.

"Get going Bamfa. That's an order!"

"Right, Prez," Bamfa grumbled, stumbling down the porch steps. He was halfway down the garden path when Mack called him from his bike.

"Hey Bamfa, it's always an honor having a brother like you in my pack. Ride safe!"

Mack headed to Portland, parking up on Ari's driveway where his former marriage counselor was packing the car for what appeared to be a camping trip.

"Taking a trip?" Mack said, frightening the man with his presence.

Taking a step back, the counselor froze to the spot as Ari waltzed outside with an extra sleeping bag. "You never know how co—" She stopped in her tracks, staring at Mack and back at her new boyfriend.

"Oh, calm yourselves. If I wanted him dead, Ari, he would be." He turned to the counselor. "She's your problem now, man. You may just survive the fecking year if you're lucky!"

"What do you want Mack? You shouldn't be here!"

"I can be wherever I fecking want, Ari. Now I've come to see my daughter. I'm taking a trip to clear my head of all the shite we caused, and I want to cwtch my baby before I go."

"Cwtch," Ari mocked. "B's grasp on you is stronger than ever, I see. Heard she survived."

Mack's pupils dilated: nostrils flared. "Take her fecking name out of your filthy mouth. If I ever hear you even whisper it again, mother of my child or not, I'll fecking kill you, Ari! And my mark better be removed from that filthy body of yours."

Ari gasped. "What the hell is wrong with you, Mack? She turn you down again? I'm just glad I don't have to put up with your shit anymore."

Mack darted towards her, spitting as he spoke. "You are what's fecking wrong with me! You entered my life and fucking ruined everything! The price I paid for my son: you're fecking poisonous, Ari."

Ari trembled, looking at her new boyfriend for support.

"Don't expect him to help you. He's about to shite himself. Look at him. Worthless! I should—"

"Daddy!" Alexandra screamed. The delight glowed on her face as she rushed from the house with Remy trailing behind her.

Mack opened his arms, scooping up his daughter, kissing her button nose. "Where's daddy's little daisy? I've missed you, sweetheart!"

She giggled into his neck, as Mack kissed her cheek and felt the warmth as he cradled her in his arms. "Daddy wanted to come and see you really quick. I have something for your camping trip," he said, walking to his bike and reaching into his knapsack, retrieving a stuffed, fluffy bunny.

"Here you go, princess. Mr. Snuggletoes will keep you company until daddy sees you again, okay?"

"Okay, daddy. When will you come back? I see, Junior and Aunt B, too?"

A single tear escaped from Mack's right eye, igniting concern in Ari's tone. "Say bye to daddy now. We're going to be late for our trip." Snatching Alex from his grasp, she handed her to Remy. "Place her in her car seat."

"Bye, angel. Daddy loves you." He watched his daughter wave until she was out of sight.

"Remy," he called.

Remy popped his head above the roof of the car.

"Look after Junior while I'm gone, would you?"

Remy nodded, his words escaping him.

"What the hell is going on, Mack?" Ari snapped, distracting him.

"Feck off, Ari. I came to see my daughter. You think you can up fecking sticks and steal my daughter away from me? You should know the lengths I go for family. Only you're not family anymore, are you?"

He climbed back onto his bike, fixing his helmet. "Look after my daughter while I'm gone, and fair warning, the club is watching your every fecking move."

Revving his engine, he blew a kiss to baby Alex and sped out of town, leaving Ari distraught.

CHAPTER EIGHTY-EIGHT

Bamfa was readying himself for another trip to Sunnyville when his cell phone rattled against the keys in his pants pocket.

"Yeah?"

"Bamfa?"

"You got some fucking nerve calling me, Ari."

"Bamfa, please just listen. Something's wrong with Mack?"

Bamfa narrowed his eyes. "Mack's the problem? It's my understanding that you dropped your panties for the counselor. Sounds like a you problem, not Mack's! After everything he did for you."

"No, that's not what I mean. Mack's just been here, threatening to kill me. He's unhinged. His words… something's off!"

"Listen, Ari. Just allow him the quality time with Alex. A few days with his daughter will be good for him."

Ari paused for a moment. "What are you talking about? He's not spending time with Alex. He stopped by to give her a gift before taking a trip."

Bamfa's heart skipped a beat. Silence loomed down the line as echoes of Ari's voice rang in his ears.

"Bamfa!!"

"Yeah, I got to go Ari, I'll sort it alright."

Hanging up the phone, he tore the envelope from his inside pocket, ripping the letter open.

Studying the handwritten note, his shaking hands couldn't contain his fear.

Holy shit, Mack. No!

Dialing Mack's number, he waited for his answer phone to kick in. "Prez, I don't know what's going on, but I need you to call me ASAP."

Flicking through his contact list, he found Frankie's number and hit the dial button. The panic tearing through his existence threatened to kill him where he stood.

"Kind of busy here, Bamfa. I've told you multiple times. Let Mackie sulk. He and B will come around. They both just need space right now."

Bamfa's voice wobbled. "We might not have a few days."

Frankie sighed. "What's that supposed to mean?"

"Mack's in trouble and this time it won't end well."

CHAPTER EIGHTY-NINE
Bitch Slap!

Ray interrogated B in a nearby family room while Erik was being prepped for surgery, almost pushing her to the point of exhaustion with his extensive questioning. B explained she did not know how the building caught fire and only escaped with Erik after the electricity failed, releasing her from her cell. She further explained how they hailed down a passing stranger who brought them to the rest stop so she could call home. Ray left to gather more evidence and informed B they would investigate her abduction and Mateo's demise to the fullest extent of the law. Ray reminded her of the ramifications of withholding evidence or impeding the investigation.

"Hang on a minute. Last time I checked, someone abducted me on my wedding day. Good boy. I watched him being shot before being carted off to be drugged and forced to fight for my life. And you're telling me I can be in trouble for potentially impeding an investigation?" she growled.

"Now, Mrs..."

"Don't Mrs, me, Sunshine. I wasn't lucky enough to say I do before being torn away and I haven't even seen my children yet, as I'm bloody dealing with the ramifications of this fucking drug. How fucking dare you accuse me of anything when I've fought like fuck to stay alive! And for the bloody record, I hope he is dead because what he did was inhumane."

Ray's sympathetic eyes bored into her retinas. "I understand you've been through hell, Mrs... uh, I mean Blethen. Understand, I'm trying to establish the truth."

B shot up from her chair, forcing Frankie to restrain her. "The truth, you fucking idiot. I'll tell you the truth. A bloody nut job rocked up to my wedding, shot up my family for God knows what reason and dragged me off, treating me like a fucking lab rat. They tortured me and forced me to fight for my survival while big wigs from across the globe watched for fun and made bids for my ownership."

Ray's slack-jaw expression didn't stop B from continuing her wrath upon him.

"Let me ask you something?" she said, breathing her dragon fire into his personal space. "Imagine going through all that, thinking your almost husband is dead, not knowing if your family is safe. Imagine having untested drugs pumped through your system to the point your body strips you of your muscle and who you are and every week you have to face off with the biggest, nastiest bastard to survive. How would you fare Mr. Fucking Police Officer? Because let me tell you something, good boy. I guarantee a slimy fucker like you wouldn't last two seconds."

"B," Frankie shouted, trying to snap her back to her senses.

"I understand you're upset..." Ray tried.

"Upset!!" she shrieked, only stopping when Zander entered the room, tracking his movements as he stood between her and Ray.

Glaring into Ray's now frightened eyes, he puffed out his chest. "I dinnae appreciate anyone upsetting my old lady," he growled. "Especially cops who dinnae investigate properly."

Ray trembled backwards as Zander stepped forward.

"Oh, fuck!" Frankie said, releasing B to grab Zander. "Come on, Prez. Let's not cause a scene in the hospital."

"I'm no' causing a scene, pal. I'm explaining to your old colleague here that if he so much as looks at my Welsh Cake the wrong way ever again, I'll slice his fucking throat and just like he failed to find her, I can guarantee no fucker will ever find what's left of him."

Ray gulped, backing toward the door.

"I'm no' fucking done!" Zander breathed, halting Ray. "My lassie has told you the truth. She's informed you of what happened, yet you dinnae want to believe her. Her pal is awaiting fucking heart surgery because of what Mateo did, and she's been through enough. Do I need to remind you that her lawyer friend is the best in the fucking country, so if I dinnae kill you, he'll have your fucking throat? Now do your job and find out what that bastard ran through her veins. We need answers and I am no' a patient man."

Ray gave him a nod before scurrying out of the room.

Zander shrugged from Frankie's remaining grasp. "Get to fuck, will ya? I'm no' stupid Frankie. If I wanted to kill him, I wouldn't do it at the hospital. It's way too convenient for the fucker I'm trying to kill."

"Perhaps you should tell B that. She may have lost half her body weight, but it still took everything to prevent her from smacking him."

Zander kissed B's cheek. "That's my girl."

B glared at him, her eyes still fiery from her encounter with Ray. "What's this? multiple personality day? Earlier you stomped off sulking and now you're defending my honor. I can't keep up with you."

Zander pursed his lips in embarrassment. "I'm sorry, darling. I'm just trying to allow my brain to catch up with the evolving situation and, every time I see you with Leif's boy, I fall into a jealous rage."

"For fuck's sake, Scottie. Don't I have enough to deal with without a jealous Prez? How many times... nothing happened between us? He helped me survive so I could return home to you. Erik is my friend."

Zander caressed her cheek. "I know. I'll get my shit together, promise!"

B dragged him to the hospital chairs as Frankie slipped out of the family room. Ushering him to sit, she stood between his legs, allowing him to wrap his hands around her, stroking her back. Running her fingers through his hair, she released a guttural sigh. "Scottie, I'm exhausted. I just want to fetch the boys from the airport and head home. Not to the club, home. Only I can't relax until I know Erik is safe and I'm about to be hooked up to another IV."

Zander gazed up at her with puppy dog eyes. "Aye, I understand, darling. I am trying no' to be an asshole. I just want you to be safe and have you all to myself with the boys, too. The anxiety I'm feeling right now is crippling. I was so scared I'd lost you forever and now that I have you, I'm terrified I'll lose you again."

B kissed his lips. "I promise, I'm not going anywhere ever again. No more putting myself in dangerous situations. I won't lose anyone again."

"Promise?"

"Promise, big guy. Just allow me to help Erik through this, please?"

"On the condition you dinnae leave my side. We go everywhere together."

"Agreed. I need you, Scottie."

Doctor Cassimino managed to sweet talk the hospital into allowing him to conduct Erik's aortic valve replacement that afternoon, and once Erik had undergone his pre-op routine and seen his family, the time for his surgery had arrived.

B sat outside Erik's room with a cup of tea following her treatment, studying Erik with his family. It bothered her how his mother and father fussed over their firstborn without acknowledging Tyr being in the room. B wondered if their bond with Tyr would unify after losing Ragnar. Only Revna treated him like a stranger. It angered B, forcing her to squeeze her hot tea, scalding her hand and spilling it everywhere.

"Careful darling," Zander said, mopping up the spillage with the paper napkin he had left over from his cookie.

"I want to bitch slap her back to Viking land!" B said through gritted teeth.

Zander rubbed her back. "I assume we're talking about her selective maternal tendencies?"

B's eyes remained fixed on Revna. "Damm right. Look at her. She's not said one word to Tyr since she arrived. She didn't even embrace him. When did she last see him, huh?"

B's temper rose to a boiling point, forcing her to her feet. "God, some people don't deserve kids. I get she's lost Ragnar, and Erik is about to go under the knife, but her baby is right there, worried and hurting too. He needs support just as much as the rest of the family."

"Then go, give it to him. She's no' his mother, darling. You are, and you have been since the moment you laid eyes on him. If she cannae see what she's losing, then fuck her!"

B's head whipped toward Zander as if a penny drop moment struck her like a bullet, before storming into the room.

"Alright, my lovely," she bellowed to Erik, kissing his cheek. "Do us a favor and hurry the fuck up with the surgery. We got shit to plan."

"Got it, Dragon," Erik said with a chuckle.

Revna's evil eyes tried to stare B down, making her smile as she wrapped her arm around Tyr. "And you, good boy? How are you holding up? I'm so proud of the person you've become, after overcoming so much. You, my boy, are the light of my life, just as Madoc, Rhys and Prez are, and never bloody forget it. You know this boy took a bullet trying to defend his Prez and rescue me?"

Tyr's face beamed, flushing red. "Thank you, Móðir he said to B, surprising Revna, while Leif didn't appear the least bit surprised, and Zander grinned from the doorway.

"Dragon." Leif said, acknowledging her presence. "Thank you so much for paying for Erik's surgery. We are in your debt now."

B rested her head on Tyr's boulder-like chest. "Unnecessary, good boy. Erik helped me survive and Tyr here is the older son I never had. You owe me nothing. However, I would like to offer my condolences regarding Ragnar. I know we didn't see eye to eye, but I am sorry for your loss."

Leif reached for her hand, squeezing it. "Thank you, Dragon. You are as honorable as your Celtic Warrior."

B provided her best smile, casting a glance at the scowling Revna as she continued. "I've expressed an interest in doing business with your club now that Mateo is out of the picture.

Leif snapped his head toward Zander in the doorway, gesturing back to B.

"Dragon. I am so humbled by your generosity towards my family after the trouble we caused. I am sorry for my dishonesty and ruining your wedding."

B blew air from her cheeks. "We've both sustained losses. How about we start over after Erik has healed?"

Doctor Cassimino entered the room wearing his blue scrubs, interrupting their conversation. "Ready Erik?"

"As I will ever be. My life is in Odin's hands now."

"I think you'll find it's in mine. Odin can wait," the doctor said, ushering the porters to wheel Erik to surgery.

Leif and Revna panicked, embracing their son as Erik gave Tyr an encouraging wink and grabbed B's hand. "You'll be here when I wake? Fighting for my life without you will be strange. I'd like to see your face when I wake, Dragon."

"Don't worry, Boyoh. I won't let you sleep too long. I'll shake you awake."

B and Zander held Tyr as Ragnar and Revna escorted Erik to the operating theater. Leif embraced Tyr, kissing his forehead as Revna continued to ignore him, stroking Erik's head, infuriating an already nervous Erik.

B exhaled a long, nervous sigh, knowing Erik was about to undergo lengthy surgery to save his life. She was about to suggest they all visit the canteen when Frankie and Tiny came hurdling down the corridor towards them.

"B!!"

"D-R-A-G-O-N!!"

CHAPTER NINETY
Love Letter

The color drained from B's face seeing Frankie and Tiny race towards her.

What's he done?

Panting, Frankie, and Tiny struggled to get their words out.

"Mackie… fuck! He's…" Frankie tried.

"Stupid cunt!" Tiny panted, clutching his injured side.

"Tell me what's bloody happened!" B demanded; the fear in her soul leading the charge as she attempted to extract answers.

Frankie handed B her phone, showing a photograph of the handwritten letter.

Taking the phone, B used her pinching fingers to enlarge the image to read Mack's letter.

My Beautiful Fiery Dragon,

I've really fecked up this time, haven't I?

God knows, every attempt to do right brings harm to you.

I've hurt you and damaged our bond more times than I can count, and you never deserved a damn ounce of the trouble I've caused.

I can only thank you for the love and forgiveness you provided when I couldn't see the wood from the trees.

You were right, Dragon. You said Ari would be the end of us, and I didn't listen.

I take full responsibility for the Cascade of Lies I brought upon our family, and I'll no longer watch my enemies come for you, knowing you are the single most important love of my life next to my kids.

My enemies have always known it's you, Dragon. You are the fire in my soul, and that puts you in danger every waking minute of your life.

I understand you want everyone on Ari's list to die Dragon, only I fear these clubs are like you: cut off their heads and two come back. They'll keep hunting you as their prey; to watch me suffer like I made them suffer, and you've already endured too much from the war I started.

You, Dragon, are the sole reason my heart beats, and I almost lost you to yet another enemy.

NO MORE!!

I will always love you, Dragon. The sad part is, despite choosing Zander, I honestly believe you love me back at last, and I wanted to say that's okay.

Zander, a great man, would sacrifice himself for you, as will I.

By the time you read this, I would probably have already met my maker doing something I love. Diving into my death for you is an honorable duty I must undertake to prevent the Cascade of Lies from killing you.

Once I'm gone, you'll be safe and at peace from the destruction I've caused.

I apologize with all my heart, Dragon. I love you too much to see anything else happen to you. These past weeks have torn me inside out and back to front. I didn't want to live without you, but I know you're strong enough to live without me.

I love you, Dragon. Always have, always will.

I know you're gonna be pissed with me for quitting on you as your best friend, but I promise you, this is the only way to keep you safe. Please just promise me you'll guide Junior through his grief, like you did with me. You're the only person he'll listen to.

Dragon, I will forever carry the biggest torch for you. I'll light the stars for you whenever you're down in the dark. Look at the night sky and you'll find me.

Please forgive me and remember... if you're too much, tell them to find less!

Fuck anyone who doesn't treat you like a God damn fiery queen of the dragons.
Love you always, my beautiful, fiery fecking Dragon.
All my love, your best friend forever,
Mackie
Xxxxx

B's bulging eyes threatened her with floods of tears until her fight-or-flight response kicked it. The all too familiar vexation rose from the pit of her stomach, forcing any tears to suck back inside her head, allowing her inner dragon to rear its ugly head. She dialed his number, reaching Mack's voicemail.

"His phone is off, B," Frankie said.

She pursed her lips. "Tiny, where's your bike?"

"Parked out front."

"Good. You're the fastest fucker I know, and I might need you to haul Mack's ass down from the bridge?"

Everyone cast crazy glances at her.

"The blue bridge. You read the letter?" she said to Frankie and Tiny, her words lost on them. "Bloody hell, he's at the fucking blue bridge. The one place he knows scares the fuck out of me. Next to the enormous cliffs he jumps from?"

"Oh, shit, B we need to leave now!" Frankie said.

Zander stepped in between them. "Whoa! Hang the fuck on. This is fucking Irish we're talking aboot. He's had paddy's for as long as I've known him; spat his fucking dummy out for twenty years! He'll no' do anything stupid."

B glared at him, angered by his misunderstanding of the severity of the situation. "He will for me, Scottie."

"What's that supposed to mean?"

"He loves me, Scottie, and he thinks he's saving my life. If he's gone, the Cascade of Lies will end. Mackie will dive from the blue bridge this evening unless I stop him. Now step aside."

B turned to Tyr, the worry on the poor young man's face aging him with rapid succession. "I understand I made a promise to Erik, but I must go to Mackie, Tyr. If I'm not back by the time he wakes, tell him I'll return, okay?"

"Erik will understand. Go. Save your best friend."

B kissed Tyr on the cheek before turning to leave, forcing Zander to block her path once more. "Your no' going on Tiny's bike, darling. You're supposed to be remaining in hospital but if you're adamant on going, we'll all drive up."

"I haven't got time for the Prez shit, Scottie. Tiny can get me there quicker. Besides, seeing us together might trigger him. I'm going with Tiny, and I will gut anyone who stands in my way, including you. You want to support me, follow in the truck," she huffed, pushing past him to enter a sprint down the corridor with Frankie and Tiny in tow.

Tiny raced like a bat out of hell, swerving through traffic to save his friend.

Adrenaline continued to make B its enemy, making her feel nauseas. Holding onto Tiny, her body threatened her with unconsciousness. Fortunately, as B's consciousness wavered, Tiny bellowed at her, snapping her back to her senses.

"Fuck, Dragon! You nearly went then. Hang on, we're almost there," he said, reaching his arm behind himself to steady her and almost crashing.

"What the fuck are you doing, Tiny?" Frankie roared through his mouthpiece. "B's no good to Mackie dead."

"Dragon almost fell off. I had to grip onto her."

"Fuck's sake. Let's get there in one piece." Frankie snapped.

The night sky drew in as the heavens opened upon them, making them slip and slide along the lethal highway. Motorcycles skidded along the highway as B as the wolves raced against time to save Mack. They could see the infrastructure of the blue, weathering steel bridge in the distance, which encouraged them to battle through the incoming storm, with the slick tarmac toying with their control on the road. Tiny pulled down an access road to enter the bridge while B scanned ahead, praying for signs of Mack.

"There!" she pointed, noticing Mack standing on the wrong side of the bridge, hands gripping the railings and staring into the vicious ocean. "Pull up here. I don't want to scare him. I'll talk him down from the bridge."

"No, it's too dangerous. I'm not losing you both tonight," Tiny said.

"Tiny, he'll only listen to me. Please?"

"Fine, but I'm getting close enough to help if required," he said, pulling to the side of the road.

Tiny and Frankie parked close to the barrier, allowing B to rip off her helmet and approach him on foot. The driving rain and whistling wind attacked her with their might, making it almost impossible to walk. The world seemed to hold her back, trying to seal Mack's fate. B fought on, glancing over her shoulder to discover an entourage of both Sunnyville and Uskiville bikers had amassed next to Tiny and Frankie, with Zander's face full of worry staring back at her, watching her approach her best friend with caution.

"Mackie!" she called, catching his attention.

His head jerked in her direction, tracking her approach to the barrier and climbing over to join him. "Dragon, no! What are you doing here?"

Her hand slipped, almost tossing her into the sea, forcing wild gasps from the pack behind them, as Mack gripped her wrist, placing it on the barrier.

B clambered up, catching her breath, throwing an encouraging glance back to a roaring Zander and MC pack and trying not to look down at the crashing waves beneath her.

"You think you can leave me a shitty goodbye letter explaining you're quitting on me, Mackie? No chance, good boy. Best friends never quit!"

"Dragon, I'm sorry. Please, get back over that barrier. You're terrified of heights."

Tears rolled down her weathered cheeks. "No, Mackie. I'm more terrified of losing you. You go; I go good boy. That's the only way this ends. It's your choice in which direction." She slid her feet closer to him, trying to reach him.

Panic washed over Mack's terrified face. "No! No! Dragon, fecking stop! Don't move a muscle," he said, shuffling his feet toward her. "Please climb back over the barrier, Dragon, please?"

B's ears rattled as the waves battled it out with the seabed, swirling giant waves into great heights and smashing them into the boundary rocks. The thunderous sky roared, pelting down rain like icy bullets, as if God was angry with humanity this evening.

"It's not your time, Dragon, please?"

"Not without you, good boy. Mackie, I can't get through this without you. I'm sorry, I never meant the shit I said. I was tired and angry. Please, Mackie, let's go home!" The desperation in her eyes pleaded with him.

Mack placed his head on hers. His hands squeezing the railings. "Dragon, you will never be safe as long as I'm breathing. I won't be responsible for your death. You need to let me go, beautiful!"

B removed a hand from the railing, gripping his soaking wet, flannel shirt. "How can I let go of the man I've always loved? Mackie, you're my best friend. I won't live in a world without you."

Mack stared into her eyes, speechless, as he digested her words.

The icy rain declared war on them as if it was trying to slice them as meal prep for the ocean.

Mack closed his eyes in defeat. "Alright Dragon, you win. Let's get off this fecking bridge!"

"You're not fucking with me?" she asked.

Mack shook his head. "No. I can't allow you to hurt yourself anymore for me. I'll travel back to Sunnyville in the truck, and we'll work this shit out."

B smiled into her tears as Mack kissed her cheek, watching her hesitantly swing her right leg back over the barrier, hauling herself over the railings. Ensuring she had two feet firmly on the ground, he followed suit, embracing her.

"I'm sorry I scared you Dragon, my fecking head went at the thought of never seeing you again." He wrapped an arm around her, ushering her toward their pack. "Let's get you home.".

They walked until they were within hearing distance of the pack of relieved wolves.

"At a boy, Mackie. We'll sort this brother," Frankie encouraged, smiling at him.

Mack smiled back, stopping B, and taking her hand after glimpsing a nervous-looking Zander.

"Dragon, I understand we could never be, while you're in love with Zander. I understand he provides the maturity I never could. You've always loved me in your unique way, but we both know it's not enough for us to be together."

B broke down in tears; the unfolding events too much for her.

Mack hugged her, rubbing her back and whispering into her ear. "It's okay, Dragon. He worships you as much as I do, and I take comfort knowing you'll be happy. It's all I've ever wanted for you."

"Mackie…"

"What I'm trying to say, Dragon, is I only bring death and destruction into your life."

"That's not true!"

Mack chuckled. "Come the feck on, Dragon. I brought a cascade of lies that should have killed you three times over. Look at the fecking state of you. I need to make that right, and I promise I'm gonna make it so nobody comes to hurt you again."

Removing her grip on his shirt, he placed his forehead on hers, taking her hands in his once more. Closing his eyes, he sighed. "Oh, Dragon, I will love you in every lifetime. Best friends never quit, especially us."

Planting a soft kiss on her lips, he lulled her into a softened state before snatching his hands back and sending her stumbling back.

As B tried to collect her bearing, Mack raced towards the barrier. Screams of panic ripped through the air as the wolves chased down their Prez in slow motion. B witnessed the horror unfold before her devastated eyes; Mack had reached the barrier before B's fragile mind could comprehend the reality of the situation.

Using his hands to propel him, Mack dived over the barrier, headfirst into the turbulent ocean.

B raced to the barrier; her frantic eyes searching the sinister seas for her best friend, just as his brothers in arms did. Frankie, Tiny and Bamfa called out to him while the rest of the pack sprinted to the rocky shoreline right of the bridge, using their cell phone flashlights to search for him.

Zander cradled B just as her legs buckled beneath her with the chilly night's reality striking her like a double-decker bus. Mack had done the unthinkable. The one thing he promised never to do: Mack had quit on his best friend.

The End

www.ingramcontent.com/pod-product-compliance
Lightning Source LLC
Chambersburg PA
CBHW020514080526
44583CB00013B/596